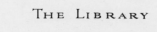

CONQUEST BY TERROR
The Story of Satellite Europe

By Leland Stowe

CONQUEST BY TERROR
TARGET: YOU
WHILE TIME REMAINS
THEY SHALL NOT SLEEP
NO OTHER ROAD TO FREEDOM
NAZI MEANS WAR

The Story of Satellite Europe

CONQUEST BY TERROR

Leland Stowe

RANDOM HOUSE · NEW YORK

FIRST PRINTING

For

All those who wait for freedom;

Especially to those

For whom freedom will come too late.

CONTENTS

ACKNOWLEDGMENTS

FOR THE FACTS AND INCIDENTS RECORDED IN these pages I am indebted to an exceptionally large number of persons, both in Europe and America. Most of all to the members of satellite Europe's underground, the bravest reporters in today's world. Under constant risk of torture and death they continue to smuggle out most revealing information from inside the Kremlin's Curtain. To these unknown heroes, nameless to me as most of them will be on freedom's honor roll, it is impossible to express my own debt or that of all free peoples. One can only hope that this book may contribute in some measure to their struggle for freedom from Communist rule by terror.

The information and research staffs of Radio Free Europe have given me invaluable assistance. They have often worked many hours to obtain or to confirm certain specific data. Without their generous co-operation, and that of many others in various fields and places, this report could not have been assembled. Any appreciation which I might try to voice would be inadequate.

I am also indebted especially to DeWitt Wallace, editor of *The Reader's Digest*, whose personal interest and support made it possible for me to take the time necessary to transform a prolonged research into this book. In preparation of the manuscript I have been helped enormously by the suggestions of Paul Palmer and Robert N. Linscott; and notably, in its final form, by the latter's masterly editing.

Portions of Chapter II are based upon my article, "Satellites in Arms," published in *Life* magazine on December 17, 1951.

LELAND STOWE

New York City, February, 1952

Foreword

I THINK YOU MIGHT BE INTERESTED TO KNOW
how this book came to be written.

It is a direct result of my belief that the so-called "Iron Curtain" has many crevices, cracks and gaps in it; and that we in the West have actually been putting a lot of unnecessary iron into it—by failing to tap, correlate and publicize many important seepages of information from Eastern Europe. This conviction had grown ever since I spent five months reporting from several of these Soviet-captive countries in 1946. We could and should know a great deal more about what the Soviet Communists are doing in the Red-ruled half of Europe. A remarkable amount of factual data has been available. It simply hasn't been pursued with sufficient effort, method and persistence

I became equally convinced that we need desperately to know much more precisely how the Stalinists are nailing down their conquest of six and one-half foreign nations (including Eastern Germany), that the preservation of our own freedoms depends on such knowledge. Exactly what are the Communists' methods of control? How are they capturing or subjugating *people* in Eastern Europe? I couldn't get any rounded conception from our press or radio—just fragmentary and scattered news items. The real meaning to us very rarely seemed to come through.

The Korean invasion posed some new questions. After all, Moscow possessed larger and much more strategically placed puppet armies in Eastern Europe than in North Korea. What were the Soviets doing with these satellite armed forces? What was their combined strength? How well-trained were their divisions? Were they larger or growing faster than General Eisenhower's defense forces in Western Europe? If the Kremlin chose to put them into action, how dangerous would they be? It seemed to me that the answers to these questions added up to one of the most important unreported stories in the world.

There also appeared slight reason to expect that the Western democracies' news agencies or newspapers would go after this story, at least not before many months. (More than seventeen months later this still had not happened.) Their editors were understandably concentrating on big headline events in Korea. But there were other and deeper reasons which persuaded me that a free-lance writer might still have a job of real reporting to do.

So I decided, in September, 1950, to try and get a maximum of available facts about Russia's "armies of Eastern Europe." That's where the much neglected holes in the Iron Curtain come in. You can actually seek out numerous sources of information. Among them: journalists in exile (some of whom I had known in Eastern Europe); members of these countries' National Committees-in-Exile; specialists associated with the Mid-European Studies Center; former career officers in the captive nations' armies, now in the West; former cabinet ministers; recent refugees from inside the Curtain. The National Committee for a Free Europe generously placed invaluable contacts and material at my disposal. Radio Free Europe, operated by the N.C.F.E., provided the most important co-operation of all. It obtains an exceptional amount of information from inside the Curtain countries. Its highly qualified research staffs, one for each Communist-ruled nation, are probably unmatched anywhere in the West.

From the beginning of January, 1951, this self-assignment soon occupied virtually all of my time. I consulted all the above sources and others; interviewed many specialists; studied hundreds of underground reports. By April the factual material in hand began to piece together like a jigsaw puzzle. It showed that Moscow's build-up of the satellites' armed forces had reached surprising dimensions since Korea. The over-all picture was much more serious than I myself had anticipated. The results of this investigation were first written for *Life* magazine; later revised and up-dated as Chapter II of this book.

But as a by-product my research had amassed much new (and sometimes jolting) material regarding many other Communist doings in the Curtain countries. This data confirmed emphatically the basic premise which had prompted my inquiry regarding military matters. What was needed was not merely a rounded report on the Soviets' expansion of the puppet-state armies. A documented, detailed report on the sweeping sovietization of the whole of Eastern Europe was even more urgently needed.

People often asked me: "But are things really so bad behind the Curtain?" Actually, as I had learned conclusively, things are a thousand times worse in these Red-ruled countries than the average American conceives of—or perhaps is prepared to believe. But why should most of our citizens remain so perilously ill informed or ignorant? That concerns the deeper reasons I mentioned earlier. As I analyze it, these are the main reasons:

1) Western news agencies and newspapers, both American and European, have attempted to report Iron-Curtain developments since 1945–46 largely with pre-Curtain journalistic methods. But you cannot adequately or accurately report events in a shut-off area by the same routine news-coverage procedures which work well enough in free, democratic countries. They logically demand radically revised journalistic techniques— and added expense. To defeat the Communists' new screen against information *more time, effort, and expense* obviously needed to be expended in new ways. Was this not, from the outset, a very difficult task requiring full-time Iron Curtain specialists?

I do not know of any Western newspaper correspondent who has been assigned to patrol as a full-time assignment the European periphery of the Iron Curtain, from Finland down to Greece and Turkey, back and forth. If two or three American news-agency correspondents had done this over the past two

years, most of our newspapers would have reported many facts
which are pretty certain to surprise you—perhaps alarm you—
in the chapters of this book. They have been waiting to be told
fully. This is part of what I mean by pre-Iron Curtain journalistic
methods.

2) The reporting we get about satellite Europe is much more
fragmentary and confusing than is necessary. This is due to
certain long established habits of Western journalism. In order
to be "news" something must have just happened. But suppose
nobody could learn about it until much later? That has proved to
be the case in regard to Russia's secret post-Korea mobilization
and build-up of the satellites' armies. Because it was a prolonged, cumulative process it was not treated as news. All that
was "news" was yesterday's doubling of length of army service
in Bulgaria, or 400 Soviet tanks just sent into Hungary. Those
items, if learned, were lost in a few lines at the bottom of an inside page. Gather twenty such items—about ten or more major
Soviet fields of conquest in all Curtain countries—over a period
of weeks or months. Then you have a dozen major, solid dispatches of commanding interest. In reality they are far bigger
news. But until now our vast, normally efficient news-gathering
organizations have concentrated chiefly on the scattered and
smaller "spot news" events. While reporting the trees of Red-
ruled Eastern Europe they have too often missed the big Red
forest—the key developments which are really the big stories.

3) Most citizens in the West are also ill informed about the
wholesale sovietizing of Eastern Europe because our media of
mass communications (from press to magazines, radio and television) operate predominantly on the theory that whatever has
been told once, or partially told, is "old stuff." (Several chapters
which follow were rejected, in outline form, by magazine editors
for this reason—more politely expressed.) Consider the known
fact that Russia's M.V.D. police are active in the Curtain countries. Consider the further fact—certainly unknown at this writing to most Western editors as well as the public generally—that
the Communists' internal police armies total more than two mil-

lion in all of Eastern Europe. How are they organized? How do the Soviets control them? What are the various types of police armies? There is a considerable difference between these two sets of facts. Because we know about a few fleas on an elephant's back, do we incline to think that we know all about the elephant?

Like the Fascists, the Communists understand perfectly that anything that is vitally important (to them) *has to be told over and over again*. Because their "facts" are chiefly fantastic lies, repetition is absolutely essential. But the totalitarians recognize clearly that most people have to have things—fact or fiction—driven into their heads. Nobody ever really learned grammar or geometry by skimming through the lesson. The Communists continue to plant their ideas in millions of minds *inside the free countries* simply because they repeat incessantly everything they want to stick in people's minds.

Is it less important that inestimably vital facts which would awaken the free peoples and strengthen their resolve should be presented repeatedly with an insistence equal to that of the Communists? The executives of the free world's media of communication very often seem to side-step their great public responsibilities. Save for notable exceptions, they appear to lean over backward to make things easier for the Kremlin.

I submit that there is an enormous distinction between such facts as these. On one hand, the general knowledge that there are slave-labor camps in Eastern Europe today. On the other, the generally unknown fact that more than one million persons are *now* being slowly worked to death in hundreds of these camps; the further fact that the Soviets are building scores of new and much larger camps to serve as death-coops for far greater numbers of slaves in the next few years. This is not "old stuff." It is a bigger story than anything on the subject (which is shamefully little) that I have yet seen in our daily press. You cannot get such abnormal realities indelibly into the minds of a majority of still complacent Western citizens with one or two newspaper or magazine articles—nor, alas, with this one book.

We must deceive ourselves no longer. *We do not yet begin to possess adequate knowledge about Communist methods of conquest* to be adequately equipped to prevent or check Russia's formidable expansion. A revolution *moves*. But defense of democracy cannot possibly move with equivalent counter-effect without the incentive of a much better informed public opinion than exists now.

4) Finally, most of us have remained seriously ill informed about what the Communists are really achieving, because of another pre-Curtain habit of Western journalism. Almost all developments in the Reds' puppet states are reported in separate, tight *national* compartments. Instead of reporting satellite Europe as a whole, our news agencies report Polish news, Hungarian news, etc. But the Soviets are not treating Eastern Europe as separate nations. They are applying identical tactics, identical programs, identical methods to all of Eastern Europe. Theirs is an *all-satellite program*, and this serves as a model and a prelude for a *world-sovietizing program*.

In terms of Western journalistic practices this, again, is reporting puppet-state trees instead of Eastern Europe's Russianized forest. What we most need is *all-satellite reporting*, co-ordinated all-East European information. What is really enlightening is not isolated Communist actions in Rumania or Czechoslovakia. It is the unity and uniformity of Stalinist actions in the entire region of captive Europe.

The rips and gaps in the inaccurately named "Iron" Curtain are large and numerous. But the information gatherers of our media of mass communications have been assigned to keep their eyes glued to only a few cracks at a time. The results are inevitably diminishing and distorting to the bigger facts and the Big Truth. For everything of first-rank importance which the Communists are doing in various puppet states demands *correlation and co-ordinated presentation* in terms of all Eastern Europe.

It is only when Soviet actions in the entire Curtain area are correlated that the frightening proportions of their menace to our own free institutions become clear—that they can assume a truly personal meaning. This kind of new approach, it seems to

me, offers our only opportunity of achieving a necessary awareness. On the day when a bomb destroyed Hiroshima it also
destroyed any justification for thinking of our world in anything less than regional terms—regional as an absolute minimum.

This is how this book came to be written. It has had to be
written to meet a deadline necessary for early publication. That
limitation, combined with my own, must be accepted as largely
unavoidable. Nevertheless, the report which follows is an effort
to tell what the sovietizing of Eastern Europe is really like; how
the Communists have developed their methods of conquest by
terror; how these same techniques are in no sense limited ge-
ographically; why they could be, and may be, applied eventually
in every quarter of the globe; most of all, *their meaning to you.*

The researches on which this report is based have required
the major portion of eighteen months. The facts which I have
found have surprised me repeatedly, even though I have followed developments behind the Curtain as closely as possible
since 1946. But nothing in these pages has surprised me so much
as would be my surprise if you should fail to find in them many
important facts of which you have not previously been aware.

LELAND STOWE

New York City,
January, 1952.

CONQUEST BY TERROR
The Story of Satellite Europe

CHAPTER ONE

The World's Greatest Plot

How to Enslave Everybody IS A CONTEMporary tragedy, written in Moscow, produced and directed by Soviet Russians, and now being played throughout Eastern and captive Europe—with a cast of 90 million persons.

Its trial runs are rapidly nearing completion. The performance will be close to letter-perfect, by Kremlin standards, within a very few years. The tryouts are now being refined and polished in every detail. *How to Enslave Everybody* could be moved onto the main stages of Western Europe, the Middle East or Asia at any time. Its Cominform directors confidently predict world-wide productions in all languages.

In several respects this tragedy surpasses anything ever known before. Its plot is unquestionably the greatest in the world's history. It contains infinitely more murder and robbery, more terror and torture, more villainy and heroism, more mockery and heartbreak than all of Shakespeare. It is exceptionally designed for universal performance.

It is no indulgence in rhetoric to state that Soviet Communism constitutes the greatest plot the world has ever seen. In what previous age have expectant conquerors organized fifth columns on every continent, in almost every country on earth? What Alexander or Caesar, what Genghis Khan, Napoleon or Hitler ever trained millions of foreign citizens to do his bidding and to betray their native lands? What conspirator in all the recorded past has devoted more than thirty years to the systematic enlistment and instruction of legions of co-conspirators inside foreign states? When before, as in Eastern Europe today, have 90 million *foreign* people been subjugated without resort to open war; without firing a shot in battle; without dropping a single bomb? This record has no rival. It belongs uniquely to the Soviet Communists.

Because the great Red plot is unequaled, both in its scope and in organized detail, its implications are terrifying for every free society. The place to see it, for what it is and what it threatens to become, is where the Stalinists are already scoring remarkable and ominous successes; where the techniques of Soviet world conquest are being perfected—in satellite Europe. For the ways by which half of Europe has been enslaved are precisely the ways by which the Kremlin expects to enslave the remainder of the world. These are the identical methods by which Western Europeans, North Americans, South Americans and all other free peoples *can* be enslaved. Iron-Curtain Europe is nothing less than a preview of world conquest by Communism.

What have the Soviets already accomplished in Eastern Europe?

They have organized such vast police armies and regular armies that half of Europe cannot be liberated by any discernible means short of a third world war.

They have made the Eastern European countries economic prisoners of the Kremlin. Their entire economic systems are sovietized. Their production and national resources are directed solely to the build-up of Soviet power.

They have controlled and regimented the life of every individual—from infants to great-grandparents, from workers to women, from bankers to beggars, from peasants to poets, from teachers to preachers, from contraltos to coffin-makers.

They have suppressed the independence of churches of every creed, and are subverting religious organizations to the political objectives of the Kremlin.

They have placed more than one million citizens in prisons and slave-labor camps, and are expanding such accommodations toward an indicated goal of several million more slaves.

They have destroyed all political opposition, and are now embarked upon wholesale liquidation of the upper and middle classes through slow starvation, mass deportations and by universal death-sentence "justice."

They have perverted education to a monopoly instrument of Communist indoctrination.

They are "Russianizing" the cultures, history, literatures, science, arts and traditions of the East European nations.

They are well advanced toward communizing Eastern Europe's younger generation—nearly 20 million young people below the age of 21, some 20 per cent of the total present population.

Eastern Europe, in sum, has already entered its final stages of sovietization. In the few years since 1945 the supremely individualistic Iron-Curtain countries have been unrecognizably remodeled after the Soviets' master pattern by the Kremlin's plotters. What is the over-all meaning of these startling achievements? In reality Poland, Czechoslovakia, Hungary, Rumania, Bulgaria, Albania and Eastern Germany have been unofficially annexed to the Soviet Union. In reality Soviet Russia extends today to Berlin and Vienna. The Red Russians hold and rule far more of Europe than the imperial Turks at the apogee of their militarist aggression. In reality, and most significant of all, sovietized Eastern Europe now emerges as a grave threat to the freedom of all Western nations—to American and British Commonwealth freedom as much as to Norwegian, French or Italian freedom. We must examine much more fully this new menace of a predominantly communized Eastern Europe. But an immediate question is posed:

How could the Stalinists so quickly enslave six nations?

The answer lies, I think, in our own widespread underestimation of Communist capacities and their methods. I confess that

I was also guilty in this respect in 1946. After five months in
the Iron-Curtain countries I had no doubts about the Kremlin's
long-term objectives. But I underrated very considerably the
Stalinists' tempo of execution. In Budapest that summer I met
one official who judged the Russians' abilities more accurately.
Father Istvan Balogh was then an assistant secretary of state.
He possessed an extremely acute political mind, the most gar-
gantuan stomach I've ever seen, a notoriously Rabelaisian repu-
tation—and has since, not surprisingly, become a renegade in
Moscow's service.

"The Soviets are the new *Herrenvolk*—the new master race,"
Father Balogh declared. "Eventually they will dominate Europe."

"But are they efficient enough to organize half of Europe?" I
objected.

First, a knowing smile above his astoundingly huge midriff.
Then a confident declaration. "They don't have to be very
efficient. . . . They will *smother* all of Eastern Europe."

The smothering of satellite Europe required no more than
another five years—not perhaps seven or eight, as I had imagined.
In this brief period the Russian Communists proved themselves
much more efficient than Father Balogh himself seemed to anticipate. Not in Western terms of technical organization and
production of goods. They proved themselves highly efficient in
creating extensions of their police-state machine; in exporting and
expanding their own slave-state system—much more so, in fact,
than the Nazis ever were. This is something we need desperately
to understand. It explains why Russia's Red totalitarianism is a
greater, more universal menace than Germany's Brown totalitarianism was at its peak. Having seen the Nazis take over the
Danubian countries in 1940, the contrasts strike me with particular force.

Maybe it was largely due to one fact. Hitler's Nazis were
handicapped by being engaged in a great war, so they never
sought to impose absolute controls on all sections of conquered
civilian populations. Save for the Jews, they cultivated the support of Eastern Europe's capitalists and free enterprisers. They

played up to the aristocrats and feudal landowners. They scarcely interfered with the churches. They left most civil servants and white-collar workers undisturbed in their jobs. So long as middle-class citizens remained passively neutral they were relatively unmolested. The Nazis had neither the time nor the personnel to enslave entire populations; and they could not afford to attempt it then. Near-normalcy and a pronounced surface show of courtesy were two of the neatest tricks of Nazi domination. Their Gestapo brutalities and crimes were concealed so successfully that I met many Hungarians and Rumanians, in 1946, who still believed that Nazi incineration camps were products of Western propaganda.

But Russia's Communists did *not* come as superficial, old-fashioned space conquerors only. Their revolutionary drills and dynamite charges were directed at the social, political and economic foundations of Eastern Europe's nations. Their basic structures must be leveled and replaced—and the Stalinists knew from long experience and training exactly how this should be done. After the first months of dissimulation and under-cover maneuvering the Red "liberators" had no reason to placate the ruling classes. Their objective was to gain absolute power. And the Moscow-trained Communists had precise orders how to do it—orders which are still good for application anywhere in the world. On May 9, 1941, these same orders were delivered by the Comintern to Tito in Yugoslavia. That date is revealing. It was not only six weeks before Hitler invaded Russia. It was exactly four years before the war in Europe ended. But it still remains:

The official Kremlin blueprint for Communist seizure of power in any foreign country.

These are the major points in the Cominform's instructions to Tito, directly quoted: *

* As published in 1948 in *Kommunist*, official organ of the Yugoslav Communist Central Committee, along with other documents concerning their seizure of power.

1. "The time has come when we must take new decisive steps toward *world revolution.* [All italics used in this book are the author's, unless otherwise stated.]

A) "The Communist world revolution *must be presented as a series of measures to achieve 'real democracy'* . . .

B) "The government of the Soviet Union may also find it necessary to make some temporary concessions . . . to promote the revolutionary cause in those countries where conditions warrant it.

C) "The Communist Party, until the seizure of power, should be careful to maintain, in the countries where the revolution is being prepared, good relations with patriotic and religious circles. No discrimination should be made against the churches. . . . National tradition should be respected. Wherever necessary . . . representatives of the churches should be allowed to contribute in the preparation and carrying through of the revolution. *Their numerical strength should determine the rate at which church influence is later to be eliminated from state affairs.*

D) "The press should be used . . .

F) "Immediately after the seizure of power the Central Committee will set up a new government. This shall be representative of the broad masses of the people *and appear democratic.* . . .

G) "Opponents of the new administration . . . should be removed as soon as possible, but in democratic fashion—that is to say, be brought to trial before a regular court or a People's Court. The latter should comprise one known member of the party and two secret members or sympathizers. . . .

2. "The country should not apply for inclusion in the Soviet Union until instructions to this effect have been received from the . . . Comintern.

4. "Traitors to the party are to be liquidated without trial once their treachery has been submitted to the party organization. . . . The death penalty is prescribed for treachery of any sort against the interest of the Communist revolution.

6. "The term 'class enemy' comprises the following groups:

members of ideological movements of a nationalist or religious character, priests, members of the police force, officers, diplomats and civil servants when they refuse to side with the revolutionary forces; all members of dynasties, any individuals known to have opposed the preparation or the carrying out of the revolution.

7. *"After the party has seized power, it shall dispose of funds, separate from state funds, taken from the following sources:* property belonging to class enemies who have been liquidated, or whose possessions have been confiscated . . . ; property belonging to hostile movements and organizations; property confiscated from the churches, the ruling dynasty and war profiteers."

This is the nature of the greatest plot in the world. The Comintern's official chart for the internal betrayal and conquest of foreign nations speaks for itself. In its organized precision, duplicity, brutality and cynicism it has certainly never been exceeded by any group of political gangsters in any century; certainly never approached in its world-wide scope of projected application. Every detail of the Comintern's instructions has long since been executed in each Iron-Curtain country. The satellite nations have thereby been transformed into the Kremlin's first great foreign training ground for global domination.

But there's another notable distinction between the Nazis' frenetic, space-grabbing methods of conquest and those employed by the Reds. The Soviets do not aim merely to get more and bigger pieces of real estate—and this is where you come in.

The Communists grab people—and all the people.

No one is too small or insignificant, too young or too old, to be shackled and regimented or pauperized and destroyed. You are *It*—simply because you have two legs and walk upright. The Kremlin's assembly line treats people exactly as the Ford assembly line handles metal parts of automobiles. Once the Stalinists thoroughly enslave a nation's people they automatically get the real estate, most of the private real estate as well as the national. The Bolsheviks' master plot is focused on everyone, everywhere. It aims to possess the earth's people as well as the earth; step by step and region by region. By its all-encompassing timetable sooner or later it has to reach *you*.

This fact directly concerns the big mystery of the world's greatest plot. Why should you or I, or any citizen of a free country, imagine that we are somehow peculiarly immune? Why should we assume that the Communist slave state cannot finally engulf us? No Western peoples are more patriotic, more courageous or more staunchly individualistic than the East Europeans have proved themselves to be in scores of wars over a score of centuries. None had greater love of freedom, nor greater desire for democratic self-government, than they had as World War II ended. Nevertheless they were swallowed by a boa constrictor possessed of consummate guile and insatiable appetite. When the Soviets swallowed up 90 million people in a flicker of time they demonstrated convincingly that they know how to eat their way around the earth. They need only more time and propitious circumstance—plus the continued complacency of their prospective victims. They are exploiting time. They are experts at creating the necessary circumstances. And they have as their chief ally the blind complacency of legions of free Western citizens, wrapped in delusions of geographical immunity.

But the Russians now control one-third of the earth, more than one-third of its population, and are organizing the collective resources of some 800 million people to a formidable degree. Everywhere under their rule they are arming and militarizing people. Most intensively of all they are arming and militarizing half of Europe. They are welding the satellite armies of Eastern Europe into new instruments of very serious potential aggressive power. They are building these armies so fast that they more than counterbalance the Atlantic Pact defense forces in Western Europe in manpower; are already much more integrated, and are definitely superior in some kinds of weapons and training. So the Soviet Russian armies still stand virtually un-diminished in strength, with some 175 to 200 divisions available to them for combat in the West. The great gap between the free West's combat forces *in being* and the Soviet East's armed forces *in readiness* is barely beginning to be reduced, painfully and slowly. At this exact juncture the free nations of the West enter:

The period of greatest danger—1952 to 1954.

This is true not merely because Marshal Tito has warned that 1952 constitutes "the danger point." It is true for reasons as obvious to every Western military authority as to Yugo-slavia's war-experienced leader. Because of the Soviet-satellite coalition's temporary but grave preponderance of armed power on the ground and in the air. Because Moscow can already use, whether in combat or for other purposes, approximately three and a half million satellite men under arms. Because N.A.T.O.'s Army of Western Europe must remain seriously inferior in strength and weapons throughout 1952, and most of 1953. In short, because these years must inevitably be a period of unique aggressive temptation to the Kremlin. If the Soviets are to seize Western Europe by force, their only real chance will exist in the period which will expire late in 1953 or early in 1954.

I do not mean for a moment that war with Soviet Russia is inevitable. America's vast superiority in atomic bombs and long-range planes with which to deliver them should logically continue to be a potent deterrent, unless the men in the Kremlin are mad. America's startling progress in the perfection of tactical atomic weapons, for direct use against land armies, may eventually be able to save the world from catastrophe. Senator Brien Mc-Mahon, chairman of the Joint Congressional Committee on Atomic Energy, describes these developments as "a revolution in deterring power." But this deterring power, in terms of im-portant quantities of new weapons immediately available, lies

several years in the future. It is in this present interim that, by
recognition of our most responsible leaders, anything may happen—indeed, *may* be most likely to happen.

We can be certain of very little. But if war does come, we
can be sure that no one can now predict accurately what it
would do to all of us. We can also be sure about this. The men
in the Kremlin, so long as they live, will never again have so
much temptation to armed aggression as during the eighteen to
twenty-four months which date from the late spring of 1952.
This is the "danger point"—because this is the period when
they might most easily, or most desperately, *miscalculate* an
enormous risk. They are likewise committed to the "certain
destruction" of Yugoslavia's heretical Communist régime—the
most dangerous menace to Kremlin domination of Communist
parties in all foreign lands. The satellites' armies could be used,
à la Korea, to eliminate Titoism while Soviet Russia again
maintained a studied pose of "neutrality."

We are brought back sharply to the mounting threat of
sovietized Eastern Europe. Moscow is now in a position to
provoke another world war over Yugoslavia, to adventure in
Iran and much of Asia, to menace Western Europe with an early
blitzkrieg conquest—precisely because she has communized and
militarized the satellite nations so rapidly and to such an alarming degree. Because its hold on Eastern Europe is physically
absolute, the Kremlin is at last in position to blackmail free
Europe and the world. By consolidating Soviet rule to the western edge of the Iron Curtain the Russians are entrenched in
forward posts of inestimable strategic value. Behind these advanced lines they are mobilizing all of Eastern Europe's human
and material resources, against many obstacles, but with remarkable speed. The mobilized power of satellite Europe is the
spearhead for Moscow's ultimate employment of Soviet aggressive power. Without a sovietized, mobilized Eastern Europe the
Russians could not challenge the West or fight a war with the
West. In reality, the United States is spending at the rate of
some $70 billion or more per year for defense purposes primarily

because of what the Soviets have accomplished in the satellite countries, and of what they are now energetically pushing toward completion there.

This means that certain things are equally true for the citizens of all the Western democracies. Our common fears and uncertainties, the higher prices and ever heavier taxes we pay, the shrinkage of goods and pleasures we can afford, the gradual decrease in our standards of living—all are directly linked to Russia's progress in sovietizing Eastern Europe. We pay an extremely high financial, material and psychological price for Russia's absorption of these tragic lands. But above all the Communists' conquest of satellite Europe is *a warning to the West*.

This is how Soviet Communism infiltrates and undermines; how it betrays and contaminates; how it dominates people, governments and all forms of administrative machinery; how it enslaves and destroys people; how it organizes every aspect of society; how it perverts patriotism, family loyalty, personal integrity and morality; how it cripples minds and poisons hearts; how it harnesses all of a nation's human and material resources to the purposes of slave-state power. This is how Stalinism expands, conquers and perpetuates itself.

But exactly how do the Communists accomplish all these things?

Strangely enough, the *how* of Soviet conquest remains perhaps the least reported, certainly the least studied and least understood phenomenon of our times. It must be examined where and as the Kremlin's plotters operate—sector by sector. The place to begin is where the Communists themselves always begin—with the armed forces and the secret police, the sources of absolute power.

CHAPTER TWO

Mobilization under Wraps

THE SOVIETS CAN BOAST OF BEING THE ONLY government in modern times to mobilize hundreds of thousands of men and create the framework of powerful *surplus* armed forces without the rest of the world gaining any clear conception of what was going on. Between the outbreak of the Korean War in late June, 1950, and the close of 1951 Moscow doubled or tripled the individual puppet-state armies inside the Curtain to a combined total strength of some one and a half million men. There is probably no other instance of such a large and successful veiled mobilization as this. From relatively shoestring organizations the Kremlin's "Armies of Eastern Europe" burgeoned rapidly into threatening military realities. While General Eisenhower was painfully laying the groundwork for a "blitzproof" Army of Western Europe by 1953, they held close to a two-year head start.

But Moscow's puppet armies were also being strongly soviet-ized as they expanded. This unique combination has remained perhaps the least understood aspect of the West's rearmament race with Soviet Russia. Today the satellite armies are not only heavily staffed and directly commanded by Soviet Army officers. They have been in process of intensive reorganization, equipping and training in Russian-type divisions and cadres since late 1950. This is true of the armed forces of all six Iron-Curtain countries, and of skeletal units destined soon to emerge as Eastern Germany's Red army.

When he addressed the executive board of N.A.T.O. (the North

Atlantic Treaty Organization) in October, 1950, General Eisenhower warned that "the future of Western civilization is at
stake. . . . The threat is great and the time is short." His
forces were still extremely inadequate. They faced, he stated, a
minimum of four million men under arms in the Soviet Union
alone. In addition there were the satellites' much increased
armed forces which, another N.A.T.O. general reminded, "we
certainly have to watch." Precisely what does N.A.T.O.'s Supreme
Command have to watch?

In the other half of Europe, as of that date, the Kremlin had a
minimum of approximately three and a half million *non-Soviet*
men under arms, including more than two million in the police
and internal-security armies of the Red-ruled captive nations.
They have continued to increase in numbers since then. The
satellites' regular armed forces, as distinct from internal police,
seem certain to reach or pass the two-million mark by 1953.
At the beginning of 1952 they possessed more than 60 Soviet-
type divisions, nearly one-fourth being motorized or partially
armored. Of these somewhere between 36 and 48 divisions were
then described as fairly well armed and trained. There are additional satellite guerrilla, paratroop and cavalry brigades,
mostly well trained. In manpower alone the satellite armies
nearly counterbalanced N.A.T.O.'s Army of Western Europe in
January, 1952. But they were much ahead in supranational integration. Actually they can be incorporated into the Soviet Army
at any time by a mere order from the Kremlin.

How can one reach a reasonably reliable estimate of the satellite armies' over-all strength? The average size of each country's
military classes is definitely known by former career officers,
now in exile. Since early 1951 Bulgaria and Rumania have maintained three full age-groups in service; Rumania large parts of
two others. Poland, Hungary and Czechoslovakia each retained
two full draft classes, plus the rough equivalent of a third class or
more. With an average Polish draft group of 150,000 it is clear
that Poland's army must very considerably exceed 450,000 men.
All regular officers and large numbers of reservists called up

since Korea must be reckoned in each puppet-state army, above
the draft classes themselves.

Table I
Over-all Strength of the Satellites' Armies
(As of late 1951)

Poland	500,000
Czechoslovakia	175,000
Hungary	195,000
Rumania	350,000
Bulgaria	160,000
Albania	50,000
Total	1,430,000
Eastern Germany's "Alert" Cadres	55,000
Grand Total	1,485,000 (exclusive of air forces and naval units)

Table II
Size of Satellites' Yearly Draft Classes
(Averages as confirmed by exiled officers)

Poland	150,000	to	170,000
Czechoslovakia	50,000	to	60,000
Hungary	50,000	to	55,000
Rumania	120,000	to	145,000
Bulgaria	30,000	to	45,000
Total	400,000		475,000

Various Classes Reported in Active Service
(As of November, 1951)

Poland: Full 1929, '30 and '31 classes; parts of 1927 and '28 classes believed retained in service.

Czechoslovakia: Full 1929 and '30 classes; part of '31 class reported; large numbers of reservists called up regularly.

Hungary: Full classes of 1929 and '30; those of 1927 and '28 reported not released; great numbers of reservists called up steadily in rotation from 1910 class upward.

Rumania: Five age groups of classes of 1928, '29, '30, '31 and '32; nearly 80,000 from each reported now in service; reservists being constantly reactivated.

Bulgaria: Full 1929 and '30 classes; five classes of reservists reported called up in July, 1951; rotation of reservists to continue from 1917 class upward.

Note: Most privates as reservists are called up ostensibly for from 45 days to three months, but in several countries few have been released. Large numbers of reservist officers have been reactivated on a permanent basis.

Table III
Divisional Strength of Satellite Armies

(As indicated by consensus of underground and other information, November, 1951)

	Over-all Strength Divisions		Those Better Armed and Trained
Poland	16	(Of which 4 motorized, 2 light-armored)	12
Czechoslovakia	14	(Of which 2 or more armored)	8
Hungary	12	(Of which 2 to 4 partially armored)	8
Rumania	16	(Of which 2 motorized, at least 1 armored)	10
Bulgaria	10	(Of which 4 motorized)	8
Albania	2		2
Total	70 *	(Of which 13 divisions or more motorized or armored)	48 *

(* Average size of Soviet-type division—10,000 men)

	Other Special Units **		Guerrilla & Int'l Brigades. (Average size: 3,000 to 5,000)
Poland	3	Cavalry Brigades	2 (1 guerrilla, 1 Int'l)
Czechoslovakia	4	Artillery "	1 "
Hungary	1	Artillery "	4 "
"	1	Technical "	
Rumania	2	Mountain "	2 "

Bulgaria	3 Cavalry Brigades	4	(1 guerrilla, 1 Int'l)
"	3 Anti-Aircraft Brigades	1	" (Albanian)
Total	17 Special Brigades	3	" (Greek
			Commu-
			nists)

Total   17   Brigades.

** Although paratroopers are being intensively trained in all satellite countries, no reliable indication of their numbers has been obtainable. It appears that there must exist a number of paratroop brigades.

The total strength of satellite divisions reported (Table III) accounts for roughly 700,000 men, while over-all totals reach 1,430,000 (Table I). The reasons for this seeming discrepancy are:

1: At this writing the Russians have reorganized only part of the satellite armies into divisions. A very large part of puppet-state troops are in brigades, battalions and other smaller special formations—possibly by Moscow's preference, since they can be more easily incorporated into Soviet Army cadres. 2: The guerrilla, cavalry, paratroop and other special brigades and formations which I have cited definitely do *not* represent all those which exist in each satellite's armed forces. I have only listed those which have been identified by several sources—underground, exiled military experts, etc. 3: It is also true that the Soviets can conceal the build-up of the satellite armies much more effectively by organizing scores of units smaller than the division, which they have done. 4: Great numbers of reservists are serving for three to six months, *in rotation*. As far as can be learned up to now, they are seldom trained in permanent divisions but in whatever units are most convenient. It appears unquestionable that the rotating reservists in training in satellite armies add a combined total of several hundred thousand men to those under arms during a given year.

L. S.

The figures and factual data which I use here are also based upon hundreds of underground reports from inside the Curtain countries, from a composite of information from East European career officers in exile and similar sources. After the most careful cross-checking and an investigation covering more than a year the startling growth of captive Europe's armed forces is indisputable.† Moscow's progress toward sovietizing her puppet

† In May, 1951, a well documented survey, published in the Polish weekly *Wiadomosci* of London, placed the satellite armies' total at 1,280,000. In its June, 1951, publication Britain's Royal Institute of International Affairs concluded an independent inquiry with the statement that their total armed strength "can be safely estimated at 1,500,000." The particularly well informed Yugoslavs placed the satellites' total at 1,880,000 as of September, 1951.

auxiliary armies is equally impressive, and in some respects ominous.

These fast developing transformations of satellite military strength contrast vividly with what I observed in the Iron-Curtain countries in 1946. The Communists were then just completing or midway in their purges of career officers. The regular armies were undersized and disorganized. It seemed that much more than five years would be required before large satellite armies, capable of offensive action beside Soviet troops, could be created. But Brigadier General Cortlandt Van R. Schuyler, chief of the United States Military Mission in Bucharest, declared clairvoyantly: "The Russians' program for Rumania is to go all the way." It is true that Moscow's maximum program for expansion of the puppet-state armies is by no means realized as yet. There are still serious discrepancies in certain respects. Even so the Russians have already gone a surprisingly large part of "all the way." Their new Red auxiliaries constitute a mounting threat which commands constant consideration by the West's strategic planners.

The Kremlin's success depended on establishing *absolute control* of all armed power in the Curtain countries. It was achieved step by step.

Step One: MOSCOW'S POLITICAL-MILITARY FIFTH COLUMN

By 1945–46 m.v.d. officers and native "Muscovite" Communists had monopolized key police and government posts in Poland, Rumania, Bulgaria and Hungary. Everywhere Communists were ministers of defense and interior, controlling both the armies and police; also of national economy, information and communications. These Moscow-trained Red leaders were also Soviet citizens: Dimitrov and others in Bulgaria; Emil Bodnaras, Ana Pauker and company in Rumania; Rakosi, Zoltan Vas, Ernö Gerö in Hungary; more of the same stripe in Poland. The Kremlin's agents held all the levers of power, with Czechoslovakia later on the timetable.

Step Two: THE SOVIETS CAPTURE THE SATELLITE ARMIES

The Russians had prepared a remarkably effective military fifth column for Rumania and Poland. From war prisoners, screened in Russia, the M.V.D. formed two communized Rumanian divisions (Tudor Vladimirescu and Horia-Closca-Crisan); also the Polish First Kosciuszko Division—actually nearer an army corps—under the Polish Communist General Berling. Men from these Red élite forces replaced purged Rumanian and Polish career officers. Several thousand Russian officers, serving with Berling's Poles, were granted Polish citizenship on Moscow's demand. Thus the two largest satellite armies were taken over at the outset.

For Bulgaria and Hungary no pre-indoctrinated former prisoners existed. So local Communists, of scant military experience, were shunted into key commands. Thereafter expulsion of career officers became wholesale. More than 15,000 were reported purged in Rumania; at least 8,000 in Poland; nearly 3,000 each in Bulgaria and Hungary, while "cleansing" of Czech officers still continues.

Step Three: INFILTRATION OF SOVIET OFFICERS

Puppet armies need tight controls. The November, 1949, appointment of Soviet Marshal Rokossovsky as commander-in-chief of Poland's army and her Minister of Defense meant just that. Soviet Marshal Ivan Konev soon spent long periods in Czechoslovakia. In Budapest a mysterious, non-Hungarian Red known as "Lt. Field Marshal" Mihaly Farkas (originally named Fuchs) is Minister of Defense; the army's chief of staff, "Lt. Field Marshal" Bata, also speaks Hungarian with an accent. In Bulgaria Lt. General Peter Panchevsky, Minister of Defense, is a Moscow-trained veteran of the Spanish war. The commander-in-chief of Bulgaria's army (since August, 1951) is a General Antanasov—a Soviet citizen of Bulgarian origin. Colonel General Bodnaras, of Ukrainian descent and a long-time "Muscovite," runs Rumania's defense ministry.

Since 1948 Moscow's military fifth column has multiplied like rats in a derelict grain ship. A reliable Czech reports via the underground: "Soviet officers keep appearing in our garrisons in ever increasing numbers. Our army will soon be entirely controlled by Russians." Underground sources say that 5,000 to 10,000 Soviet officers now serve in the Polish Army; some 2,000 in Hungary's; nearly 3,000 in Bulgaria's. Knowledge of the Russian language by satellite officers, for planning and operational commands, has been obligatory since 1950. Satellite troops are increasingly required to learn Russian military terminology. Their uniforms have been changed to Soviet-type tunic blouses, with almost identical epaulets and insignia for officers.

A list of *Soviet* officers appointed by Marshal Rokossovsky to top posts in the Polish Army in mid-1951 is revealing: Chief of Staff, General Korczuk; Deputy Chief of Staff, Major General Sirocchi; Chief of Staff of Ground Forces, Major General Siennicki; Commander of Armored Forces, General Suchov; Chief of Intelligence, General Kaszinkov; Chief of Signal Corps, Major General Tychonczyk; Commander-in-Chief of Polish Air Force, Major General Kadazanowicz. The Polish names in this list were assumed to conceal Russian or other Soviet nationality.

During the 1950–51 satellite maneuvers the Soviet High Command's close supervision could not be disguised. Marshal Malinovsky repeatedly visited Poland and Czechoslovakia; Marshal Sokolovsky commuted to Rumania and Bulgaria; Marshals Vasilevsky and Budenny likewise to Rumania; Marshal Voroshilov to Hungary. The satellite armies have been fitted into the chain of Soviet command. They are integrated into overall Soviet strategy. Their general staff officers are chiefly Russians.

What Russian monopoly control of the satellite armies' major commands really means

These developments are all interrelated. They provide the mechanisms for final integration of the puppet states' armed forces with the Soviet Army and the Kremlin's military planning. To grasp how advanced this process already is one must imagine what an equivalent situation would be like in Western Europe today. There would already exist, of course, a 40- to 60-division "European Army" fully functioning, not on paper or in prospect. In every country from Norway to Portugal and Italy the governments, ministries of defense and interior would not only be ruled by Totalitarian Party Z. The "Z Army's" officers would monopolize the general staffs of all Western Europe's armed forces; would control all their top echelons; would staff thousands of operational commands. No possibility of independent military decisions or actions would exist. No opposing policies could be voiced in national parliaments. Public conformity would be assured by two million strongly armed police troops—the rear guard of the Z Army.

There would also be no multinational representation in a genuine sense, such as was true of General Eisenhower's N.A.T.O. command from the start. All of Western Europe's military forces would be tightly locked into the Z Army's rigid controls; tied into its front and rear organizations; subordinated utterly to its unique strategy. General Eisenhower was obliged to launch Western Europe's military integration at a snail's pace, by joint participation, joint discussion and eventual mutual compromise. But Moscow's "Armies of Eastern Europe" are integrated by iron-fisted compulsion. These facts indicate the dimensions of Moscow's new armed menace in Eastern Europe.

The Korean War pushed the button for Russia's all-out expansion of the satellites' armies, probably history's least visible and least known mass mobilization. I did not conceive of its actual magnitude until I had sifted through hundreds of underground reports and thousands of pages of documents based on information smuggled out of the Curtain countries since June 25, 1950. Then Moscow's secret orders, in close paraphrase, were clearly revealed by a whole series of events, much of which had been screened from public knowledge in the West. They began, quite obviously, with:

"Mobilize! Call up reservists! Build new divisions!"

Immediately after the Korean invasion the Kremlin launched its maximum program to prepare large satellite armies for possible war. In the first weeks Hungary called up reserve officers while Bulgaria summoned reservists up to the age of 45. By October the Czechs activated reservists "under every pretext," including officers over 45. Both Rumania and Poland extended their length of military service, called up two new classes, and retained parts of classes due to be released. In January, 1951, Bulgaria doubled its length of service to three years. Everywhere the closely curtained mobilizations proceeded without interruption. By July 1, 1951, four new Hungarian divisions, ordered by Moscow the previous October, were completed. Later in the year seven additional Polish divisions and four new Czech divisions were reported in formation.

What is the object of these intensive mobilizations? In his Order of the Day (November, 1950) "Lt. Field Marshal" Bata bluntly declared its goals: to inculcate Soviet military science, and to make every recruit "a convinced Communist with but one desire—to resemble the warrior of the glorious Soviet Army." That confirmed another Kremlin command:

"Indoctrinate by Soviet saturation methods!"

Unlike Western armies' organization, the Communists' military system concentrates emphatically upon killing two birds with one stone. *The Soviets' first objective is to make convinced Communists while making capable soldiers.* Communize them as you militarize them! It's all one process. This explains why Soviet-style political commissars have played a major role in all satellite armed forces from the outset. On October 1, 1950, special officers' indoctrination schools and "evening courses" were inaugurated in Poland, Czechoslovakia, etc. Even satellite generals and staff officers attend four-hour courses twice a week, study Stalin's *History of the Bolshevik Party*, write political essays and must pass *written* examinations.

Soviet ideologists rightly show deepest concern over Eastern Europe's peculiarly resistant peasant soldiers. They are subjected to four hours per week of Marxist lectures by the so-called "cultural and information officers"; to seminars with party leaders; obligatory subscriptions to Communist newspapers; group readings of party publications; propaganda films and other "opinion molders." The Polish Army's daily shriek, *The Soldier of Freedom*, stresses that the duty of party cells (existing in every military unit) is "to train soldiers to be Communists." It demands ceaseless vigilance of every man in uniform "as long as the class enemy exists. . . . That means to hasten the extermination of the imperialists."

Yet despite these pressures and the risk of death sentences hundreds of Hungarians, Rumanians and Bulgarians have fled their armies into Yugoslavia; Poles and Czechs into Western Germany. Here are direct-quote reasons which they give for deserting: "My parents are half-starving since they collectivized the land. . . . They arrested my brother. . . . My father is doing forced labor. . . . They took our horse and cows. . . . Why should I fight for them?"

To re-enforce the communizing process, during their first year's service recruits get no leaves, for whenever they see their embittered families, hounded by quotas and work credits, the peasant soldiers' natural antagonism to Communism is inevitably inflamed.

Today's satellite soldiers, in great majority, are far from being "politically reliable" also because they have had but a few years of Red schooling. For the same reason their family and religious loyalties are less undermined. As a result Moscow must fear to trust a large proportion of personnel in the puppet states' armed forces for several more years. But the Stalinists are focusing their ideological pressures especially upon some ten million youths, male and female, from age ten to 18. An exiled

Hungarian leader warns: "By 1954 age groups will enter the army who have had nearly ten years of Communist indoctrination. By then I estimate that Hungary's army will be a reliable Communist army, willing to fight and die for the Kremlin. We would commit a grave folly if we failed to recognize this prospect now."

Another order from the Kremlin concerns a related aspect of sovietization:

"Reorganize the armies into Soviet-type divisions!"

The Soviet Army's structural pattern is being universally imposed. Satellite divisions are everywhere in various stages of realignment to the Soviet model, aimed at establishing similar proportions of combat infantry, artillery, anti-aircraft and other units. Much unevenness probably still exists. But this standardization process should have progressed notably when it enters its third year during 1953. Already satellite divisions closely approximate the Soviet division's peacetime strength, averaging between 8,000 and 11,000 men. Already uniformity of organization, by Red Army pattern, increasingly improves co-ordination in all commands, in training, supply and the like. This gives the Soviet-satellite armies an important advantage over the West's armed forces. As Drew Middleton points out, N.A.T.O.'s Supreme Command "faces the prospect of faulty tactical co-ordination because of the differences in organization between United States, British and French divisions." *

The Russians significantly introduced a similar reorganization of East Germany's "People's Police" early in 1951. Their military *Bereitschaften*, or "Alert Units," were reformed into 24 combat cadres. Newly armed with Soviet T-34 tanks and artillery, the cadres participated with Soviet forces in spring maneuvers. Each combat cadre, originally of 2,000 men, is reportedly scheduled to be doubled. They provide the hard core for a future

* *The New York Times*, June 13, 1951.

East German Army of 24 divisions, or some 250,000 men. Along with these purposeful military reforms came another Moscow command:

"Train satellite troops in Soviet techniques!"

In tactical operations the Red Army employs many highly specialized methods. I learned this as a war correspondent with the Finns in 1939–40 and with the Russians on their central front in 1942. Many German generals who fought in Russia have since verified where and how the Soviet Army fights with greatest effectiveness and skill. These specialties are notably stressed in current training of satellite troops. Basic training manuals for both officers and men are virtually direct translations from the Soviet manuals.

Experienced Russian combat officers direct or supervise most training of puppet-state units. Tactics which the Russians used most tellingly against Hitler's *Wehrmacht* have top priority. These include exceptionally heavy concentrations of artillery with infantry; the launching of multiple or "storm-wave" attacks—as by North Korea's Reds. Rigid high command controls are maintained in traditional Soviet Army fashion—an inflexibility which often proved excessively costly to Soviet operations in the last war. Another dubious practice—interference by political commissars—is described as "characteristic" in some satellite armies. This will probably continue because of justified Communist distrust of many officers' and most soldiers' reliability. But where Soviet tactics excel they excel most dangerously.

In camouflage: Of the seven different national armies with which I served as a correspondent in World War II none, except the Finnish, could rival the Russians in the arts of concealment and ambush. All Western armies were decidedly inferior. The Germans contracted a deadly fear of Russian ruses. The same Indian-style exploitation of terrain and subterfuge are now taught the satellites' combat forces. The Soviets also extract the maximum from peasant soldiers' extraordinary endurance. East Europeans are being hardened by twenty-mile "alarm marches" at night; by Soviet-Army-style "bad weather" operations and infiltrations.

Guerrilla warfare: In all Communist armies this is a highly developed successful military instrument. Fourteen satellite guerrilla brigades were reported as of January, 1951. Eleven belong—significantly—to Yugoslavia's neighbor states; four each to Hungary and Bulgaria; two to Rumania; one to Albania. About 32,000 anti-Tito Yugoslavs, thoroughly trained in Russia, were reported to be in Hungary a few months later. Several Greek Communist brigades also exist. By September, 1951, several international partisan brigades participated in Hungary's biggest postwar maneuvers. Moscow obviously plans to employ guerrilla tactics very extensively in event of war. Satellite units can be used with paratroops behind enemy lines for commando operations and for the toughest harassing activities. They are highly communized shock brigades, of unique value in offensive warfare and a choice Soviet instrument against enemy communications.

Abnormal amounts of artillery: Stalin strenuously applies his oft-quoted maxim, "Artillery is the god of war." The Soviet Army employed more guns, more profligately, in the late war than any army on record. The Russians sometimes used as many as 400 or 500 guns on one mile of vital front. Former Soviet officers, now in the West, place artillery as 35 to 40 per cent of Red Army combat strength. This obsession with massed firepower is being transferred to all satellite armies. Their artillery reservists have been called up in great numbers. A recent report fixes artillery at about 25 per cent of the Hungarian Army's combat strength. The Soviets form entirely separate artillery divisions or brigades, as well as unprecedentedly heavy proportions with infantry divisions wherever possible. This eventual goal appears much short of realization in the puppet-state armies as yet. But a steady build-up toward it is unquestionable. It is related to Moscow's further command:

"Standardize satellite weapons!"

Up to mid-summer, 1950, Eastern Europe's nations, especially the Hungarians, Rumanians and Bulgarians, got along chiefly with weapons left over from World War II. These were confusing mixtures of German, Czech, Italian and French arms. But lack of uniformity in weapons caused numerous complications during the first joint Soviet-satellite maneuvers. So the Kremlin abandoned its previous marked antipathy to equipping the "colonial" troops with Soviet arms on a large scale.

Large shipments of Russian tanks, artillery, mortars and other matériel have flowed steadily into the puppet states since Korea. Underground reports confirm this graphically. From Bulgaria (October, 1950): "Enormous quantities of Soviet arms have arrived over the past several months. By ship to the ports of Burgas and Stalin (Varna); also to Rushchuk on the Danube." From Hungary (in November): "Very heavy traffic in Soviet military freight trains. Especially tanks and artillery." From Poland (in December): "During the past week 400 T-34 tanks were shipped to Czechoslovakia; 800 more to Hungary and Rumania. More tank shipments are being directed south and west. A small number of 57-ton Stalin III tanks is reported sent to Hungary." From Poland (March, 1951): "Tanks distributed sufficient for training three Polish armored divisions, but none are yet fully armed." From Hungary (in April): "War matériel for complete equipment of ten divisions has arrived from Russia. It passed through Csap where weapons, ammunition, uniforms and trucks were transferred from wide-gauge Soviet trains." (It is interesting that two Hungarian officers, who escaped in July, 1951, estimated that Hungary must then have "nearly ten tank divisions, at full strength." Their testimony was so surprising it seemed to merit being treated with reservations. Yet Russia may well possess tens of thousands of excess tanks. She is in a position to startle the world by the magnitude of her build-up of satellite armored forces.)

One fact is most thought-provoking. *Russia obviously now possesses such huge amounts of tanks, artillery and other arms as to be able to push forward a program for equipping six satellite armies, plus the East Germans.* Even so, it appears that the demonstrably heavy arms shipments up to now do not yet begin to fill the requirements. Meanwhile, however, more and more satellite divisions are being mechanized or armored. Sufficient arms have been supplied to facilitate enormously the stepped-up training of satellite troops. That accounts for another post-Korea order:

"Build a Stalinist élite of satellite officers!"

Here the Kremlin is up against a major weakness of today's puppet-state armies. Despite many thousands of Russian officers in their upper commands, they still suffer from an acute shortage of native officers and noncoms who are both militarily efficient and dependably communized. This may prove to be the Achilles heel of the satellite armies' efficient development for a considerable time. Even though they remain highly suspect politically, thousands of once-purged Eastern European reserve officers have been reinstated to meet this emergency. Nearly half of Rumania's dismissed career officers are reported back in service. The Reds had no immediate alternative. Constantly enlarged armies require thousands of additional officers. But the Russians have also inaugurated a much more practical, long-range answer to the problem.

Several thousand satellite officers, from lieutenant-colonels down to noncoms, completed courses in Soviet military academies during 1951. Thousands more are now attending them under a rotation system. Underground sources report that 2,000 Poles were sent to Russia in this period; 1,500 Bulgarians (making a reputed total of 9,000 Bulgarians so dispatched); and 4,500 Czechs. In July, 1951, a large group of Hungarian officers, from generals to lieutenant-colonels, returned from a staff officers' school in Leningrad. Other Soviet military schools in the Moscow and Kiev regions operate for specific satellite nationalities.

Courses last from six to nine months. "Ideological and military
re-education" is their announced purpose. Eastern Germany's
"Alert Units" are now being trained by 150 German officer
graduates of Russian academies. On August 1, 1951, a satellite
staff officers' school was opened in Moscow. It is reported to
be operated by the G.U.K. (Command of Cadres of the Soviet
Army), under Marshal Govorov. Its three-month courses mark
another step toward standardized training of top-level Comin-
form-nation officers in the Soviet pattern.

No less than 3,000 young Rumanians, trained in Russia for
two years or more, returned in June, 1951. They were assigned
immediately to army units as officers, replacing career officers
who were dismissed for the second time. These communized
new officers are described as intended to form "the backbone of
the new Rumanian Army." This is how an élite corps of Soviet-
schooled, Red-indoctrinated satellite officers is being created. By
1953 or 1954 the puppet-state armies may be notably strength-
ened, both ideologically and professionally, by more than 20,000
Red Army graduates. But Moscow's need of completely reliable
medium and junior officers in the "colonial" armed forces is so
great it probably can only be filled over a period of several years.
This may explain why the Kremlin continues to rely predominantly on its own Soviet Army units throughout Eastern Europe,
dictating the order:

"Build special stockpiles for the Soviet Army!"

From Poland down to Bulgaria the Russians have established
scores of separate supply bases, designed to support heavy
Soviet re-enforcements at any time. Huge shipments of arms,
spare parts, trucks and uniforms are delivered to strategically
placed depots for the Red Army. These so-called "Voy-Mags"
are always strongly guarded by security troops, commanded by
Soviet M.G.B. officers (foreign branch of the M.V.D.). In Hungary
a dozen or more major Russian supply bases have been greatly
enlarged since Korea. Similar depots, holding fuel and food as

well as weapons, are dispersed across Poland, Czechoslovakia, Rumania and Bulgaria. In regard to extensive Soviet depots at Burgas, Stalin and Rushchuk, a Bulgarian informant reports: "The large size and steady increase of Soviet shipments seems a sure indication that they cannot be meant exclusively for a campaign against Yugoslavia. Much recent equipment is new and comes direct from Soviet factories."

Another fact demands forceful emphasis. *The Russians in Eastern Europe are perilously far ahead of our Western coalition in modernized air bases.* For the dangerous years 1952–53 the Soviets not only outnumber the combined Western Air Forces in operational planes by a very serious margin; since Korea they have constructed literally scores of new air fields behind the entire length of the Iron Curtain—more modernized and expanded fields in Poland or Hungary alone than may be operating in France by 1953. In any early conflict it appears quite possible that the Soviets might be able to put ten or twenty Red planes, predominantly jets, into the air for every Western plane—for lack of Western facilities as well as combat planes.

The Soviets have only started to build up the satellite air forces since 1950. Their commanders and staffs are chiefly Russians. Red Air Force men have appeared in large numbers in the captive nations. But for the first time satellite pilots are being trained in considerable and increasing numbers. Their fuel supply is strictly limited so they cannot fly West. But satellite air forces have already received at least several hundred Russian jets and medium-sized bombers. Even during 1950 Poland is stated to have obtained about 100 in these categories.* Training of Polish fighter pilots was tripled in the first months after Soviet General Torkil became chief of Poland's air force in the spring of 1951. The build-up in Hungary and Czechoslovakia is also impressive.

Throughout Eastern Europe the Russians have constructed scores of new air bases and scores of troop barracks. They are

---

* See "One World For Stalin," by Cmmdr. William T. Greenhalgh, U.S.N. *The Reserve Officer* magazine: September 1951.

continuing at this tempo. Building seems scarcely able to keep
pace with the expanding armed forces. A new Soviet base at
Miskolc in northeastern Hungary is exceptionally important.
After more than a year thousands of slave laborers remained
actively at work. Miskolc is the Russians' main transportation
and supply-distribution center for all of central Europe. Some
reports say it may become the Soviet Army's general headquarters for this vital region. It has unusual four-way communications: directly from Russia through the Carpathians and with
Poland, Czechoslovakia and Rumania.

Close by Miskolc, recently taken over by the M.V.D. as mid-
European headquarters, is the super-plush prewar pleasure resort
of Lillafured. The Miskolc and adjacent Trans-Carpathian-
Ruthenian region is rapidly becoming the Soviet Army's key hub
for military operations and controls throughout the entire mid-
Danubian area. Hungary seems in process of development into
Russia's great forward bastion between Poland and Bulgaria.
An earlier Kremlin order has already been fulfilled to a remark-
able degree:

"Tie Eastern Europe strategically to Soviet Russia!"

One must consult a map to see how the Russians have transformed the strategic communications of Eastern Europe since
1946, and how their more ambitious plans are being pushed forward. By constantly expanding rail and highway networks they
have linked Eastern Europe's countries far more tightly to
Russia than ever before. For military purposes this revolutionary
development is of enormous consequence—especially because of
the progressive extension of Russian broad-gauge railroad lines
into all satellite countries, toward the heart of Europe. It has
already profoundly altered the strategic realities and war-waging
possibilities in half of Europe.

For the first time Moscow now has Russian-style, broad-gauge
rail lines running directly from White Russia and the Ukraine
across Poland—into Czechoslovakia—into Hungary—across most of

northern Rumania—across southeastern Rumania into Bulgaria. This is indeed a revolutionary transformation of immense portent; a Soviet rail-line invasion of Europe, apparently scheduled to be pushed as far westward as Iron-Curtain limits will permit.

The key to the Kremlin's momentous communications offensive is Carpathian Ruthenia, better designated as Trans-Carpathia. It used to be the eastward-thrusting tail of Czechoslovakia, stretching across the Carpathians toward the Ukraine. In 1945 Moscow forced the Czech government to cede Trans-Carpathia to the u.s.s.r. That gave the Soviet Army the westward slopes of the Carpathians—a Russian bridgehead assuring the Soviets of military domination of all Central Europe. What the Kremlin's big brass had in mind is now confirmed by Soviet actions. A close look at the drastically altered railroad maps of this whole region tells the story. (See end paper map)

Three railroad lines from new Soviet territory, formerly Polish, pass through the Tartar, Verec and Uzhoc passes of the Trans-Carpathian mountains. Since 1947–48 all have been changed from standard European to Russian broad-gauge tracks.

1) Take the line which runs from Lwow through the mountains to Mukachevo and to Csap, now the Russian border town opposite Zahony in Hungary. The Soviets have extended this new broad-gauge line from Csap to Miskolc, their big army base in Hungary. From Csap, during 1951, they were also broad-gauging another line southward through Debrecen and Bekescaba toward Szeged, main military headquarters in southern Hungary. This means that *the Soviets will soon be able to deliver both arms and troops, on Russian trains, directly from the interior of the Soviet Union to deep inside Hungary—within a short distance of Yugoslavia's frontiers.* Nothing like this has been possible before. Hitler never undertook anything like it.

2) From Soviet-annexed Stanislawow (formerly Polish) Russian engineers, early in 1952, had nearly completed the final broad-gauge sections of a second Trans-Carpathian line. It runs down through Jasinja, on the Czech-Polish border, to Sighet and Baia-Mare in Rumanian Transylvania and is Russianized that far at least. By the time these words reach print it should be completed through Dej to Cluj—a key junction on the Bucharest-Budapest line. Broad-gauging from Cluj into Budapest is a logical future step.

3) But the Russians, by late 1951, were believed to have completed an entirely new rail line through the Carpathians, equally of primary military value. This route is a direct link from Russia's southern Ukraine through the Rumanian city of Jassy near that border across Transylvania to Dej and Cluj. The western three-quarters was reported completed early in 1951 eastward through the mountains to Gura Humorului. By-passing Bucharest far to the south, Russian military traffic to central Europe will be shortened by fifteen to thirty hours or more.

4) The Soviets already have two main lines Russian-gauged virtually across Poland. The first runs from Brest-Litovsk southwesterly through Deblin and Kielce to Wroclaw (formerly Breslau). The second runs from Brest-Litovsk straight west through Warsaw and Poznan. The final section into Frankfurt-on-the-Oder in Eastern Germany was reported nearly finished late in 1951.

5) Simultaneously the Czech underground indicated that the rail line from Uzhorod in Soviet Trans-Carpathia was being Russianized through Presov and Zilina to Prague. Another link-up from the Czech-Soviet border station of Cierna pri Cope to Kosice in eastern Slovakia was said to be nearing completion.

6) A southern Ukraine-to-Bulgaria line of great strategic use was virtually finished during 1951. From Soviet Bessarabia the new broad gauge crosses the top of the Danube delta to Tulcea, by pontoon bridge or ferry. It parallels the Black Sea coast, through Babdag and Medgigia to connect with Varna in Bulgaria. This is the first direct, through rail route from Russia's Ukraine into Bulgaria. In that country itself five new branch or cut-off lines have been built; four more are known to be under construction—two leading to the Turkish and Greek borders.

7) Another Rumanian broad-gauge railroad of great importance now carries oil directly from Ploesti's fields through Buzau and Braila to the Soviet border at Galati. In addition all Rumanian railroads have been changed over to the Russians' red-and-orange signal system.

Russia's new military highways in Eastern Europe

One of the latest, designed to connect Slovakia with the u.s.s.r., will be called "The Highway of Friendship and Peace." But there are dozens of other military highways already completed, or nearly so. All roads in Hungary's Miskolc region linking it with Soviet Trans-Carpathia have been rebuilt. This network is said to have occupied 10,000 slave laborers for many months. All satellite arteries leading toward Yugoslavia—such as the Budapest-Mohacs highway—have been modernized. In Bulgaria alone at least six new military roads have been constructed leading to the Yugoslav, Greek and Turkish frontiers. Bulgaria's heaviest fortifications, called the Christo Botev line, parallel the Turkish border. New supply roads link this region to Burgas, Plovdiv and Stara Zagora.

Since 1946 the Russians have constructed heavy fortifications along the entire Baltic coast, near Constanta on the Black Sea and around Bulgaria's ports. V-2 and V-3 rocket sites exist along the Baltic; others have been reported during 1951 on the western slopes of Hungary's Vertes mountains and in her Bakony forests. An expelled Italian engineer states that a submarine base at Tulcea, completed in 1950, accommodates 25 small submersibles. Soviet engineers have also constructed a submarine-mounting base at Sozopol, Bulgaria.

The Kremlin's strategic integration of Eastern Europe must be expected to continue unslackened for an indeterminate number of years. But the whole of Eastern Europe is already bound to Russia by communications arteries as never before. The new map of the Red-ruled half of Europe is predominantly and increasingly a war-purpose map.

The Soviets' wholesale mobilizing and militarizing of the Iron-Curtain countries compels a reassessment of the urgency and magnitude of the tasks confronting the Alantic Pact's defense forces in Western Europe. They demonstrate convincingly that Western publics, beginning with Americans, must understand the necessity of greater, more persistent and long-term efforts. For although the Red puppet-state armies are still handicapped by certain serious weaknesses and limitations, they are nevertheless gaining formidable dimensions and increasingly dangerous potentialities. They will certainly become more so with every year.

Moscow's "Armies of Eastern Europe" hold definite and marked advantages over the N.A.T.O. Army, and may retain most of them in important degrees for several years.

1) The satellites' armed forces constitute the largest, most thoroughly *internationalized* army ever created.

2) They are held together by a common indoctrination system, bound to become more effective year by year.

3) They are the only international armed forces with one common language (Russian) for operational commands.

4) Their general staffs and strategic plans are entirely controlled by one sovereign, master army—a monopoly which no single Western army could exercise over its allies.

5) Their uniform Soviet-type divisions and cadres are already formed; in structural integration they are far in advance of the heterogeneous N.A.T.O. Army.

6) Normal nationality barriers, which harass N.A.T.O.'s Supreme Command at every turn, are largely eliminated through the Communists' rigid controls.

But how effective are the satellite armies for combat purposes, as of today?

I have not found any exiled East European officers who would presume to essay the relative fire-power of an average satellite division with that of a United States, a French or a Russian division. No one this side of the Curtain knows exactly how much specific arms equipment most satellite divisions have now, nor exactly what proportion of each puppet-state army is well-trained or fairly so. All satellite armies are *in process* of being supplied with standardized weapons, of being trained in Soviet methods; and both processes increase from month to month.

Nevertheless, certain known facts and factors permit a broader but still useful evaluation. First, the hard core of the present satellite armies consists of those units which are best armed and better trained. They include between 36 and 48 divisions, now from two to three years old; they also include from 20 to 30 guerrilla, paratroop, artillery and cavalry brigades. It appears that most of these could be used in any war emergency.

Second, informed military specialists are unanimous in the conviction that the "hard core" satellite divisions of 1952 rank below the average Soviet divisions, or the best Western divisions, in all-around equipment and training. Where each infantry division has one artillery regiment, it is predominantly horse-drawn. Most satellite infantry divisions still had considerably less artillery than a Russian division, and were correspondingly less advanced in gunfire training.

An acute shortage of motor transport also afflicts every satellite army. The total of both military and civilian vehicles available for army purposes in Bulgaria, Rumania and Hungary is placed at about 10,000 each; only some 40,000 in Poland; perhaps 65,000 in Czechoslovakia. The pronounced lack of professionally schooled officers has greatly retarded mass production of well-trained divisions. But a fair number of élite units in each puppet state cannot be discounted. Bulgaria's army is generally regarded as the most developed, with Poland's next.

A prudent estimate of the satellite armies' current effectiveness must conclude that about half of their approximately 70 divisions may compare rather favorably in training with the 1952 average division in most Western European armies. Special guerrilla and some other units may rate definitely high. But what the over-all satellite armed forces still lack in arms, armor, firepower and training they will assuredly get a great deal of during the next two or three years.

Former career officers from Eastern Europe warn strongly against underestimating the present capacities of the captive states' armies. Their lacks and disabilities will be steadily reduced. These informed career officers insist it would be dangerously unsound to assume that few, if any, satellite divisions could be counted on to fight well under Russian command. That would depend primarily on where and how they were used. It is the general practice of Western officers also to estimate the probable performance of troops according to the circumstances and conditions under which they are used.

Hitler proved decisively what the conqueror's bandwagon means and accomplishes. Many Rumanian divisions, totaling several hundred thousand men, fought hard and well in Russia—so long as the Germans were winning. Thus, exiled officers draw a well-justified distinction. If the Soviet Army were to drive swiftly and triumphantly to Europe's Atlantic and Channel coast, we must expect that many East European divisions would fight very well alongside the Russians. But should Soviet forces be checked and then smashed backward, the reliable support of many satellite troops would certainly dissolve, quickly perhaps; in the end, extensively. There is also the very pertinent matter of:

The Soviets' "sandwich tactic," and why satellite divisions can be forced to fight effectively beside Russian troops.

Why should many puppet-state units fight strongly as Moscow's allies under almost any circumstances? Highly communized élite formations and shock brigades will unquestionably do so. Fanatically Communist, Soviet-trained North Koreans have proved this—to the extent of dying in battle by hundreds of thousands. Satellite élite divisions and brigades have been getting the same intense training and indoctrinal adrenalin for a long time now—and they consist of nationalities with far greater fighting traditions. These are still definitely a minority, but not an inconsequential one. We should be willfully blind if we underrated their possible contribution. But we must also consider another serious possibility.

Could the Russians use many satellite troops in such a way that they would have no alternative except to fight well? The fact that Eastern Europe's armies are now organized into Soviet-type divisions permits the Soviet High Command to "sandwich" satellite units between Red Army divisions or to incorporate them into Soviet Army Corps. They are being prepared to be used in such fashion, even to familiarity with operational commands in Russian, and increasingly by the soldiers' obligatory study of Russian. The satellite forces' training is also entirely tactical and not designed for large, independent operations.

How does the Soviet "sandwich tactic" work? Consider the troop dispositions near the Hungarian-Yugoslav border. Near the frontier, Magyar troops—behind them, Soviet M.V.D. troops and armored units. Behind these, Soviet paratroops in Hungarian uniforms. In an attack Russian paratroops would be dropped *ahead of the Hungarians—who would then have Soviet combat forces both in front of and behind them.* What soldier, caught in this juxtaposition, could refuse to fight? Moscow's solution for the better trained satellite combat cadres is simple: "Put them where they *have* to fight!"

The exact effectiveness of satellite divisions today, taking them as armies, is of much less importance than the fact that their better trained divisions could, right now, be used successfully. Up to early 1952 the puppet-state ground forces had also received at least 2,000—perhaps up to 3,500—Soviet tanks since Korea. Presumably, with 270 tanks per division, they may have some 10 to 15 armored or partially armored divisions with fair standards of competence.*

Aside from better trained élite units, guerrilla brigades, etc., there remain hundreds of thousands of satellite troops which may be used as forces of occupation. Many exiles anticipate that less reliable "colonials" of one nationality may be dispatched to another puppet state, to China or elsewhere. . . ."If they wanted to quit, they'd still have to fight their way home," says a former Polish general. "Never forget this. *The Soviets always intermix nationalities*, especially in foreign lands."

* As of spring, 1952.

What do maps of Soviet Central Asia, printed with Polish place names, foreshadow?

A certain proportion of every satellite army consists of soldiers and many officers whom the Russian Communists still deeply distrust. Such troops will never be used in or near combat zones, unless in a great emergency. This is particularly true of great numbers of fiercely patriotic Poles whom the Soviets both hate and fear. With this in mind consider the personal experience of a Polish soldier who escaped to Vienna in March, 1951.

Because he spoke Russian his Polish colonel ordered him to translate Russian place names on a map into Polish. Very curiously, it was a map of Kazakhistan in Central Asia. The soldier got suspicious. He soon found other Poles similarly engaged in the cartographic section, putting Polish place names on maps of the Soviet Turkmen, Kirghiz, Uzbek and Tadzhik republics. These maps were ordered to be mass produced for Polish Army Headquarters. The Polish soldier deserted fast.

The maps in preparation covered the entire region from the eastern shores of the Caspian Sea to the borders of Chinese Sinkiang. To the Kremlin the remote heart of South-Central Asia evidently seems a safe place in which to use hundreds of thousands of recalcitrant Poles as internal troops of occupation. Polish exiles have long insisted that a large portion of their country's "captive army" will be sent to mid-Asia or the Far East in event of war. This is an old czarist and Russian custom. The Soviets have proved themselves intensely Russian. (Perhaps we might prudently ask ourselves, at frequent intervals in the course of these chapters: Who is showing the greatest foresight and the shrewdest, long-term planning in extraordinary detail— the Western democratic governments or the Soviet Russians?)

Half a million or more "not-too-reliable" East European troops, garrisoned in Soviet Asia, would release as many well-indoctrinated Soviet soldiers for combat in Europe, Iran and the Middle East or elsewhere. A second-rate Hungarian division would cause no trouble in Tomsk or Irkutsk and by policing the region it would contribute a tough native division to some Soviet front.

The satellites' internal-security troops, as yet even larger than their regular armies, re-enforce Moscow's hold on Eastern Europe in another way. The Russians do not have to weaken their combat forces for rear-area policing and guarding of communications. The security troops—intensely Communist secret-police terrorists—are supremely equipped for this ruthless job. But if war comes—given the 25 to 35 per cent Communist-voting populations in France and Italy—N.A.T.O.'s high command would have to divert many combat divisions for rear security purposes. Moscow has entirely separate satellite rear-guard armies totaling approximately two million men—about as many as all the N.A.T.O. troops General Eisenhower had available early in 1952. The regular satellite armies, for one use or another, *constitute a complete surplus military asset for the Kremlin.* They appear to come close to counter-balancing much or most of what the democracies' Army of Western Europe may be able to achieve by well into 1953. Even if they were only capable of off-setting half of the N.A.T.O. Army's combat capacities, they would still be a formidable Soviet asset.

It is still hearteningly true that the West possesses great atomic and enormous arms-production superiority over Russia and her satellites—if and when exploited to the utmost, and that the Western soldier greatly excels the Soviet or satellite soldier in average education, in technical skills, in adaptability to modern weapons and initiative. It is possible that the peace of the world may finally be saved chiefly through America's new atomic weapons for tactical use. Eventually they may be capable of nullifying, largely or completely, Moscow's present great superiority in Soviet-plus-satellite armed manpower; in tanks, artillery and air bases. Eventually the Soviets may prove to have created the most gigantic, semi-obsolete armies in recorded military experience. But the atomic artillery, atomic rockets and other revolutionary weapons which *might possibly* reduce large portions of the Russian-commanded armies to relative futility cannot be produced in the necessary large quantities before 1954 or 1955.

Secretary of Defense Robert A. Lovett felt constrained to warn on September 25, 1951, that no magic way of winning wars was yet at hand. He cautioned especially against "the exaggerated impression" that a "quick, easy and inexpensive security" could be attained in the near future. Throughout this near future—whether of two or three years or somewhat longer—the free Western peoples will remain confronted with Soviet Russia's steadily growing armed might plus the steadily mounting armed might of Kremlin-mobilized Eastern Europe.

The facts here reported about the satellite armies have been generally unknown to Western publics, or complacently underestimated by them, for a dangerously long time. They constitute a powerful and increasing threat to the freedom of all democratic nations and peoples. But they also constitute an initial revelation of how the Communists conquer, subjugate and control entire nations; of how Soviet imperialism is forging the weapons, organizations and techniques by which its leaders are convinced the world can be communized. Finally, they reveal and confirm the Red imperialists' reliance upon armed force, and a monopoly of armed force.

That Red monoply depends, first of all, upon the Soviets' export into foreign countries of their secret-police system and armies. What the Kremlin's exported M.V.D. system has done and is doing to the peoples of Eastern Europe demands a much more detailed examination than most Western citizens have yet given it. For this is where and how Communist conquest really begins and consolidates itself.

CHAPTER THREE

Secret Police or How the Communists Control Everybody

A "DISPLACED" BUDAPEST BANKER ORDERED coffee at his favorite café and started a friendly conversation with the waiter, an old acquaintance. The waiter glanced carefully around, then murmured, "Please, sir. Don't talk these days with *any* waiter!" Three waiters in Bucharest's most popular restaurants have won rather startling promotions. One emerged as a colonel, the other two as majors in the M.I.A.—Rumania's equivalent of Russia's dreaded M.V.D. Throughout satellite Europe today every waiter is compelled to serve as an agent of the secret police. He must make nightly reports of "useful information"; otherwise he loses his job.

A Prague S.N.B. officer told a meeting of Czech customs inspectors in July, 1950, that they must show their loyalty by denouncing "at least one enemy of the state each month." By January, 1951, under the slogan of "more denunciations to help world peace," each customs official was ordered to boost his denunciations to three persons per month. Failure to conform would be considered "lack of vigilance." Customs inspectors also have to eat.

Russia's Europe is infested with police spies. Hotel employees. apartment-house managers, janitors, mailmen, railroad conductors and countless others are forced to act as informers for Soviet-type secret-police organizations. Even at the risk of sounding like a circus blurb-writer, it is sober fact to state that the Soviet Communists possess the greatest, as well as the most barbaric, police system the world has ever known. It controls, watches and intimidates all persons living between Kamchatka's and Vladivostok's Pacific coast and Berlin and Vienna. It also controls much of Manchuria and unknown portions of China, directly or indirectly. No other single police-terror organization has ever dominated such a vast area of the earth, nor such a huge total of human beings. This is Terror, Torture & Murder, Incorporated—reaching one-third of the way around the world.

The Stalinist police system was Moscow's first, top-priority export into the Iron-Curtain countries. It has now been installed and consolidated in every city, town and village.* It penetrates every nook of daily occupation, every cranny of human activity or entertainment. No conquered nations have ever been so utterly and inescapably police controlled as the so-called "liberated people's democracies." The Kremlin's M.V.D. network reduces Hitler's murderous Gestapo to a second-rate status by a wide margin. It is much more all-embracing, more tightly organized.

The Security Police and other Internal Armed Forces in the Six Satellite Nations, plus Eastern Germany

(Based on underground reports and a consensus of other data and estimates, as of 1951)

Poland (approximate combined strength):	565,000
Czechoslovakia " " "	391,000
Hungary " " " (probably low)	115,000
Rumania " " "	447,000
Bulgaria " " "	198,000
Albania (estimated total):	50,000
Eastern Germany (estimated total): at least	400,000
Over-all approximate total:	2,166,000

* The town of Hlucin in Moravia, Czechoslovakia, has about 5,000 inhabitants. Before World War II Hlucin's normal police staff consisted of five policemen. Today the town has two s.n.b. police stations, manned by 30 police. In addition militiamen frequently patrol the town. The total of Communist secret agents in Hlucin and vicinity is unknown.

Breakdown of Satellites' Security Police and other Internal Armed Forces

(Based on 1951 reports and estimates)

	Minimum	
Poland		
Security Police (U.B.)	250,000	
Internal Security Corps (K.B.W.)	100,000	
People's Militia (M.O.)	150,000	
Frontier Guards	50,000	
Railroad Guards	15,000	
	565,000	565,000
Czechoslovakia		
Security Police (S.N.B.)	125,000	
Internal Security Corps (S.T.B.)	100,000	
People's Militia (L.M. & R.M.)	150,000	
Border Guards	12,000	
Railroad Guards	4,000	
	391,000	391,000
Hungary		
Security Police (A.V.O.)	100,000	
Workers' Militia	?	
Frontier Guards	10,000	
Railroad Guards	5,000	
	115,000	115,000
Rumania		
Security Police (M.I.A.)	160,000	
Internal Security Units (P.A.Z.A.)	60,000	
Workers' Militia (G.M.)	180,000	
Frontier Guards	35,000	
Railroad Guards	12,000	
	447,000	447,000
Bulgaria		
Security Police	80,000	
Motorized Militia & Cavalry Units	12,000	
Communist Armed Cadres	30,000	
Workers' Brigades	35,000	
Frontier Guards	35,000	
Political Commissars' Corps	4,000	
Railroad Guards	2,000	
	198,000	198,000
Albania		
Estimated total of all Internal Forces	50,000	50,000
Eastern Germany		
Estimated minimum of all Internal Forces	400,000	400,000
Over-all Approximate Total of Satellite Security Police and Internal Forces		2,166,000

The Stalinists have five major and separate police-control organizations in every satellite country in addition to many subsidiary "special services."

1) *The Security Police*, identical with the Soviets' M.V.D., are both highly political secret agents and the specialists in mass arrests, purges, interrogations, torture and executions. Their alphabetical designations are the U.B. (in Poland), the S.N.B. (Czechoslovakia), the A.V.O. (Hungary), the M.I.A. (Rumania), etc.

2) *Internal Security Corps*, which are uniformed, strongly armed adjuncts of the security police, equipped to maintain public order with many weapons. These are the Polish K.B.W., the Czech S.T.B., the Rumanian P.A.Z.A. and the like.

3) *The People's or Citizens' Militia*, used chiefly for ordinary public surveillance, somewhat parallel to state police or gendarmeries, but always subject to call by the security police.

4) *Frontier Guards*, heavily armed units whose duty is to keep all borders sealed and to prevent "liberated" citizens from leaving their country.

5) *Railroad Guards*, who maintain rigid controls of everything pertaining to rail transportation.

At the beginning of 1952 the combined strength of these five varieties of police and internal armies for all of satellite Europe totaled approximately two million men or more. They are definitely *armies* in structure, training and equipment. The Red régimes actually list their security troops as a part of their armed forces. Special security-police units possess armored cars and tanks, sometimes light artillery. They are being increasingly supplied with Soviet weapons. Their separate units are much more heavily armed with sub-machine guns than regular army companies. Every man in a company often has a tommy-gun. All police and militia formations are organized on common Soviet patterns. Many could be incorporated into the regular armies in an emergency; but their main job is to control and intimidate their home populations. Militiamen usually patrol the villages in pairs, due to their unpopularity.

Although the Red régimes' internal armies are abnormally large, they are abetted by numerous special control agencies. In Czechoslovakia an organization called the D.O.Z. (Officers for Defense of the Nation) provides an extreme security control over the entire military establishment, also over civilians for their political attitude, and over all foreigners. It employs great numbers of secret agents; next to the S.N.B. security police it is the most feared. In all puppet states the Communists have created "economic police" who are extremely active. Thousands are placed in factories to guard against sabotage; notably in all plants which produce for military purposes. But the economic police serve a most important purpose as raiders and robbers. For more than two years they have invaded the homes of all likely prospects, seizing gold, silver, jewelry and similar private property. It has been decreed a crime for individuals to possess capitalistic valuables of this sort; even gold fillings in teeth are now forbidden by law in dental offices. Upper and middle-class citizens have been robbed of possessions worth millions of dollars in this manner. In conformity with the Comintern's blueprint instructions regarding disposition of "property belonging to class enemies" the loot accumulated by economic "policemen" goes to swell the Communist Party's "separate funds."

In Poland, and probably in other satellites, the Stalinists have created an institution called "Piony." This places four Piony representatives—one from the security police, one Communist Party official, one trade-union member and one official of the competent ministry—among the executives of each industrial plant, each office, each political, social or cultural organization. Both the security-police member and most party members serve as spies. In fact, all four Piony representatives are required to fill their "norm" of accusations. They hold a police whip over every factory management, over the administration of every type of organization permitted to exist under the Red régimes. Supposedly, this inside police surveillance is intended to build efficiency as well as to ferret out anti-Communists and un-reliables. Actually it results in such a competition to keep in

right with the police that fear-ridden executives report an endless variety of mistakes, omissions and abuses by others, often
making an efficient operation virtually impossible. But the police
state's first aim and necessity is fulfilled. Fear and suspicion
abound. The police have their fingers in everything.

How many spies and informers do the satellites' secret police employ?

The cadres of the main security-police organizations are
never static in membership. Their numbers are always on the
increase. The recent ratio of expansion has apparently averaged
around 200,000 a year. In a single year Rumania's M.I.A. was
enlarged by 80,000. But of course the Communists do not
publicize the size of their plain-clothes armies. These run into
hundreds of thousands, from Eastern Germany down to Bulgaria's Turko-Greek frontiers. Beyond all these, however,
are legions of police informers—both paid and unpaid.

Millions of wretched or trapped individuals serve as secret
agents for the satellites' M.V.D. system. Great numbers are
youthful Communists and misled children, acting from sincere
but fanatical motivations. Far more are fear-obsessed, pitiful
creatures who have no real choice—people who desperately need
to keep their jobs. There are also large numbers from the lowest
10 per cent of humankind—natural-born bootlickers, opportunists and traitors who would betray anyone for a little cash
or a slight privilege. Finally, those whose families desperately need more food or clothing; those impelled by impoverishment and want; or those whose thirst for some few luxuries
makes them willing tools of police oppression and murder. The
Communist state is a permanent condition of fear, coercion and
privation or destitution for some 80 to 90 per cent of its population. Its very condition breeds informers like maggots in a mass
burial pit.

When the extraordinary circumstances and compulsions are
considered it is not at all surprising that neither waiters nor

workers, train conductors nor customs men—and vast numbers of other average citizens—escape being coerced or lured into the role of party spies. In a conquered population of 90 million it seems safe to estimate that at least ten million persons either belong to official police organizations or serve as informers and spies in varying capacities and degrees. That means approximately one police agent of some sort for every nine inhabitants. Under wartime limitations the Nazis never remotely approached such percentages of police-and-informer activities in their occupied countries.

The Stalinists have simply exported and expanded their M.V.D. system with a methodical thoroughness which is almost inconceivable. From the beginning this vast operation has been directed and controlled in each satellite nation by top-level M.V.D. generals and colonels sent from Russia. In every puppet state the Communists demanded and got one of their party leaders as minister of interior—the department which controls all police formations. The Communist minister of interior was native-born, but trained in Moscow. Behind him, and at first hidden from the public, a group of Russian M.V.D. officers really ran the country's police system. It was a very tight, well-masked inside job until the Communist régimes became solidly entrenched. Then the M.V.D.'s "occupation" of Eastern Europe's police organizations began in earnest.

Today the professional experts of the Kremlin's secret police empire, many thousands in number, completely dominate and direct all major police operations in the six satellite countries and in Eastern Germany. Soviet General Kurinsky occupies the key post in Hungary's ministry of the interior; in Bucharest another Russian, Colonel Borisov, commands all of Rumania's police services. Soviet M.V.D. officers are everywhere in top commands, and now have large numbers of their own countrymen as assistants and subordinates in each puppet state.

How the Soviet M.V.D.'s "occupation" of captive Europe operates

This secret-police invasion has been very much enlarged since Korea. Its build-up continues to coincide with the expansion of the satellite armies, and with the intensification of Russia's grip on Eastern Europe's populations. In the latter part of 1950 Moscow ordered a drastic tightening-up of police controls in the puppet states. Their security police and all other police organizations were purged and reorganized. A great new influx of M.V.D. officers from the Soviet Union followed, virtually unreported in the West, as so many of the Kremlin's most significant measures of conquest have been.

The process of Russian secret-police infiltration works in this fashion. A group of 30 to 50 M.V.D. specialists is assigned by Moscow to reorganize Poland's, Bulgaria's or another satellite's police armies. Forty new M.V.D. officers assumed key posts in Budapest's A.V.O. headquarters in January, 1951. The Hungarian A.V.O. officers whom they replaced were dispatched to Russia for "re-educational courses." They included four generals and twenty-two colonels. Education—of a kind—never ends under the hammer and sickle. The nature of this particular "re-education" is revealed starkly by satellite victims of police torture who escape to the West. Hundreds of security-police officers from Eastern Europe are reported in training, in regular relays, at the Yezhov Police School in Russia. The Soviets are transforming all the upper-echelon satellite secret police into M.V.D. graduates. Admittedly there is no other police instruction to compare with it. But even this is not enough to accommodate the Kremlin's psychopathic distrust and fears. So the Russians are also producing:

Thousands of Red terrorists in satellite police-training schools.

Of all police-state bureaucracies the police itself is naturally of supreme importance. The more people are enslaved, the more police and police agents are needed—especially in foreign lands. For this reason Eastern Europe's security organizations recruit new members virtually without interruption. Underground reports show that a dozen or more secret-police schools now function in the Iron-Curtain countries. Like all Soviet institutions, they are highly specialized.

A Czech training center for security-police officers has operated near Moravska Ostrava since mid-1950. Its courses were mapped out by an M.V.D. commission sent from Russia. Simultaneously 250 Russian special agents from the U.S.S.R. and Eastern Germany screened high-ranking officers in the Czech Army, civil service and the party. Hungary's A.V.O. conducts a school for police terror brigades in a cavalry barracks at Debrecen. Enrollment is maintained at 600 trainees. They are equipped with the latest Soviet infantry weapons. In addition certain "technical courses" are given to a carefully selected number of party members, including a considerable number of women. Rifle-shooting exercises for the Hungarian police are held on army training grounds at Nagyteteny.

The great majority of security-police recruits are young Communists between the ages of twenty and thirty with reliable party records. In two months they graduate with the rank of lieutenant. It is reported that nearly 90 per cent of Rumania's secret-police rookies are taken from the working class. In all satellites the percentage of those selected from the working class is very high; notably in the case of candidates for careers as prison guards and in slave-labor camps. The toughest, most fanatical young Communists are chosen, and usually those of lowest intelligence. They qualify most quickly for beating and torturing of prisoners. The Communists' police schools produce agents of every category and specialty.

Among other police-training centers are those for various kinds of intelligence work. Sofia has a school for industrial agents, or factory spies. In Ceperka Castle near Prague a school trains Czechs as secret agents. At Repy, also near Prague, M.V.D. experts instruct young Communist women to serve as spies for the S.N.B., D.O.Z. and S.T.B. Training of satellite women, particularly young and attractive women, as intelligence agents and informers everywhere is emphasized and developed energetically under Soviet guidance.

It is impossible to learn the total of M.V.D.-type graduates for all the satellites annually, save that they number many thousands. The gruesome rate at which new prisons and slave-labor camps are being built further verifies the steady expansion of police personnel. The demand for brutal interrogators, guards and wardens increases as deportations, arrests for sabotage and drives to force resisting peasants into collective farms accelerate. But Communist régimes create larger and larger police armies without difficulty. The Red slave state requires slave-masters above all else. The inducements to join this most privileged service are exceptional. The security police are much better paid, in all grades, than any other state employees in Red-ruled Europe. High-ranking officers, like other party leaders, possess handsome private houses confiscated from the wealthiest of "class enemies." Secret-police generals, domestic or Russian, also have appropriated luxurious country estates or castles from princes, barons and former industrial millionaires who have been jailed or liquidated. But lower officers and even the slave-camp guards receive higher wages, better food and other rewards than they could obtain elsewhere. Some of the more notorious extra-curricular privileges have been so abused, however, that they are now considerably restricted.

Only the very big Reds can have mistresses.

That is, in the secret-police organizations. This unusual limitation on the personal freedom of the official freedom-suppressors developed only recently. High life had been their monopoly, along with the élite of Communist leadership, for years. But the Kremlin has had ample opportunity to observe how absolute power can corrupt an all-powerful police system. Members of the satellite police organizations long profited by

their unique license to indulge in drunkenness and affairs with
women when off duty. Heady with power, many guardians of
proletarian justice became increasingly involved in drunken
brawls in public places. The prettiest, most enticing young
women in every city and town were also at their mercy. Communist ministers of the interior have uniformly set an example
for wholesale coercion of attractive females into their palatial
residences and their beds. But top-level Red high-jinks are something else; the recognized prerogative of the rulers. When
such practices became prevalent among secret-police officers of
much lesser rank the Soviet M.V.D. chiefs cracked down.

An order was issued by the chief of the Czech secret police in
April, 1951, prohibiting S.T.B. men from having mistresses. The
risk of security officers and militia members whispering boudoir
confidences had become too great. Severe disciplinary measures
were also taken against excessive drinking. A Czech S.T.B. agent
now faces expulsion if he separates from his wife. One Red de-
partmental chief, Joseph Urbanek, was sent to hard labor in the
mine pits for six months for mistreating his mate. The leaders
of history's greatest criminal organization actually issue solemn
pronouncements that the party's "high moral standards" must
be upheld.

Perhaps the most cynical joke of all concerns the puppet
states' Communist big brass. Most of them, of course, are
"Muscovites"—the popular term for domestic Reds trained in
Moscow. But despite their presumed authority and favorable
status they are strictly controlled by the Russians. Satellite pre-
miers, cabinet ministers and army generals are surrounded and
watched by representatives of the M.V.D. Since late in 1950 top
Communist leaders in every puppet state have been made literal
prisoners of the Russians, on the pretext of "security precautions." This is the final triumph of the Soviet slave-state system.
Its chief foreign propagators are bound by police coils.

A Soviet "experts' commission" arrived in Prague in the
spring of 1951 and privately delivered certain strict instructions
to a very few Czech officials in the Ministry of State Security.

Not even Premier Zapotocky himself was consulted. Underground information insists that he knew nothing of what was afoot. Security-police guards were suddenly assigned to every cabinet minister and his family. They were also quartered in each Communist minister's home and ordered to accompany him wherever he might go. Premier Zapotocky was treated exactly as all the others. A notorious bibber, he is said to have reduced his habitual guzzling by a marked degree since the decree prohibiting private drinking parties among Red bosses.

Of all the satellite big Reds Matyas Rakosi of Hungary appeared for years to hold the most solid position with Moscow. Nevertheless his regular secretaries were replaced overnight by unknown "private secretaries" who, ever since, stick to him like shadows. Before Rakosi leaves the party headquarters in Budapest an alarm bell rings. All traffic is stopped for five minutes, both in the halls and for one hundred yards on Akademia Street outside. Then the titular Communist ruler of Hungary emerges under armed guard. Most of these guards are Soviet citizens. They accompany him everywhere. While ostensibly protecting Hungary's Communist leader, they also know everyone he sees, everything he does. In private Hungarians smile wisely and wryly. There's a certain satisfaction in knowing that the Red betrayer of his country may be in a worse spot than they are.

Quite aside from their terrorist activities, the security police, people's militia and other police organizations constitute powerful military forces. They can be used to suppress ruthlessly mass uprisings of any dimensions. But they can be used, in very considerable proportions, as military re-enforcements for the armies as well. In any war emergency they would serve as home-based troops—an invaluable protection for the rear of Soviet and satellite armies. By their armament and training they are specifically prepared for these purposes. They control public order on this basis at all times.

With some two million men in their secret police and related internal armies the Communist régimes have 2 per cent or more of Eastern Europe's population enrolled in security units. Their power of mass enslavement is fearsome. The M.V.D.-type formations and Internal Security Corps consist chiefly of extremely brutal elements, virtually all fanatical Communists and mostly callous killers. Their commanders are veteran inquisitors and executioners, Russian or "Muscovite." When millions of individual spies and informers serve such large and ruthless police forces, their omnipresent reach and capacity for intimidation can scarcely be exaggerated.

CHAPTER FOUR

How Satellite Civilians Are Trained for War

"YOU REMEMBER THE BEAUTIFUL ROLLING countryside along the highway from Pilsen to Marienbad," a Czech friend in exile says. "It is still a favorite region of our young people. On almost any week-end you see them hiking, marching or playing games in the fields. In certain places, back from the road, there are always groups of boys and girls in a kind of throwing contest. From a distance you might think the Czechs had invented a new kind of baseball. Then you see they are throwing things of a different shape—made of metal. They are practicing with non-exploding hand grenades. That's part of the regular program for Communist Youth members. They have Sunday outings especially. In that way the party leaders keep the young people from attending church."

This particular youth-training exercise is confirmed in numerous reports from other satellite countries. It seemed, when I first heard about it, like a long shadow from the past. During the first months of Hitler's régime I had learned of identical grenade-throwing games in the schoolyards of Berlin. I also learned much else about the Nazis' wholesale militarization of civilians, copied straight from Bolshevik models in Russia. In November, 1933, I wrote a small book called *Nazi Means War*. (Less than 650 persons bought it in the United States, about twice that number in Great Britain and France.) I thought then that the Nazis were the greatest organizers of human cannon-fodder of this century. This is the only respect in which that

1933 report erred. Time and the Kremlin now show the Soviets to be far in the lead.

Of course the Nazis had completed an amazingly thorough job of militarizing the not-unwilling German people by August, 1939. Their accomplishment in only six years may possibly be unique. Moscow's program for all-out militarization of Eastern Europe dates in its application, however, from the Communists' absolute control of the puppet states' governments—in most cases from 1949. When their initial six-year period expires, in 1955, Russia threatens to surpass the Germans' achievement by a wide margin in many respects.

One notable difference commands our serious consideration today. Hitler's Nazis never succeeded in militarizing large proportions of any *foreign* nation's population. They confined their war-grooming arts to Germanic peoples. But the Communists are already proving themselves remarkably efficient at the military indoctrination of key segments of foreign populations, despite the pronounced anti-Communist and anti-Russian sentiments of the great majority in these countries. This is a lesson from our contemporary history worth noting and heeding. The Kremlin's techniques of mass militarization, unlike those of the Nazis, are *exportable*—exportable anywhere.

What, exactly, are the Soviet Communists doing?

They are training Eastern European civilians, in increasingly great numbers, as reservists for incorporation in the Red armies in the event of war. Since the Korean War began they have expanded these activities strikingly. It is an *all-satellite* program, revolutionary in concept. Yet it has forged ahead virtually unnoticed and unreported in the Western democracies. This despite the fact that it is seriously diminishing our relative strength in case of an East-West conflict.

To understand the Kremlin's present and growing mass militarization of Eastern Europe's civilians one must try to visualize an unrecognizable United States. The American Boy Scouts, Girl Scouts and similar groups would be merged into Communist youth organizations. More than 12 million of our young

people between the ages of ten and 19 would be receiving various
degrees of military instruction. All physically fit boys in our
high schools, as well as in our colleges, would be taking mili-

Communist Para-Military Organizations Specializing in Training of Satellite Civilians

(Where official figures are given the year precedes the total. Other
figures are composite but conservative estimates—as of 1951)

Special Military-Purpose Party Organizations and Volunteer Civilian Reserves

Volunteer Civil Militia Reserves (O.R.M.O.: Poland)	500,000
Czechoslovakian Aero Clubs	5,000
"Fighters for Freedom" (M.S.H.S.: Hungary, 1951)	150,000
"Ready to Work & Fight" (M.H.K.: " ")	450,000
"Ready for Work & Defense" (G.M.A.: Rumania)	300,000
Nat'l Defense Volunteers (Bulgaria, 1951)	100,000
"Fighters against Fascism" " "	130,000
Total	1,635,000

Communist Youth Organizations

Union of Polish Youth (Z.M.P., 1950)	520,000
Service for Poland (S.P.)	750,000
Pioneers (Polish) (Z.H.P., 1950)	1,000,000
Union of Czech Youth (C.S.M., 1951)	1,000,000
Pioneers (Czech, 1951)	146,000
Union of Hungarian Youth (D.I.S.Z., 1951)	620,000
Pioneers (Uttorok, Hungarian)	300,000
Union of Working Youth (U.M.T., Rumanian)	420,000
Pioneers (Rumanian)	350,000
Union of Working Youth (D.S.N.M., Bulgaria, 1951)	737,000
Pioneers (Bulgarian)	200,000
Albanian youth organizations (Estimate)	75,000
East German youth organizations "	800,000
Total	6,918,000 *

* An estimated 876,000 Pioneers—those below the age of ten, who receive
very slight pre-military training, are deductible. This leaves—

Communist youths receiving training, approximately	6,042,000
Special military-training organizations	1,635,000
Approximate total, definitely receiving various degrees of military training	7,677,000

Other Communist Organizations Giving Military Training to Portions of Their Membership

Communist Nationalized Sports Organizations

Nat'l Com. for Physical Culture (G.K.K.F., Poland, 1949)	4,400,000
Polish People's Sports Teams (L.Z.S., 1951)	574,000
Czech Sokol Gymnasts (C.O.S.)	1,500,000
Nat'l Sports Association—Rumania	400,000
"Ready for First Aid" (G.A.S. ")	150,000
People's Sports Association (P.S.A., Bulgaria)	200,000
Eastern Germany's Sports Association	?
Total	7,224,000 *

Communist National Women's Organizations

League of Polish Women (L.K., 1951)	2,000,000
Union of Czech Women (C.S.Z.)	500,000
Democratic Association of Hungarian Women (M.N.D.S., 1951)	697,000
Union of Democratic Women (Rumania, 1951)	2,100,000
Union of Bulgarian Women	450,000
Union of German Women	?
Total	5,747,000 **

* Among more than 7,224,000 in the satellites' nationalized sports organizations it may be safely estimated that some 10 to 20 per cent receive actual military training in some degree. This means somewhere between 700,000 and 1,400,000.

** Among well over 6,000,000 satellite women in Communist national organizations (not including Eastern Germany)—the great majority under 40 years of age—it seems certain that from 25 to 40 per cent are receiving some degree of pre-military or war-service type of training. This means somewhere between 1,500,000 and 2,400,000 women.

tary instruction for many hours per week. In addition, at least several million adult Americans would be serving in "voluntary" reserve corps and in a workers' militia—including large contingents from the A.F. of L., C.I.O. and other unions. In our major industrial cities American workers would march from their factories to drill grounds several nights a week. In every state large numbers of citizens in the 20-to-40 age bracket, as members of "Anti-Fascist" or "Defense of America" political organizations, would be obliged to take regular, specialized military courses.

All phases of American sports and American women's activities would be revolutionized. Every game, from baseball to ping-pong, would be "nationalized" and tightly controlled from Washington. Sports games for the fun of it would be abolished. The chief object of every sport program or contest would be the hardening of muscles in preparation for future military service, together with political indoctrination. Meanwhile thousands of American women's federations, associations and clubs would have utterly disappeared as independent entities. Millions of American women, absorbed into a single nation-wide organization, would be enrolled in various categories of war-service instruction or in outright military training.

All of these drastic changes have been imposed by Moscow through its régimes since 1948 or 1949. Militarization of the majority of their able-bodied citizens is by no means complete as yet. The quality of present training, in different sectors of the population, varies greatly. It would appear that several more years would be required before something like uniformly effective results could be produced. But if these same Soviet-type, para-military programs had been actively applied in the United States since 1948, much more than our civilian habits, our personal timetables and our easy freedoms would have been radically altered. As of today (in proportion to what Eastern Europe's Communists have already accomplished) the United States armed forces would have *a new reserve of partially trained civilians* conceivably totaling 15 million persons or more. On a proportionate scale this is being done, and steadily increasing, in the Red half of Europe. Taking the Soviet empire as a whole this much is a factual statement: Nowhere on earth, at any period of history, have so many millions of people been subjected to mass militarization as those now living beneath the shadow of the hammer and sickle; and nowhere by methods of such thorough organization.

Take Poland as an example. More than two million young

people receive various degrees of military instruction in three major Communist youth organizations. It must be estimated that at least one million more are given intensive training in Polish high schools and universities. Quite aside from the People's Militia, the o.r.m.o. (Volunteer Civilian Reserves) includes approximately another 500,000 Poles. The People's Sport Teams enroll another 574,000. It is probable that a minimum of one-fourth of the League of Polish Women's membership takes military-purpose instruction of one kind or another, which means another 500,000. More than one million Poles are either in their armed forces or in the security police and other internal armies. Out of Poland's total population of 25 million approximately 4.7 million are in regular armed services or are receiving military training or pre-military education in varying degrees. Translated into an equivalent percentage of the United States population, nearly 30 million Americans would have to be engaged in similar war-preparedness service and training.

These may be no more than close approximations of exact percentages. Nevertheless the facts in regard to Communist militarization of a single satellite nation are rather startling— startling because we have remained so dangerously ignorant both of their existence and their progressive increase in size and long-term significance. But the facts concerning Eastern Europe as a whole are more startling, and most revealing. How do the Communists' para-military programs operate? To what extent are their purposes being achieved? Actually the Kremlin's systematic militarization of puppet-state civilians is being expanded energetically through six major types of organizations. It begins where the Stalinists always make their most intensive and rewarding efforts, with:

The military training of satellite youth.

In hundreds and thousands of localities in each puppet state teen-age boys and girls are perfecting their skill at throwing hand grenades, at using firearms and in many other military requirements—week after week, month after month. The Nazis began with the same malleable youthful material. At the end of 1933 they had 1.5 million boys and girls enrolled in the Hitler Jugend. By 1939 they had several times that number—and Germany's youngest generation fought for Nazi totalitarianism with unswerving loyalty through nearly six years of war. The Hitler Jugend and its military indoctrination paid enormous, if tragic, dividends in extraordinarily effective cannon-fodder. In the Iron-Curtain countries the Kremlin's unions of satellite youth serve identical purposes, are providing the same military instruction are creating the same blind loyalties.

Throughout captive Europe, including Eastern Germany, Communist youth organizations had an over-all total membership—at the end of 1951—of at least seven million boys and girls; possibly much more. Nearly half of these are between the ages of 15 and 19. Therefore they will be eligible for service in the puppet-state armed forces by late 1954. These youth union members belong to the z.m.p. and s.p. in Poland, the c.s.m. in Czechoslovakia, d.i.s.z. in Hungary, u.m.t. in Rumania, d.s.n.m. in Bulgaria and to Eastern Germany's "Free Youth." With their total enrollment of some 3.5 millions of Eastern Europe's youth, aged 15 to 19, these organizations probably equal or exceed in number the Hitler Jugend of 1939. In another few years Moscow will have many more of Red-ruled Europe's young people prepared for war service than Hitler had in all of Greater Germany when he went to war. That fact merits some serious thought in the free West. Especially because of one further fact. The 1951 *reported* memberships in the unions of satellite youth are capable of being doubled or tripled by 1954.

Intensive communization of the puppet states' youth unions is accompanied by organized programs for military instruction. All of the male members, and a large percentage of the girls, are drilled to serve as a future Red élite in the armed forces when they reach military age. In addition to infantry training and target practice the tactics of guerrilla warfare are taught with pronounced emphasis. Communist young people also receive

constant military discipline—in labor brigades, in tractor stations, or serving as guards for arms and supply depots.

As in Russia, the Young Pioneers include boys and girls from
six to 15, but pre-military instruction begins at the age of
nine or ten. Memberships claimed for the Pioneers in Hungary,
Czechoslovakia, Rumania and Bulgaria—as of 1951—were abnormally low. This may be due to inadequate information; to
deliberate Communist deception; or possibly because the Russians have concentrated first on organizing the older boys who
will soon be candidates for the draft. Boy Scout and Girl Scout
organizations have everywhere been absorbed by the Communist
Pioneers, whose first members were recruited from workers'
children. From the age of ten Pioneers are taught the use of
firearms. They take special courses for "junior policemen";
serve as messengers and cyclists for military or party formations. Older Pioneers are among those who qualify for hand-
grenade practice.

A second category of militarization has been introduced in
the captive nations' high schools, technical schools and universities in sweeping compulsory fashion since 1950. As a result
several hundreds of thousands of boys are given thorough military courses in satellite high schools—possibly more than one
million. Training for girls was introduced in Poland in September, 1951. Reports from Gdynia, Zakopane and elsewhere describe high-school girls turning out for target practice with
machine guns as well as rifles and carbines; also grenade throwing. In Hungary male high-school graduates may qualify for a
lieutenant's commission with an additional six months of training.

Captive Europe's universities now serve as officers' training
camps for almost all physically fit students, save those preparing
for fields where they are urgently needed. Students are required
to devote two or three times as much work to military subjects
as is usual for American students in reserve training units. At
Prague University (in 1951) students preparing for teaching
were obliged to take twelve hours of military studies and drills
per week; also to serve for two months in army training camps

each summer. After four years they receive an army commission with their diploma. Polish universities require from sixteen to eighteen hours of military instruction weekly, including field exercises on Sundays. In from three to five years students qualify as cadet officers. Other East European youths, who are not taking advanced education are not overlooked, however. They are enrolled in:

Special organizations for civilians' military training.

These are Communist shock brigades bearing such names as the "Hungarian Fighters for Freedom" (M.S.H.S.); "Ready for Work and Defense" (G.M.A.) in Rumania; or Bulgaria's "Fighters against Fascism" (U.F.A.F.). The total membership of these three approaches or exceeds 600,000. But they are much more important than their considerable numerical size for two reasons: their members are strongly communized; they are also intensively trained as military units in selected fields of specialization.

Hungary's M.S.H.S. contained more than 150,000 youths by 1952; both males and females between the ages of 18 and 21. Like G.M.A. and U.F.A.F., members are trained with infantry weapons, in reconnaissance, in operation of clandestine radios and in military intelligence. After its April, 1951, national congress, M.S.H.S. launched a nation-wide program. New shooting ranges, motorized and radio units were created under direct army supervision. Since Korea paratroop training has been greatly increased everywhere. The official publication of "Fighters for Freedom" reported on May 4, 1951:

From all over the country leaders of parachute troops [!] are assembling. They meet here to improve their techniques by practicing jumps. The frame of mind of the comrades in the magnificent Maszoviet planes is excellent. They jump with automatically opening parachutes. . . . Jumping with parachutes opening almost above the ground was a practice in which Soviet partisans showed greatest skill. M.S.H.S. members will be trained for just such purposes.

This is a frank admission of the Communists' true objectives in the accelerated build-up of their para-military organizations. Hungary's Reds have set an enlistment goal for M.S.H.S. of "hundreds of thousands of workers, in the first place young men and women" and a doubling of membership to 300,000 by 1952. It is probable, although confirmation is lacking, that this figure was reached. The proportion of members being trained as parachutists certainly runs into tens of thousands for Hungary; very much larger totals for all Eastern Europe. This fact prompts a brief observation.

Parachute jumping has been an extraordinarily popular sport in Russia for at least fifteen to twenty years. In 1942 I watched hundreds of teen-age Russians clamoring for their turn to mount the 100-foot jumping platform in Moscow's Park of Culture and Rest. No Luna Park or Coney Island ever rigged up such a double-purpose amusement device as this. Young Muscovites got a tremendous kick out of parachuting for the fun of it—but they were also getting very valuable pre-military training. This was a favorite Soviet sport. By now the Kremlin may well have at its disposal one million or more parachute-trained young men and women. It certainly must have many times the number presently existing in the West. But despite this, paratroop training of satellite youths has become a notable Russian program. It seems to indicate that Moscow has grandiose plans for use of air-borne troops and for unprecedented behind-the-lines guerrilla operations, if war comes. The possibilities for these and other tactics are improved through:

*Workers' militias and "voluntary" civilian reserves
in the puppet states.*

On April 23, 1950, regiments of Rumania's Workers' Militia paraded in Bucharest. The display included units equipped with light armored cars, with field artillery and some tanks. So far as I have been able to learn these heavily armed formations may as

yet exist only in the puppet-state capitals and a few large industrial centers. But all workers' militias are thoroughly trained
as infantrymen, and well armed with rifles, pistols and sub-
machine guns.

The workers' shock brigades actually serve as a special
punitive force available to the Communist leaders and the security police in any emergency. Their personnel consists chiefly
of carefully screened, strongly communized proletarians. They
serve as re-enforcements for the M.V.D.-type armies, are on call
to suppress any chance popular uprising or rioting; are sometimes
employed to enforce grain and crop collections from unwilling
peasants. The majority of medium-sized and large factories have
militia units—with their weapons kept on the premises. The
number of militiamen varies from a few dozen up to some 5,000
in Czechoslovakia's big Skoda arms plants. After work they
march to nearby drill grounds several evenings each week, and
are often given longer training on week-ends. Most satellite
militia units receive many more hours of instruction, per week
and per year, than are averaged by United States National Guard
units. Since Korea their training schedules have been much increased. The workers' militias could be incorporated into the
satellites' regular or secret-police armies at any time.

An eye-witness report from Prague describes how employees
of the Vlatava Stone Industry Works are drilled by S.N.B. police
officers on each Monday and Saturday. Their militia group consists of 28 men and four women. "There is normal jumping with
rifles. A special feature is jumping off a truck which is in motion,
followed by immediate assumption of firing positions. The shooting range is at Kobylisy nearby. . . . Volunteer women members of the Workers' Militia are enthusiastic Communists and
particularly dangerous." (Received in September, 1951)

In October, 1950, the Budapest régime ordered the induction
of 350,000 factory employees into the Workers' Militia. Training exercises were imposed from 6 to 8 P.M. every evening
—meaning a minimum of ten hours per week. Officers trained
in Russia command the larger, key formations. Instruction is

divided into special groups and courses; for infantry, for guerrilla warfare, for demolition, counterespionage, etc. By early 1952 underground information indicated that the satellite militias must total something like 800,000 in strength. They are a special category of reservists; professionally trained and well armed.

So-called "civilian volunteers" serve as another shrewd Communist device for mass militarization. In Bulgaria they are called "National Defense Volunteers" (N.D.V.O.); in Poland, the "Voluntary Civilian Militia Reserve (O.R.M.O.). It is not clear whether similar organizations as yet exist in the other satellites. But the Communists are impressively consistent in the uniformity of their organizational methods. In every country under their control they have duplicated virtually every major Soviet instrument for political, military, propaganda and other purposes. Poland's O.R.M.O. is recruited from all classes in its population and had a 1951 minimum enrollment of about 500,000. Members perform auxiliary police duties. They are on call by the People's Militia at any time, and constitute a powerful reserve force in any local or nation-wide emergency.

Mobilization of sports for war preparedness

Sports for fun have been completely abolished by Eastern Europe's Red régimes. No game is tolerated unless it serves both immediate political purposes and ultimate military purposes. To this end all forms of sport and physical education are nationalized —under direct control of ministries or committees of physical education. The Communists' objective was stated plainly by Radio Bucharest in regard to the January, 1951, Winter Sports Games: "The participants will be called to fight against imperialists and warmongers, the foes of youth, culture and sports." Thus a contest for the ski championship of Rumania is promoted and extolled uniquely as a means for patriotic hardening of muscles for a possible future conflict with the West.

By making sports a state monopoly the Stalinists, in reality, have seized control of all sport-loving, sport-practicing persons in the captive nations. This gives them an additional and tremendously effective hold on many millions of Eastern Europeans between the ages of 14 and 40—especially those of military age. It was accomplished quite simply between 1949 and 1951—merely by setting up duplicates of the Soviets' "G.T.O." sports system and its "State Sports Complex" in each satellite country. All existing sports organizations were merged under National Committees for Physical Culture. These committees direct the creation of sports associations by districts or provinces; establish sports circles in all schools, and "sports collectives" on collective farms and in rural regions. Members must be indoctrinated "in the spirit of unswerving faith in the victory of the *international* proletariat . . . and Socialism throughout the whole world." *

Another task of the State Sports Complex is to combat "servility toward the decadent sports of the West." The extraordinary reach of the Soviet sports-monopoly system is indicated by the fact that Poland's Committee for Physical Culture claimed a membership of 4.4 million as far back as 1949. Its active People's Sports Teams (L.Z.S.) totaled 574,000 in 1951. When the Reds seized power in Czechoslovakia (1948), its world-famous Sokol gymnastic societies possessed an astonishingly large membership in proportion to the country's small population—about 1.5 million persons, male and female. Such a huge, juicy apple as this must be eaten into and devoured. The Sokol (C.O.S.) has been nationalized; its administrative leadership strongly communized; its entire membership exposed to unceasing party propaganda. Czech exiles believe, however, that as yet only about one-tenth of Sokol members are Communists.

In Rumania the Stalinists merged the National Sports Association with a party mass organization, "Ready for Work and Defense" (G.M.A.)—a combined reputed strength of perhaps 700,000. Similar mergers put party officials in control of the sports complexes in Hungary and Bulgaria. Military-training courses and creation of parachutist units are universal in the

* From the Bucharest régime's *Official Bulletin*, February 2, 1950.

satellites' nationalized sports systems today. Hungary's "Ready to Work and Fight" (M.H.K.) was established on Soviet lines in 1949. By the following summer it operated 16 paratroopers' camps near Budapest alone. Courses from two to four months were given, averaging between six and eight hours per week. Factory workers were induced to sign up through rewards of extra food rations.

The Kremlin's sweeping organization of sports and physical education throughout Eastern Europe can only be explained in terms of extracting maximum military strength and reserves from the "colonial" populations. How are these objectives attained? In February, 1951, Hungary's National Commission for Physical Education and Sports radically revised and expanded M.H.K.'s program. All sports and trade-union clubs were "required to make the M.H.K. system the basis of their physical training." The M.H.K. curriculum was also made obligatory for secondary and high schools. Plans for training new instructors were drafted by the department for "training of cadres." The Ministry of Health was ordered to check regularly on those engaged in the program. The National Commission's propaganda section was ordered "to enlighten workers on the role to be played in the new M.H.K. system." The program's requirements were ordered to be communicated to students by the heads of sports departments in all Hungarian schools. Sports committees of counties, districts and towns were invoked to discuss application of the new system. In sum—a most illuminating demonstration of high-powered, all-inclusive Communist organizational techniques. In streamlined mobilizing Hitler's Nazis seldom rivaled this performance.

Why the all-out urgency of this sports drive? The new M.H.K. curriculum proves to be chiefly concentrated on military discipline and instruction. Membership is compulsory for Hungarian school pupils and trade unionists. The National Commission declared that M.H.K.'s existing membership of 400,000 should be doubled or tripled by spring, 1952—a remarkably high goal in a population of 9.5 million. The Ministry of Health announced that

5,000 new instructors would be distributed around the country. The dead earnestness of this program shows what the Soviets are planning to achieve by mass militarization through sports. Within a few years they will have built up several millions of additional partly trained reservists inside the Curtain—in the name of sport. Along with this the Communist régimes specialize in:

Military training of satellite women.

Eastern Europe's women are being trained to perform as many vital wartime functions as Soviet women, who worked so amazingly in World War II. In Russia in 1942 I learned what a tremendous role women of peasant origin, well-trained and disciplined, can play in a nation's armed forces. Nowhere else, from Britain and Norway to China, had I seen women in uniform on such a scale, nor in so many kinds of army jobs usually held by men. In addition most of Soviet Russia's food production, and much of its transportation and communications systems were in female hands, plus great numbers working in war plants. Millions of Soviet men were thus released for the combat services or the ever expanding M.V.D. Eastern Europe's robust women are as strong-bodied and capable as Russian women. The Kremlin now trains them by hundreds of thousands to fill the same war jobs which Soviet women carried out with impressive ability.

It's as easy to militarize women in any Communist state as it is to militarize the youth, the workers or sportsmen. The only existing organizations for satellite women are party monopolies called The Union of Democratic Women, the League of Polish Women, and the like. Their total membership, including Eastern Germany, approached seven million as of January, 1952. Since the majority of their members are below the age of 40 it seems certain, by conservative estimate, that from 25 to 35 per cent of them are involved in some form of para-military training. Underground reports show the typical Soviet thoroughness with which Moscow's programs for women are being conducted. They fall into specific categories for specific purposes:

Girls in the 15-to-18 age group are trained for field brigades, for military communications, commissary work, tractor-station service or as air-raid watchers.

Young women 19 to 21 are instructed especially as spies and informers, and for guerrilla operations; also as nurses, ambulance drivers, military police, radio and telephone operators.

Women from 22 to 32 are trained as streetcar motormen, bus drivers, locomotive engineers and truck drivers; also as prison guards and concentration-camp supervisors.

Women from 33 to 45 are trained as factory foremen, as members of municipal councils and district supervisors, as junior civil administrators, hospital attendants, etc.

Full companies of women soldiers, marching with rifles, have become a common sight in Hungary. In Gdansk, Poland, women in uniform belong to the Harbor Guards. In addition to their port duties, they practice with sub-machine guns and at grenade throwing three times a week. The Communist régimes have had large numbers of younger women under military-purpose instruction since 1949, and possibly earlier. The size of their specialized squads and categories increases every year. Judged by the Kremlin's demonstrated skill at putting women to greater, more varied war-purpose or wartime use than any other government in today's world, only one conclusion is possible. Eastern Europe's women will soon be equipped to add the equivalent of nearly one million men to the puppet states' armed forces. Several millions more are being rapidly prepared to fill war-purpose roles in other important fields.

How many satellite citizens are now in the armed services, in the police armies and internal militia, or are receiving a serious degree of military-purpose training?

At this point some simple arithmetic seems in order. Suppose we take the official Communist figures where possible, and the most careful composite estimates available, as of 1951. These figures cannot possibly be absolutely exact under Iron Curtain conditions. Nevertheless I have made a scrupulous effort to consult all best-informed sources I could reach in regard to each Eastern European country. Where estimates were unavoidable they have been cross-checked as far as possible. Above all, it has been my endeavor to avoid any sensationalism; to select the more conservative figures or estimates where any reasonable doubt existed. It may be that a few figures cited here are still too high. After a full year of research and study, however, I believe that in the great majority of cases they are not exaggerated. It is also true that some figures for separate Communist organizations in various satellite countries which I have used are definitely too low in comparison with identical organizations in other puppet states. Errors in certain individual estimates should be largely compensated in the over-all totals. On this basis the following items—again as of 1951—seem to me to merit recording as an ensemble:

Strength of combined satellite armed forces. Over	1,300,000
Security Police and internal armed forces. At least	2,000,000
Special military-trained units & civilian reserves	1,600,000
Communist youth unions & Pioneers (age 10 to 19)	5,800,000
Estimated ¼ of Communist Party Sports Complex members	2,000,000
Estimated ¼ of members in Women's Unions	1,700,000
Approximate grand total of satellite citizens under arms, in police and militias, or under partial military or military-purpose training	14,400,000

It is my conviction that the figures in these six categories are, on the whole, conservative and reasonably accurate. They indicate that approximately 14.4 million persons out of satellite Europe's 90 million people were either under arms in regular formations or undergoing some degree of military-purpose training, as of January, 1952. That would constitute nearly one out of every six persons in the Iron Curtain populations. Admittedly, this seems almost incredible. I did not dream that anything approaching these proportions already existed when I began these investigations. I can no longer doubt it.

But suppose we make a very generous allowance for misinformation and other errors due to circumstances. So we deduct 2.4 million from the grand total above. That leaves roughly 12 million satellite citizens in some form of military service, police armies or military training or instruction—or one out of every 7.5 persons in Eastern Europe.

This is *mass militarization* on a scale and intensity never paralleled in modern times, save in Soviet Russia itself. What does it mean in terms of Communist-ruled, mobilizable manpower and womanpower available to the Kremlin in event of war?

Some 3.3 million men are in the combined satellite armed forces, police and other internal armies. It seems conservative to estimate that nearly half of the civilians in para-military organizations or under military-purpose instruction—close to four million in any case—may already qualify as partly trained civilian reserves. They could certainly provide the material for very greatly enlarging the satellite régimes' armed forces, as they stand today. But we must also keep in mind the fact that most of these countries have had compulsory military service for many years or decades. They have large numbers of World War II veterans, plus those who have completed their terms of military service since 1945.

How many trained reserves are available to the puppet-state governments? Former East European army officers and other military authorities in exile supply reliable data on this point. According to their consensus, the five main captive countries (not including Eastern Germany) possess a minimum of two million trained reserves, possibly more than 2.7 million. Perhaps a major portion of these trained reserves are today in the internal police armies or undergoing part-time training in para-military organizations. In the workers' militias, the M.H.K., G.M.A. and other special para-military organizations, they serve to make over-all training far more effective.

What do the civilian-training programs reported in this chapter mean to Soviet Russia's war-waging potential? Obviously, they already increase very considerably the potential over-all strength of ground forces under Kremlin command available in connection with any possible Soviet assault against Western Europe, southeastern Europe or Turkey. But Eastern Europe's millions of trained and partly trained civilian reserves are far less important as a military factor today than they will be in another two or three years. The standards of para-military training will improve. The civilian cadres will become increasingly efficient. In another few years eight million or ten million civilians—men, women and youth—will be militarized as never before in the history of their countries. Great numbers among them will be equally sovietized. Whatever else they may be ordered to do, these militarized and communized 10 or 12 per cent of their populations—not counting the standing armies and police armies—can well be sufficient to keep half of Europe permanently Communist, short of another world war. This is a Kremlin goal now almost within reach.

I hope I may be pardoned for re-quoting here the concluding sentence of *Nazi Means War*, as written in 1933: "The happiest denial which the facts set forth in these pages could possibly provoke would be the historical proof, in two years, or ten, that they do not mean what every rational deduction today makes them appear inevitably to mean."

One further direct quote speaks for itself.

In the course of a lecture to candidates for Communist Party military specialists in Czechoslovakia a Red officer declared: "In Spain a 'People's Army' resisted trained military experts for more than two years. . . . Experts are not enough. The Americans propose to fight mostly with machines. *They will lose, for war is waged by people.*"

Millions of East European civilians are being militarized to this end—to wage war *as people* in behalf of Communist conquest.

CHAPTER FIVE

Crime Legalized

WHEN COMMUNISTS OR FASCISTS CONTROL A nation's government they do what any other gangsters would do if they got a chance. They pack the judges' benches with members of their own gang, and they make their own laws by decree. In that way intimidation and persecution, extortion and robbery, vengeance and murder are legalized for leaders and adherents of the totalitarian party. License for the ruling gang becomes law. Freedom for everyone else is swiftly strangled. In their first months of power I watched the Nazis transform German justice into noose, chains and mockery. The Communists have done the same thing in every Iron-Curtain country. But their cynical perversion and manipulation of all legal mechanisms has been carried to almost inconceivable extremes. Laws in the Stalinist version concern themselves with astonishing regimentation and coercion of the individual citizen, down to the smallest details of his daily life. Bulgaria's Conscription Act reveals both how annoying and how dangerous it is to live under laws devised by a Communist régime.

As a Bulgarian owner of a motor car or a truck you must keep it in condition for requisitioning for military purposes at any time. You must immediately report "every change of permanent garaging." You must get an authorization from the defense ministry before you can make any radical changes in your vehicle's construction—also before you can sell an old jalopy for junk. You face jail terms for violation of any of these regulations.

As a Bulgarian farmer you are under similar requirements re-

garding your horse or your mule. You must obtain a certificate
of ownership for every animal you possess; must have their
condition inspected twice a year; must deliver them—and your
car, if you have one—in time of mobilization at your own expense. If you avoid delivery of car, truck, horse or mule, you
will be sent to jail or to slave labor—for five years. The Communist government decides how much it will pay you for what
it takes by requisition.

This, of course, is a relatively lenient Red law. Selling a
broken-down wreck on wheels for junk is a crime. But suppose,
as a citizen of any satellite state, you should exclaim in an un-
guarded moment: "What can you expect while these people run
the country?" That is a subversive attack on the sacred "people's
democracy"—a crime against state security. If reported, you are
certain to spend several years at slave labor or in jail. In addition,
all of your property may be confiscated. If you are at all suspect
in the eyes of the police or some minor party official, you are
certain to lose your house, your furniture and everything you
own.

Confiscation of property as a "legal" punitive measure has
never been provided for such a multitude of offenses as in hundreds of decree laws now in force in satellite Europe and Soviet
Russia. No gangsters, ancient or modern, ever devised so many
safe and easy ways by which to relieve people of their property
and personal belongings—by the scores of thousands. A hold-up
gun is quite unnecessary. A simple denunciation to the police
does the trick—or perhaps the secret police themselves merely
like the looks of your house, and mark you down for deportation.
Whatever the excuse, the local Communists, under any Red
régime, are simply carrying out Point 7 of the Comintern's blueprint for conquest: funds for the party should be obtained through
"property belonging to class enemies . . . or [those] whose
possessions have been confiscated by the findings of a court of
law."

That final phrase sounds legal, even respectable. But what do
the Communists mean by a court of law? They mean what

their revolutionary semantics-twisters call a "People's Court." The Comintern's instructions, regarding what every good Red must do after seizing power, blandly define how a "People's Court" is constituted: "one known member of the party and two secret members or sympathizers" comprise its judges. With all three judges members of the gang, "legal" confiscations have no limits. They have provided Eastern Europe's Communist Parties with hundreds of millions of dollars worth of booty in the past few years. When you make your own laws, usually by simply issuing a decree, there is no purpose which they cannot be made to serve. This explains why:

The Communists have a law for practically everything.

The Red régimes in Eastern Europe issue decrees the way a road-mixer pours cement. There's always someone else or something else that must be cemented into the Marxist mold, and the Kremlin's legal improvisers exhibit an inventiveness far beyond the capacities or tolerance of Western juridical minds. The ingenious imaginations of Communist law-drafters defy adjectives as well as imitation.

To this end the Red puppet governments pour forth an endless succession of decrees. Their hapless populations are smothered with regulations and restrictions, prohibitions and prospective punishments. There are constant amendments to existing laws; new steel bands drawn around the regimented, shackled citizenry. These decrees, inspired by the truly "invaluable experience" of Soviet juridical science, are either direct copies or refinements which contain even more repressive teeth than the Soviet originals. Communist laws and decrees often run into scores of pages, sometimes into hundreds of pages. So many thousands of them have been proclaimed in the puppet states since 1945 that several volumes would probably be required to list them fully. They have swept away the economic, political and social structures of Eastern Europe, together with its legal standards and the most elementary protections of the individual.

It is difficult to imagine the lengths to which the Communist law-devisers go. They even pursue people into their graves. In their mania for Marxism Rumania's Reds have revised property rights in cemeteries. Owners of cemetery lots still retained a minimum of established capitalistic practice—personal ownership of a few square feet of earth. The Reds claimed they were not paying enough taxes on this private property. To eliminate this dangerous situation the Bucharest régime issued another decree. It "nationalizes" the plots of all persons—alive or dead—who are pronounced guilty of anti-Socialist behavior. The remains of those who were no longer in a position to worry about that serious delinquency were removed and dumped into common graves. Just how the Communists will use the nationalized cemetery plots is not disclosed. But under the hammer and sickle candidates for occupancy are never lacking.

Death is almost the only escape from the incredibly long reach of Communist laws. To understand how they are used, both as an instrument of Red conquest and as instruments of permanent domination, one must try to imagine the terrible power of law in the absolute control of utterly unscrupulous and astute conspirators. For the world's greatest gangsters, or for politically organized gangsters in any nation, the power to make laws by decree is an indispensable weapon. It permits and justifies all succeeding abuses and crimes. The dictators write their own tickets—as many thousands of tickets as may be opportune.

The simplest way to grasp what has happened to 90 million Eastern Europeans, and can happen to every inhabitant of free nations, is this: Suppose you were the leader of American Communists who have just seized power. You control Washington, the U. S. armed forces and our federal, state and municipal police. How would you go about communizing the United States? First, of course, you must purge all administrative departments of democratically loyal citizens. You must also transfer American industries, factories and farms to state ownership as soon as possible. But you can't dismiss millions of public employees without legalizing their purge. Nor can you grab billions of dollars in private property without laws to make your Kremlin-style reforms stick. The police are not enough. They must have laws to enforce; and you must control the courts and judges, or you can't be sure that your dictatorial decrees will be carried out. Once you make the laws, make the courts and make the judges you are really in. This is what the Comintern's blueprint demands as an initial "must"—merely orthodox Communist procedure. It has been applied with frightening efficiency in all satellite countries.

"*Pack the courts with Communist-serving judges!*"

When party members constitute only 1 or 2 per cent of the total population, as was true in most East European countries, how do the Reds find enough judges? They rely heavily on fellow-traveling "sympathizers" at first. They appoint non-Communist dupes and some party members as "people's judges" and "popular assessors." A Communist as minister of justice packs the judiciary with opportunists, anxious to curry favor with the new régime, and with "independent" citizens who are secretly Communists. In this way more than a thousand Rumanian magistrates were replaced. The Rumanian bar was abolished and Communist-run "colleges of lawyers" set up in its stead. The number of lawyers permitted to practice in Bucharest alone was reduced from 12,000 to 2,100. With similar methods the processes of law were sovietized in each captive nation. But the Communists themselves are the best authorities for explaining how they produce hundreds and thousands of Red judges with extraordinary speed. Consider the case of Comrade Schubert.

Among those who graduated from the Slovak University as doctors of Law and Government on July 24th (1951), [reports Prague's *Pravda*] there was also Comrade Ladislav Schubert. The case of Comrade Schubert is of special interest to the workers, for he is also a former worker. . . . Schubert managed to prepare himself for university studies in the one-year law course for state prosecutors. He started his studies in February, 1949. After completing the course, where he acquired a *full knowledge of criminal law* and deepened his knowledge of Marxism-Leninism, he became a prosecutor at the State Prosecutor's office in Bratislava, and soon after an assistant professor of criminal law.

Thus Comrade Schubert, with only eighteen months of university study, jumped from a factory lathe to a public prosecutor. In the first months of Communist power, however, many hundreds of others went straight from their workers' benches to the benches of "popular assessors" or "people's judges"—with only a few weeks' evening study of rudimentary Soviet law. Until quite recently appointments of magistrates in satellite countries required no more than one year in a law school. Candidates are still recruited chiefly "from the ranks of the working class." The Czech Deputy Minister of Justice announced in 1951 that more than half of the country's 40,000 "people's judges" were of working-class origin. This means that more than 20,000 workers were metamorphosed into practicing magistrates in a three-year period since 1948, in Czechoslovakia alone. The level of Communist judicial procedure and decisions can be adequately gauged by this fact. But to return to Comrade Schubert.

Pravda of Prague boasts:

He fulfilled his party pledge, undertaken at the start of his studies, to complete them by the end of 1951—and he even managed to shorten the period by five months. The great work for Comrade Schubert will begin only now. He has decided to devote himself to a pedagogical career; to show our university youth, as special assistant professor of criminal law, the road to the growth of the new Socialistic man. Such a difficult and responsible task can only be fulfilled by such people as Comrade Schubert.

Comrade Schubert will undoubtedly be a success as an assistant professor; he could succeed equally as a public prosecutor or a judge, for thousands of his ex-worker comrades demonstrate this fact. In captive Europe it takes less time to produce a "popular assessor" than a first-class tractor driver; less time to create a "people's judge" than a skilled mechanic. That a prosecutor or magistrate should possess only a superficial smattering of law is of no consequence in a Communist system. What are such half-literate administrators of the law supposed to do?

"The judge must interpret the law in favor of the party that belongs to the proletarian class," soberly states the Bucharest régime's law journal, *New Justice*. Not so much as a pretense of equality of justice remains. The former factory worker, as judge, need not have the foggiest notion of what even a Soviet law really means. All he needs to do is to use the law as a weapon of class vengeance; to serve the interests of the Communist Party and to terrorize, jail or liquidate any who may conceivably oppose it. When free legal practice was abolished by decree in Poland (June, 1950) it subjected lawyers to disciplinary measures for "acting contrary to the interests of the working class." Communist conquest of the law, and conquest by law, is virtually complete throughout Eastern Europe. Yet new decrees and amendments to decrees are issued week after week, and month after month. They serve to multiply:

The unparalleled savagery of Communist laws and courts.

We have space here only for brief illustrations in a very few major categories, although a long book could be written—and is needed—on this subject alone. It might well be entitled *What Would Happen to You Under Communist "Justice."* Here are certain varieties of Red vengeance which you would be most fortunate to escape, *if* you did:

The Communists' criminal codes: Modeled in all satellite states on that of Soviet Russia. Its Article 58 declares that: "Any act designed to overthrow, undermine or *weaken* the authority of the workers' and peasants' Soviets . . . and governments of the U.S.S.R. . . . or designed to undermine or weaken the external security of the U.S.S.R. and of the basic economic, political and national achievements of the proletarian revolution is deemed to be a counterrevolutionary act." Failure to do your work to a commissar's satisfaction, but due solely to ill health, can thus condemn you to slave labor for years.

Under the Soviets' Article 58 adult members of the family of
a member of the armed services who has fled abroad are punishable by five to ten years of imprisonment and confiscation of all
property. "The remaining adult members of the traitor's family,
and those living with him at the time of the commission of the
crime, are liable . . . to exile to the remote areas of Siberia for
a period of five years." That means slow death. A man's wife,
sisters and brothers, parents or cousins are subjected to brutal
punishment for his offense.

Anything you may do which *"leads to the disturbance of the
smooth functioning of the organs of government or of the national
economy*, and which is accompanied . . . by disobedience of the
laws *or by other activities*, causing a weakening of the . . . authority of the régime, is considered a crime" (Article 59, Soviet
Criminal Code). Deprivation of liberty "for a period up to ten
years" awaits any transport worker found guilty of infringement
of traffic regulations or poor quality repairs, "if such infringement has led *or might have led* to the damage or destruction of
rolling stock, the line . . . *the dispatch of trains or vessels off
schedule*, the accumulation of empty trucks, etc., the holding up
of trucks and vessels, and other events entailing the breakdown
(non-execution) of freight plans. . . ." Siberia hangs over the
head of every Soviet transport worker. A late train or an empty
truck is sufficient. But daily work is even more perilous for
almost every employed person in the puppet states today. In
the satellites Moscow has remarkably "improved" its drafting
of fantastically all-inclusive, most vaguely defined criminal
offenses.

As a Rumanian citizen *you can be sentenced for breaking a law
which does not even exist*. This is undoubtedly one of the most
incredible mockeries of justice ever written into law. An amend-
ment to Rumania's Criminal Code (April, 1949) stipulates that
"any action *and omission* that brings harm to the economic, social
or political structure . . . are dangerous for society. Actions
considered dangerous for society can be punished *even when they
are not expressly prohibited by law*." A Communist judge decides

that you, by *omitting* to do something or other, have caused danger to the Communist system. "The extent and limit of criminal responsibility"—your responsibility—"is to be determined *in accordance with the legal provisions in force for similar crimes*." Which may very well prove, in the eyes of a Communist court, to be a death sentence; at very least a considerable term at slave labor, with confiscation of your property. This is the universal character of criminal codes now in force in the "people's democracies."

Economic crimes: Every employed satellite citizen is wide open for extremely heavy punishment under these newly refined expressions of Communist law. Dozens of varieties of actions are ruled to constitute "economic sabotage." In two 1950 decrees Poland's régime established special commissions to handle "cases of delinquency tending to harm the economic or social interests of the state." The offenses range from alleged bribery and speculation to something so mist-shrouded as "panic-mongering for the purpose of injuring the interests of the working masses." The commissions may also sentence any suspected delinquent who "*may in the future* commit a misdemeanor." You are not only a cooked goose if any chance remark of yours can be interpreted as "panic-mongering." You can also be jailed for something which the secret police or a Communist official may suspect that you *might* do, just possibly, sometime next year. It just depends on who suspects you—and how much!

Any employed person so unfortunate as to work in Rumania today may be sentenced to from one to twelve years on such all-inclusive grounds as these: For "lack of conformity to (official) orders . . . concerning achievement of the State Plan. . . . Lack of conformity to orders concerning the direction, organizing and control of production; or distribution and consumption of goods and products *of any kind, not mentioned in the State Plan*." In a Communist state that covers virtually everybody connected with the manufacture, distribution or consumption of virtually everything—including babies' diapers, which require state-controlled cloth. "Lack of conformity," of course, is what any Red bureaucrat chooses to decide that it is. You can't conceivably earn a living without being exposed to this law's "one to twelve years." This is only Article I in Rumania's Decree for Punishment of Economic Offenses. In its third article it contains five more categories of offenses, good for up to six years.

For "destruction or damaging of any instrument of production, *intentionally or by carelessness*," any Rumanian faces a possible six-year sentence. If he makes a mistake from being brutally overworked, it's just too bad. Various other offenses are punishable by from five to fifteen years at hard labor. Finally, in Article V, comes another unprecedented Soviet "legalistic" invention: "*An attempt of a law violation is punishable the same as the accomplished breach of the law.*" You shoot at a man and miss —but you're guilty of murder for all that! At this point it seems plain enough that Communists mean by "law" what they mean by "democracy," "peace" and much more—exactly the opposite from what any civilized person knows the meaning to be. Double-talk in legalized jargon forges the chains by which the whole world is eventually to be enslaved.

Crimes endangering state security, "peace laws," etc.

A sailor worked on a ship which commutes between the Czech and German shores of Lake Elbe. The security police keep a close watch on the crews of these ships. On his return one night the sailor sat down, in uniform, to dine in a Lovosice restaurant. "Are things really as bad in Western Germany as the papers say?" asked someone at the next table. The sailor replied, quite honestly, that you could find almost anything at reasonable prices in the West German shops, and anyone could buy whatever he wanted. Before he could finish his dinner the sailor was arrested. He was sentenced to six months for "spreading false rumors."

Death is a normal sentence for revealing state secrets, but what constitutes a state secret can be almost anything under recent satellite laws. A 1951 Hungarian decree declares "every official document which has been ordered to be handled confidentially (is) a state secret." Crimes which formerly brought three-year sentences now bring life imprisonment; other crimes, previously punished by five years' imprisonment, now provoke death sentences. In the name of state security the satellite citizen's personal insecurity has become enormously great.

Laws for the "defense of peace" were decreed in the satellites during 1950–51 with years of slave labor as their chief penalties. Offenses under the Polish version include "facilitating the spreading of propaganda put out by (Western) centers carrying on the campaign of war-mongering" and "combating or insulting the Movement of the Defenders of Peace." The legions of puppet-state citizens who somehow listen to Radio Free Europe, the Voice of America or the B.B.C. thus expose themselves to torture and long imprisonment. Even repeating what someone else has heard is a crime against state security.

The Red régimes' Soviet-style "Laws for Educational Labor" —meaning slave labor—are among the most important and terrible of all Communist "legal" innovations. They receive further attention in Chapter X, but the fact that the majority of persons condemned to slave labor are gradually *worked to death* or *starved to death* commands underscoring here. No more barbaric and protracted form of mass extermination of human beings has ever been invented and practiced. For 90 per cent of those sent to "re-educational labor" the true sentence is slow-motion execution spread over indeterminate years. The foremost feature of Communist laws is, quite literally:

"Death if you do!" or *"Death if you don't!"*

Suppose you accidentally drop a monkey wrench or a match. If the consequences cause fairly serious damage, you can be convicted of sabotage or plotting against the state in any satellite country—and executed. But this penalty exists not only for "sabotage against the development of the economy of the People's Democracy." In Rumania, for instance, death sentences may be handed down for "*intentional non-accomplishment of duties or careless performance of duties.*" This applies to those employed in any kind of industrial enterprises, power and gas plants and the like. A forest fire or fires which destroy railroad equipment or a radio installation, regardless of origin, can be ascribed by the courts as "sabotage against the state's economic security." Death sentences on such counts are virtually automatic.

There's another category of satellite death laws which, like many other legalistic Soviet concoctions, provides something utterly unknown in the history of jurisprudence. Death penalties are imposed for alleged sabotage "when committed *against another state* where the power is held by the working class, *or against the working class of another country.*" This is straight out of the Kremlin's top-bracket criminal minds. A patriotic Rumanian can be sent to the firing squad on grounds of having sabotaged the "economic prosperity" of Soviet Russia, of Poland or Albania—presumably, of North Korea! A worker in a Transylvanian meat-packing plant, through some mishandling of his designated operations, may be shot—for undermining the economic stability of the working class in Soviet Uzbekistan. In a Red-ruled United States every American worker would—soon and inevitably—be placed at the mercy of a similar law. When the Soviet Communists hit upon a supremely diabolical legalistic device to annihilate patriotic opposition in foreign puppet nations they use it—everywhere.

Death for this and death for that equals Communist law. These penalties are exceptionally sweeping in the recent satellite Military Justice and Military Criminal Codes. Hungary's 1948 code devotes fifteen long sections to elaborating death-sentence provisions for members of the armed services. Czechoslovakia's code contains twelve similar sections. Yet despite their terrible risks, and the brutal sentences which threaten their families, hundreds of Eastern European officers and soldiers continue to flee westward each year.

Death is both the major end product of Communist law and the ever present threat for even minor infractions. For in reality court procedures amount to Bolshevik courts-martial. In August, 1951, three Czechs, accused of counterfeiting food-ration cards, were given summary trial and shot. The purpose of Communist law is to rule through terror by perpetuating terror. To understand how this system works, backed by secret-police armies and legions of punitive laws, one need but examine how it holds every inhabitant of Eastern Europe in its talons today.

CHAPTER SIX

Food as a Weapon

So Helen and I are waiting for the police truck which will take us to a place as yet undisclosed. I leave these lines with my neighbor, G—. The blow came at 4:30 this morning. We were allowed only one hour for packing. I had to leave everything behind except a few clothes and your father's letters. We are permitted to take only as much as we can carry ourselves.

The letter is from an eighty-three-year-old lady, formerly a prominent official of the Rumanian Red Cross. One week later she sent a second letter from the town to which she had been deported: *Here is my new address. We are five in one small room in a suburban house. Unfortunately Helen was left behind in Cluj. She was unable to stand the terrible three-day journey by truck, and fainted again and again. We had to leave her at a hospital, and we know nothing further about her. I don't really expect to see her again.*

In such brief, hurried sentences a few hundreds among scores of thousands of Eastern Europe's "evacuees" manage to inform their relatives in the West of their fate. One letter from Hungary begins: *My dear brother: I think this will be my last letter. I must leave at dawn with our mother. I take only a bundle with me. The rest would be stolen anyway.*

A woman writes to her sister in New York: *Today we tried to sell all our belongings that are still left. Our winter clothes are in a pawnshop. They should be redeemed before I am deported. Deadly silence reigns in Budapest. People have long ceased going to tearooms and cafeterias. The streets have been empty for months because people*

are seized on the streets and carried off. The police raids on private
homes increase all the time at night. Everyone dreads that he may
be on their list. On the highways, all over the country, they stop
cars and search for refugees in the luggage compartments. The terror
grows and grows, and hope becomes fainter. But my instinct for life
is still alive. I will not commit suicide. If nothing happens to me, I
shall write again soon. Pray for us, please.

In innumerable cases these are the last words that sisters or
brothers, daughters or sons, have received from their families.
But great numbers of those deported by the Communist régimes
never have an opportunity to scrawl a few lines. For them, as for
virtually all deportees eventually, "the rest is silence." During
1951 somewhere between 80,000 and 110,000 Hungarians were
deported from Budapest and the border regions. Another 40,000
were deported from major Polish cities in May alone. Thousands
of Czechs, Rumanians and Bulgarians were also torn from their
homes, their possessions confiscated—transported in the night to
the endless night of Red banishment. The police divide them into
categories: first, the political unreliables destined to work as
slave laborers for the rest of their days; second, the ill and aged
who are officially doomed to expedited liquidation. One evacuated family was dumped into a single damp, earth-floored room
in a Hungarian village. The aunt went to the president of the
village council, begging for livable quarters. What happened is
reported in a letter to a relative in Washington, D. C. The Communist council head sneered: "So you want more room, do you?
There's plenty in the cemetery. When food runs out and you
can't pay rent, you'll drop dead anyhow."

Directed by Russia's m.v.d., the security police handle all details with icy efficiency. The deportees are taken originally to
"separation centers." What happens there conforms rigidly to
the system which has flourished in Soviet Russia since 1922. The
secret police have precise typed instructions on "The Manner of
Conducting the Deportation." They include a section on "the
manner of separating a deportee from his family." It stipulates
that "it is necessary to execute the operation of deporting both

the members of his family as well as the deportee simultaneously, *without informing them of the separation confronting them.* . . . Only at the station should the head of the family be placed separately from his family in a railway car specifically intended for heads of families." These are direct quotations from secret M.V.D. instructions used in regard to Baltic state deportations, but they are now applied universally throughout satellite Europe.*

Separation means what it says. It means minor children quite as much as husbands and wives and other near relatives. In Iron-Curtain countries older children are taken by the Communists and assigned to work wherever party officials may regard them as most useful. Babies and very young children are taken from their mothers and placed in state nurseries, orphanages or party schools for intense communization.

Budapest's daily, *Szabad Nep*, assures the world: "We always carefully follow the humanitarian principles. Only aristocrats, generals, etc., have been deported." How does this "humanitarianism" function in practice?

Mrs. Stephen Nagy escaped from Hungary in the summer of 1951. As a widow she had worked in a factory to support her two-year-old son, Louis. Then the régime began to establish Soviet-style women's brigades in the army. Another Communist decree was issued: children of drafted women would be taken care of by the state, and the mothers would receive special remuneration. Because Mrs. Nagy had fallen below her production quota the Red manager of her factory placed her name on the list of women to be drafted. She was assigned to the First Women's Brigade and ordered to report, with her baby, to the Rakosi Children's Home. Its officials told her that the state would assure her son's "suitable education," and would "redeem" her with the sum of 2,000 forint ($40 at the currency's true value). The mother sobbed, pleaded and fought in vain. Her baby boy was wrenched from her arms. She never saw him again.

* See *The Soviet Slave Empire*, by Albert Konrad Herling. New York: Wilfred Funk, Inc., 1951. Pp. 91–95.

When she finally fled to Austria she brought with her this official "receipt":

The Rakosi Children's Home hereby certifies that Mrs. Stephen Nagy, née Julia Kovacs, a volunteer of the first Women's Brigade of the People's Army, has this day *relinquished to the state* her two-year-old son, Louis, for the sum of 2,000 forint. She thereby gives up all parental rights, transferring the latter to the Rakosi Children's Home.

When Communist régimes forcibly and officially seize the infants of working-class women it is not surprising that they also rob deported mothers, branded as "class enemies," of their children. The Red state's kidnappers feel no compunction at paying cash for the babies of evacuee mothers. "Separation of families" is an official policy—both for revenge and to conquer the youngest generation.

Hungary's Communists published an official list in mid-summer, 1951, which purported to give final figures concerning deportations from Budapest. Among those evacuated they reported 21 former ministers under the Horthy regency; 190 former career generals; 1,012 staff officers; 274 "old-time" police officers; 812 civil-service executives under pre-Red governments; 176 plant owners; 157 bankers; 391 wholesale merchants; 347 directors of large enterprises; 292 large former landowners; 9 princes, 163 counts and 121 barons. By deporting and breaking up more than 3,900 families of the previous ruling class the Stalinists unquestionably dealt a crushing blow to Hungary's aristocratic and capitalistic élite. Their press boasted that professors, scientists and writers "have now moved into these luxury apartments," but failed to mention the party leaders who had occupied most of them. Even if the Red-listed families averaged five persons each, they would still constitute less than one-fourth of the total evicted from their homes. The remainder were middle-class citizens of modest circumstances whose only crime was the fact that they belonged to the hated bourgeoisie. They had to be destroyed before Hungary could be safely communized. Budapest newspapers carried advertisements such as this: "Apartment fully furnished; library and furniture for sale cheap due to urgent departure." Only a few persons had sufficient warning, however, to attempt to liquidate their possessions for what they could get. How do those who are not deported live?

What happens to average people under a Communist police-state government?

Every person, male or female, is registered with the omnipresent secret police. You cannot earn a living or walk the streets without having been officially ticketed, double-ticketed and reticketed—in addition to the regular identity cards which are normal throughout Europe. The satellite Communists use three further devices for absolute control of every individual: 1) Ration-card systems, by which the amount a person eats is determined either by his political status or by the degree of heavy labor required of him; 2) "Work books," without which no worker can obtain or hold a job; 3) Nation-wide registration of populations, by which each citizen is listed with the police—according to various special categories—for future reference. Along with identity cards these devices provide double, triple or quadruple cross-listings with the Red authorities for most adult citizens.

If you live in any Communist state, you cannot escape these ever present police controls. As an Eastern European today you cannot change your residence until you have notified the police. You cannot sell your own house without official permission. You may be told the price at which you must agree to sell, regardless of the sacrifice to you. You may be told to whom you must sell, or be denied the right to sell.

In order to visit a cousin in another part of your country you must obtain a police visa, just as you might require a visa to visit Argentina or Japan. In some satellites you must obtain a police travel permit to journey no more than thirty or forty miles from your home town. There are certain forbidden regions in your own country (some reserved to the Soviet Army, others for secret purposes) which you cannot enter—unless you are a Communist Party official or member, or of course, a Russian. Some of these barred areas cover thousands of square miles.

But suppose you are a Hungarian, and you need to take a train to a place more than sixty miles away. When you buy your railroad ticket you must present a stamped permit issued by your employer. In this permit you state the purpose of your trip—"to visit my cousin, Maria P—, who is very ill." You also give her address, and declare how long you intend to remain at her home. But when you get off the train in Maria's home town you don't grab a taxi. First you go to the railroad ticket office to have the exact date and hour of your arrival stamped on your permit, and signed. Then, within six hours of your arrival, you are obliged to report the fact to the local police. After that you begin to enjoy your visit—if you can. . . . Oh yes. You should, of course, have applied for your travel permit six or eight days before your departure. If Maria didn't get seriously ill that much in advance, it's too bad.

But some freedom-inebriated innocent asks: "Why not drive there in your car and avoid all that red tape?" That assumes that you belong among the few thousand non-Communists in any satellite country who possess an automobile. But even though you happen to be included among the rare and lucky few, gasoline is severely rationed—to a degree unknown in most Western nations during wartime—even in oil-rich Rumania. You probably haven't gas enough for a round trip of more than 120 miles. It's much more likely that you had to sell your car long ago in order to give your family half-enough to eat. Or that the police, or some party organization, or a Russian captain, merely took your car. Let's assume that by some miracle you have retained it. One of the easiest ways to lose a private automobile is to take a long trip. If the highway patrols dislike the looks of your papers, they're certain to take over your car. So you travel by train. But chiefly, you don't travel.

A routine journey is as complicated as this. Nevertheless, many other things are more complicated—and harder on body and soul. Including the most elementary of all things. You are at the mercy of the Communist state for every forkful of food obtainable for yourself and your family. The fixed policy of Soviet Communism, everywhere, is that:

Food and hunger are political weapons.

You eat according to how loyally you serve the Communist system; or according to how much value the Red rulers attach to your particular function in society; or, finally, according to how soon the men in the Kremlin desire to have you eliminated either as a dangerous element or as a *potentially* dangerous element. These criteria are applied as ruthlessly in every satellite country as in Soviet Russia. The new Stalinist aristocracy *determines both what you eat, and how much you may eat.* Your stomach and your appetite are absolutely at the disposition of the state. In practice it is summed up by: "Stuff the comrades, feed the fellow-travelers—and starve the bourgeoisie and other 'class enemies.'"

The Communists achieve this through their ration-card system by creating three or four separate classes of citizens. Of course the first-class citizens are Communist officials, higher level police and army officers, writers and artists who prostitute themselves for Moscow, and other sycophants of special status. Their preferential ration cards are largely supplementary in any case, for the new Red aristocrats enjoy the maximum of the conquerors' traditional wining-and-dining privileges. They also have special withdrawal prerogatives at Communist "Supply Offices"—called the u.z. in Poland. These are huge warehouses, or party stores, filled with goods confiscated from "enemies of the people" and deportees: rugs, furniture, paintings, fur coats, clothing, groceries, kitchen utensils, alcoholic beverages, etc. Members of the Communist élite merely present their cards and select whatever their fancy dictates. Everything is free—a year-round bonus for top servitors of the Kremlin.

All heavy workers in good standing also enjoy first-class

*Food Prices in Red Rumania, Showing How the Communists
Use Hunger as a Weapon of Conquest*

This table shows prices in dollar equivalents.

During this 1951 period the pay of Rumanian industrial workers averaged 18.7 ¢ per hour. U. S. industrial workers earned $1.56 an hour.

	For the privileged: (Three categories of citizens with ration card rights)	For those condemned to hunger by the state:	
		At state shops: (Profiting from the desperately needy)	Black market: (To pauperize the upper classes)
Bread: 1 lb. 4 oz....	$0.38	$ 2.80	$3.87
Flour: 2 lbs........	1.00	6.04	8.05
Sugar: 2 lbs........	2.91	10.02	....
Macaroni: 1 lb........	2.21	6.05	9.08
Vegetable oil: 1 pt.....	1.83	5.24	7.35–10.49

(*Meat:* Very rarely available, except for those with first-class ration cards)

Lamb: per lb.......	2.51	None	3.77–4.52
Pork: " "	3.02	None	6.04–6.54

Rumanian workers must pay any of these prices from average wages of $47.75 *per month.*

These food prices come from official and black-market price lists smuggled out of Rumania in 1951. They were transposed into dollar equivalents, in terms of a U. S. worker's wages, by an exiled Rumanian economist.

ration cards, although they are second-class citizens in every other respect. State employees, office help, teachers and other white-collar workers receive a second category of lighter rations regarded as sufficient for their type of employment. Below them come further reduced rations for unemployed members of families, old people, and the like. In reality there are four classes of citizenship open to ration privileges, usually with three categories of cards. But any holder of a ration card can be deprived of it for a slight infraction of some Communist regulation. The first, relatively mild, punitive blow by party officials or the police is to "hit them where they eat." In fact, your right to eat is entirely a party and state monopoly.

Provided, of course, that you are among those so fortunate as to possess a theoretical right to eat. For there are millions of Eastern Europeans who are fifth-class citizens, barred from all ration privileges. The Soviet Communists' rule for these outlawed citizens is:

"Starve them! or Starve them into submission!"

It is simple for a police state to arrange that certain kinds of people shall eat very little, and gradually less and less. The Rumanian régime's 1951 decree for food and clothing rationing shows how this is done. All private businessmen, self-employed persons and their families are deprived of ration cards. So are owners of more than two and one-half acres of arable land; employees of private farmers; retired persons, and the families of all these. Anyone is ration-outlawed who retains a slight base for independent livelihood; anyone who once had enough property or savings to hope to live modestly independent in later years. What can these people do? How do they exist?

Like those with inadequate rations they can find limited amounts of food in state shops—at prices six to ten times higher than is charged for the same products at the official ration stores. This is how it works out (by 1951 Rumanian prices). Instead of paying 38¢ for 20 ounces of bread, one pays $2.80; for a quart of milk, $2; for a dozen eggs, $6.65; for sausage (if available), $8 per pound. Those whose ration allowances leave their families still underfed must pay such prices from incomes usually averaging between $40 and $75 a month. Those without ration cards must pay such prices for everything they eat—and eat as little as possible. In all satellite countries food has been desperately and increasingly scarce since 1949 for all but the Red rulers and workers. A housewife describes the results of this in her Danubian capital:

For ten weeks we have had no meat. Neither by ration card, nor is

*there any in the state shops or the black market where only the new-
rich can buy. I wait three or four hours in line—then they have
nothing but bones to sell. I spend the whole day going from shop to
shop, standing in line. I waited with Anna for two hours. Then we
each could buy only one small fish. You can buy spinach for 75¢
a pound; almost no other vegetables—a few tiny potatoes, like we
used to feed the pigs.* [The vast bulk of Eastern Europe's huge
potato crop is shipped to Russia for manufacture of vodka.]
*Last Sunday I wanted chicken, but we can't afford to pay $7 for one.
So I made poached eggs with spinach. But in a little while we were
terribly hungry. Every day when I get home I have bought almost
nothing. My kidneys and legs hurt so much I can't stand on my feet
any more.*

In the richest agricultural countries of all Europe this has
become a permanent condition. They produce the greatest food
surpluses of the entire continent. Their markets and restaurants
normally abound with an extraordinary prodigality of staples and
delicacies—such as I have only seen surpassed in Argentina, and
seldom equaled in variety and cheapness in prewar America.
In 1940 American correspondents marveled at restaurant menus
in all Danubian countries. In 1946 I dined like a king in Budapest
and Bucharest. The daily choice ranged from caviar and numerous varieties of fish to meats of all kinds, duck, pheasant and
goose-livers broiled whole. Even most poor people, hit hard by
inflation, could still eat adequately. This was Europe's traditional
bread-basket, poultry-basket and meat-basket. For centuries its
people have almost never lacked food in peacetime, save in a few
years of disastrous drought. Yet in three years from 1946—by
the time the Communists had gained complete control of the
satellite countries' governments—food rationing was applied on a
mounting scale. By 1951 the inhabitants of these lands of agricultural abundance had become—and remain today—Europe's
most underfed and hungriest peoples.

The peasants' resistance to collectivized farms and Communist crop collections is no more than a partial and secondary
explanation of this swift transition to scarcity. The main cause

is Kremlin policy—food exports to Soviet Russia. While Eastern
Europeans are on severe bread rations, and millions of them go
meatless for weeks and months, their huge home-produced
surpluses in wheat, grain, beef, pork and poultry are delivered
to Russia in vast quantities. In Poland and Rumania (probably
elsewhere) "Soviet Offices for Meat" function smoothly. Rumania's largest meat-packing plants have worked exclusively on
exports to the u.s.s.r. for several years. Simultaneously the Russians are stockpiling great amounts of grain and food in the
puppet states for military reserves. Meanwhile the "bread-
basket" populations remain rigidly rationed. The Kremlin system requires it. Hunger is a most powerful weapon of conquest
and control.

Puppet-state rationing tightens rather than diminishes. New
reductions in Czech rations, coupled with punishing price increases, precipitated strikes and public riots in mid-summer,
1951. Six workers were killed by police and militia in the mining
town of Kladno. Security-police re-enforcements were rushed
into Brno when housewives smashed the windows of food
stores. Even the workers' militia refused to intervene against the
enraged women. But occasional courageous acts of desperation
are like tears upon rock. The Reds' police armies are everywhere
so strong that rioters can be swiftly suppressed. Meanwhile:

What happens to outlawed citizens without ration cards?

They spend the last of their savings to buy food at extortion-
ists' prices in the state shops or the black market. Then they
sell their most valuable possessions, one after the other—which
the Communists intended that they should be compelled to do.
For great numbers this is their only remaining recourse to keep
alive. Recent exiles bring pitiful reports of how this enforced
pauperization of "class enemies" proceeds:

"Every day you see people on the streets carrying rugs, pictures or fur coats; or carrying records, used clothing, almost
anything. Often the articles are of obviously little value. Very

few people have things of real value left. They go to pawnshops or to second-hand stores. They have to take whatever the merchants will give. Homes are gradually stripped of everything valuable. Thousands of families had already lost almost everything when party officials or Russians took their apartments or houses. They were only allowed to keep enough furniture for one or two rooms—and great numbers were not rich; just people of comfortable means. Now they are always hungry; so they have to sell what is left. With spring some even sell their only winter coat, and they know they can never afford another one."

All goods for clothing are now exorbitantly dear inside the Curtain. Rumania's state stores charge the equivalent of $300 a yard for overcoat material; $200 a yard for men's suit material of indifferent quality. Even with ration cards luckier people must pay the equivalent of $276 for a man's suit; $83 for a pair of shoes—and an average Rumanian worker's wages are $47.75 *per month* (1951 official figures). Retired persons and those dependent on small pensions must expect never to own a new pair of shoes for so long as they may live.

When I remember the strikingly well-dressed throngs crowding café terraces and restaurants in Bucharest, Sofia and Budapest in 1940 it seems impossible to conceive how people in these capitals actually look today. But letters received by exiled friends leave no doubt. Save for the new aristocracy, everyone wears clothes which are many years old. Middle-class citizens— from doctors and lawyers to minor civil employees and stenographers—now wear the same frayed garments week after week.

Many, in writing, crack wry jokes about each other: *Paul has had his suit taken in for the fourth time. . . . Jan looks exactly like a gypsy, including what's left of his shoes.* These are the "dangerous elements" the Kremlin is determined to proletarianize or destroy —the middle-class enemy. If you are an average American, with an income varying anywhere from $3,000 to $10,000 a year, you belong in the same Red-liquidation or down-leveling bracket. If your income is higher than that, you are definitely among the "capitalist exploiters" marked for urgent extermination. It doesn't much matter, since the end consequences for you under Communism would be misery or death in any case. As an average or better-off than average American *you have to be* on the Communists' list for ultimate, systematic impoverishment or liquidation. Eastern Europeans of similar economic and social status merely constitute the first foreign victims of expanding Soviet imperialism. They are guilty of the same unforgivable crime of which you are guilty—the crime of having known and enjoyed a far better life than the average Soviet Russian has ever known, or will ever know.

But of all Eastern Europeans those outlawed citizens, denied the right to ration cards, are the most hungry, the most cruelly doomed. It is impossible to state their exact number. Together with their families it is probable that they total at least some eight million to ten million persons in all the Iron-Curtain countries. They are reduced to slow, deliberately manipulated starvation. Soviet Communism is unique both in employing hunger as an instrument of political domination and in using food rationing for class destruction.

This method has obvious advantages over the more crude barbarism of the Nazis' incineration chambers. When people shrivel gradually into corpses over periods of months or years, there is nothing dramatic about it. They are not publicly persecuted or beaten up. There are no mass graves; no executioners who are immediately identifiable; scarcely a ripple of ugly publicity. Deaths from systematic undernourishment are obligingly scattered in time and place. Hundreds of thousands of persons— a little later on, millions—can be killed off virtually unperceived. Doctors soberly write down the causes as "tuberculosis," "heart trouble"—any number of highly respectable diseases, all devastatingly prevalent throughout satellite Europe today.

For those who plan and impose slow-motion starvation it is the least embarrassing method of human mass extermination ever devised. No fact-finding United Nations commission can possibly establish more than broad estimates of deaths so caused in the Red puppet states since 1949. It is certain that many millions of Eastern Europeans are now being gradually starved to death, or starved into incurable illnesses. In another few years the toll of the Communists' "anonymous extermination" may conceivably surpass that of the Nazi gas chambers. But there will be few, if any, glaring headlines to stir the free world's protests. What other system of wholesale murder veils itself with equal finesse? In modern times it has thrived uniquely under Soviet rule.

Why is the Kremlin bent on liquidating millions of upper and middle-class Eastern Europeans through starvation? It is because they are the only well-educated people who exist in large numbers in the puppet states. As such they have "capitalistic standards." While a few were accustomed to an extravagant life, all were used to a good life—to what, by comparison with Soviet Russia, was an incredibly good life. Therefore they are contaminated by the amenities of Western civilization. Even for what they remember with sighs or tears, they are a menace to the Communist system. All these people are equally intolerable because they have independent minds, values of their own, and bases of comparison. That makes them a permanent threat to Bolshevik rule. They are the incorrigibles. Their tastes can never be thoroughly vulgarized, nor their habits of thought reliably perverted. Unless they are destroyed Moscow can never feel sure of its grip on Eastern Europe. The Cominform's answer must be the same for all such upper and middle-class people wherever Communist rule is established: "Pauperize them! Starve them! Starve those who may survive into submission!"

A subversive rhyme, circulated in Bucharest's "New Times" factory, runs as follows:

> Stalin is so devilish smart
> He takes our food off by the cart;
> He takes our gold off by the bag—
> And leaves us only a red rag.

Inside the Curtain laughter is rare and bitter. Average satellite workers earn $45 to $65 per month. Bonuses go only to the party-favored few and to those of abnormal physical endurance.

A young Czech who escaped from the uranium mines at Pribam managed to earn $100 a month—$25 a week—but he had to produce 200 per cent of his fixed norm (quota) daily to make such big wages. After a 1951 wage increase a Bulgarian clerk earns $36.55 per month; a bookkeeper $51.39 monthly; a technical manager of a factory $71.55; an industrial director $75—or $20.24 less per month than in 1939. With prohibitive and still rising prices these are normal wages and salaries in satellite Europe's proletarian paradise. They illustrate graphically:

How people live under a Communist system.

A Communist daily in the Ostrava region of Czechoslovakia carries brief classified advertisements. Under the heading "Offered for Sale" it publishes items like these:

A motorcycle, c.z., 500 ccm; in perfect condition; 70,000 crowns. (Equivalent to $1,400)

A new fur coat, rabbit and wildcat; price 8,500 crowns. ($170)

An almost new prewar bicycle; price 4,500 crowns. ($90)

A wedding gown of lace material and slip, for 7,000 crowns. ($140)

A vacuum cleaner for 12,000 crowns. ($240)

The era of the vacuum cleaner is fast disappearing in the Red half of Europe. What housewife can dream of such luxury when a second-hand machine's purchase price equals four or five months of her husband's total earnings?

By now, of course, doctors and dentists have been "nationalized." Czech dentists work for the National Insurance Corporation, which assigns them to its district offices. In the practice of dentistry Communism has obviously far outstripped the West in efficiency. Exactly as with factory workers, the dentists are subject to "working norms." They are expected to treat four and one-half patients per hour—regardless of what may be wrong with their teeth, or of what may happen to that extra half-patient. A chief dentist, in charge of a district clinic, earns $216 per month. From this his taxes, national-insurance contribution and trade-union membership fees are deducted—leaving an actual monthly income of approximately $40 per week. That would seem to leave even a top-ranking state dental expert with quite a few living problems.

But even the dead in sovietized Europe may present serious problems. The production of coffins is also state-controlled. Coffins must be made strictly according to fixed quotas and official specifications—unless a party big-shot merits fancy trimmings for having departed unpurged. When a very ordinary citizen died in a Slovak town the state's quota-fixer had underestimated the coffin market in his district. The family was told to apply to the neighboring district's communal plant, but it was also out of stock. Burial was delayed for four days until a local carpenter was granted permission to build an emergency coffin.

The lumber shortage—in heavily forested Rumania—became so acute in 1951 that private citizens had to obtain a special permit to purchase boards of any kind. Material for coffin construction disappeared entirely, so that most deceased persons were buried in simple winding sheets. Some village churches keep one coffin on hand for use during the funeral service only. While Rumanians are deprived of sufficient boards for burial purposes Sovrom Lemn, the Soviet-Rumanian timber monopoly, produces and exports many millions of board feet annually to Russia.

The Communist press consistently ignores the callousness, abuses and injustices rampant in their régimes. Instead it chants endless paeans to the triumphs and privileges of the party-regimented societies. Where, save under the hammer and sickle, has marriage been organized on an assembly-line basis? Prague's *Lidovè Noviny* (January 26, 1951) makes the system's advantages sound almost irresistible:

Let others elsewhere think of war. Here our communal enterprise Svatka arranges weddings. Svatka takes care of getting the necessary documents. . . . During the first year of its activities it has arranged 1,700 weddings, and *saved more than 40,000 working hours for the couples*. [Italics mine—saved by getting the newlyweds immediately back to their factory machines!]

Marriages were performed even within an hour and a half. The whole wedding is arranged for only 170 crowns ($3.04). In other cases wedding bouquets, photographs, wedding parties, announcements, cars and plane tickets are provided at reduced prices. Information is also furnished on church weddings, clothing coupons, free apartments and even loans.

Svatka will now spread its organization to plants. An arrangement will be made with the managements for certain official days when the Svatka official will visit the plants for mass marriage plans. . . . This is a fine service for those who want to found a family—[in a foundry?] —and for older people who want to settle family affairs. . . . Now people will have an orderly family life, better than ever before. Svatka makes all the steps easier, saving all difficult details.

It isn't stated whether Svatka also supplies the vodka, but the Red newspaper jubilantly concludes: "The newlyweds only have to take care of a happy family life."

Zdenek Lenk and Rozena Maskova were among the first of Svatka's mass-marriage protégés. What about their chances of "taking care of a happy family life?" They may possibly manage to achieve a few isolated minutes of relative contentment now and then *if*. . . . *If* Zdenek remains an obedient conformist in his Communist union. . . . *If* he keeps his output at least equal to his norm, and never loses his job and his ration card. . . . *If* both he and Rozena never say or do anything to arouse the suspicions of the party or the police. . . . *If* they both attend party meetings and conferences several nights a week. . . . *If* they are clever enough to join an evening class in Russian. . . . *If* they become informers about fellow workers and friends. . . . *If* some envious person doesn't report, truly or falsely, that they listen to Radio Free Europe. . . . *If* the secret police do not knock at their door at three o'clock some morning. . . . *If* they live and act like automatons all their lives. . . . *If* they do not indulge in American dances, a slave-labor offense. . . . If they contrive to avoid these and many other pitfalls, Svatka's newlyweds may drag along in a gray, mechanical existence—but of course, without being able to call the interior of their four walls their own.

Privacy of the home is intolerable—and impossible.

The Communist system guarantees that family privacy, in its world-accepted sense, cannot exist. Every citizen's home is either a party peeking place or a Red agitator's meeting place. It is invaded incessantly by a succession of party canvassers, campaign leaders, block watchers, block or apartment "secretaries," janitors or building superintendents in service of the police, and spokesmen for numerous Communist organizations. In the guise of promoting Moscow's peace movement, one of the more recent tricks is the appointment of "house peace committees." Leaders of these committees combine party propagandistic work with spying and many kinds of pressures. A Budapest daily reveals frankly how these pressures operate through organized invasions of home privacy:

The peace committee regularly holds group meetings to which tenants of one floor are convened to discuss most recent achievements of the struggle for peace. At house conferences books are reviewed from which the tenants can learn best how to fulfill their duties. . . . The tenants' achievements in production are posted on the front doors. At first people thought they were thereby subjected to public ridicule. Later on they realized its stimulating effect.

This happened with Mrs. Czako, who said she was not interested in politics. But since her achievements appeared on her door she has accomplished 140 to 160 per cent of her norms. Mrs. Czako's accomplishment caused quite a commotion. Mrs. Kiss immediately asked her husband why Mrs. Czako achieved better results than he did. Since then Comrade Kiss's results are constantly rising. . . . The tenants offered [!] to economize with electricity in honor of the constitution. The economical use of electricity is supervised by a brigade of three members.—["Better turn off your lights, Mrs. Kiss!"]—The tenants entered into a thrift competition with those in two neighboring houses.

These are among the assured pleasures of Zdenek's and Rozena's "happy family life." The only thing certain about it is —never a peaceful evening, alone at home.

"Fear of informers makes life unbearable."

"Even members of the same family often cannot trust each other," says an escaped Polish sailor, Henrik Skorupka. "There are spies in every shop, in every office, in every street, in every building. Life is so hard and people desperately need so many things that someone can always be tempted by what the secret police offer as payment. It is almost impossible to know whom you can trust."

A ragged old woman, begging on a Bucharest streetcar, poured her woes into the ears of a young army officer. As he handed her some money he remarked sympathetically: "Never mind. Things will change." The beggar screamed for the police at the next stop and the officer was arrested—for subversive talk against the régime. A fanatically Communist woman boasted to the sister of an exile about this incident. "It shows how clever our police are," she said. "They even have beggars as provocateurs."

Among Western citizens who have never lived under a police-state dictatorship, one of the least understood Communist methods for ruling any nation is this: *the Red régimes deliberately and diabolically propagate fear and terror among the entire population.* They create and perpetuate a universal psychology of *permanent menace.* In every walk of life you are constantly subjected to reminders of what a false step or a delinquency may mean. No person, not even the blindly conforming party member, can be certain of his status. Every person receives countless warnings that neither he nor his family enjoy any real immunity. Nation-wide registrations, ration-card systems, "work books," travel permits, endless invasions of personal privacy multiply uncertainty and insecurity interminably. The police and the party must know everything about everybody. Each individual is made to feel that he is watched and followed wherever he goes, whatever he says.

Life is becoming more and more a nightmare, writes a Polish woman. *It isn't only that we are in material poverty—Stefa and I cannot go out at the same time; we own but one pair of shoes. But the worst is that constant, suffocating fear about our nearest of kin— about tomorrow. I thank God that Victor is far away in Wroclaw. At least I do not suffer each evening those dreadful moments of anxiety about whether he will come home.*

Bolek's fate is terrible. He was so crippled in the war that he cannot work. His wife is chained to the house, as she must care for him. They are at the mercy of their daughter and son-in-law, both of whom are Communists. Bolek and Vera talk in whispers behind shut doors and windows. They must always be on guard because of their own daughter. You remember Basia. She tells them plainly that she will not tolerate any "reactionary babbling" in her house. Fortunately, not all our young people are like that. But Poland's present rulers are devilishly cunning; they know how to corrupt youth and win them over. . . . That the end of this torment might come, at last!

The mounting toll of suicides and death sentences

The extreme nervous tension and torment, mental and physical, of existence under satellite conditions is deepened immeasurably by recurring tragedies, such as that of Stefan Scurea. A former head of Rumania's National Peasant Party, Scurea was arrested and savagely tortured for many weeks. He was finally released on condition that he serve as a police informer. Scurea, like many others, chose honor above life; he committed suicide. The number of East Europeans who have already ended their lives from sheer despair or heartbreak will never be known. Inadvertently, however, Hungary's National Council has indicated how shockingly large self-inflicted deaths have become in the Red-captive nations. Its official figures show that between January 1 and November 1, 1950, suicides in Hungary alone totaled 21,794 persons.

Communist death sentences are certainly as high proportionately; probably much higher. The annual grand total of those executed throughout satellite Europe cannot be imagined by readers of the Western press. For not one out of one hundred routine death penalties under extreme Communist laws ever receives notice in Western newspapers. They continue uninterruptedly, week after week. The percentage of victims of trumped-up charges can never be guessed, but the increased tempo of firing-squad liquidations is unquestionable. They serve to keep terror universally alive. Peasants are sentenced to from two to six years at slave labor even for illegal slaughtering of a cow or a pig. The police state makes certain that personal security, as well as privacy, cannot exist.

Fear is driving all human sentiments out of younger people, and many who are older, writes a woman of seventy from inside the Curtain. She tells in concrete terms how the Stalinist techniques of conquest effect, through mass intimidation and terror, virtually every household under Communist rule:

K— leaves at 6:30 in the morning because it takes him one and one-half hours to get to the ministry. If he gets home before 11 at night we consider it a real holiday. It is not only the office and the instructions. Every day there are meetings and conferences. He is fading before our eyes. In the past year he has lost at least twelve pounds. Not only because of hard work. It is most dreadful because of this atmosphere of uncertainty, fear and always waiting for something evil to happen.

People laugh now only when they have some drink in them. K— tells us that for every 26 officials and stenographers in his office there must be at least 7 spies; perhaps more. Brother does not trust brother. People withdraw like snails into their shells. Z— was arrested actually because his niece denounced him—and he died in prison. In our house three persons "disappeared" in one week. Sometimes I wonder why human beings have to live in such conditions at all.

If Communism seizes power in *your* country, could they really get *you?*

Unless you become a Communist, an opportunist, a bootlicker, a purveyor of hatred and lies, a spy or informer—an affirmative answer exists in the lives of some 75 million persons in Eastern Europe today. Your chances of escape—by flight only—would be roughly something like the ratio of 1,000 out of 1,000,000.

CHAPTER SEVEN

The Farmers Fight for Independence

THE TWELVE-YEAR-OLD TRANSYLVANIAN BOY was not named Paul Revere. But his mission, as he crept into the village church that August morning, was very similar. The Rumanian peasants of the Arcus region's collective farm were waiting for a signal, as other farmers once waited in Lexington and Concord. They had brought in an exceptionally bountiful 1951 harvest, after two years of poor crops. At last they would have a real surplus. Then the government's crop collectors, backed by the militia's guns, took almost everything. The boy remembered his father's bitter despair. He reached for the bell-rope, and pulled long and hard.

With that the Arcus peasants rushed from their homes. They smashed into the village hall. They tore up the records of the collective farm, the documents which listed them as members. The Communist policeman (not a native) vainly waved his revolver. Then, suddenly, he killed the boy with a single shot. Within five minutes he was beaten and kicked to death by the enraged farmers. Later that day truckloads of militiamen arrived from Stalin, formerly Brasov. They arrested several dozen peasants who have never been seen since. That ended the August, 1951, revolt at Arcus.

A few weeks earlier Bulgaria's Reds sent "harvest brigades" of city dwellers to the village of Bovatova. They damaged much machinery. Some were spies and invaded the peasants' homes, rifling everywhere for possible hoards of grain. Because they dared not leave their work, the peasants sent their wives to protest at the militia's headquarters. The Communist chief of militia quailed before the indignant cries and clenched fists of the farm women. He shouted a command. When the shooting stopped they carried away the bodies of twenty women and children. That finished what the Reds called "the uprising at Bovatova."

In the Polish village of Lutzra (also during July, 1951) a Communist tractor driver had definite instructions. He started plowing down the borders between the villagers' privately owned garden plots, their chief source of food for winter. Once these demarcations are leveled it means that the peasant's last piece of land is gone forever. The wife of one farmer saw the plow assault her family's boundary markings. She ran, wildly shouting protests at the tractor driver. Then she threw herself on the ground, crying, "You will have to kill me first." The driver cursed her roundly. She refused to budge. These villagers were devilishly stubborn. They needed an example. He threw in his clutch, and drove the tractor over her leg. It had to be amputated.

A regional Communist newspaper later published this version of what happened: A peasant's wife in the village of Lutzra was so overjoyed by their land being collectivized that she ran, with her arms full of flowers, to give them to the tractor driver. But just as she reached him she tripped, fell in front of the machine, and was accidentally run over!

Would a peasant woman risk her life for a mere patch of ground? Thousands do. For any peasant land *is* life. The East European farmers' war for freedom from communization has been raging since 1949. It increases yearly in intensity. It is war without an armistice and without an end. It promises to remain that for so long as the Kremlin battles to snatch the earth from under farm-born people whose independence is indissolubly linked to the soil which they own and love.

Why do the Soviets insist upon forcing Eastern Europe's peasants into collective farms?

Because this is the only way that notoriously independent-minded farming folk can be firmly controlled by the state.

Lenin explained it very frankly. Peasants, he said, are "the last capitalistic class." Under Communism every farmer with land enough to be his own boss must eventually be deprived of that land. Lenin cited the Bolsheviks' experience in Russia. "It was not very difficult to kick out the landlords. Nor was it difficult to kick out the capitalists." But separating peasants from their land was "the most difficult part of the class struggle—the most important part" because Communist "preservation of power" is impossible without complete conquest of the peasants. (Meaning also the farmers in any Western country.)

The Kremlin's goal is to reduce captive Europe's peasants to the status of state-chained proletarians. The Communists began with the 1945–46 land reforms which destroyed the landed aristocracy. The titled nobility and the church, especially in Hungary and Poland, had monopolized vast feudal estates for generations. Hundreds of thousands of landless peasants groaned for land of their own. The majority of great feudal landlords blindly refused to compromise in time. They invited the cruel fate which caught up with them at last. They also handed the Stalinists their most powerful weapon for winning, initially, the peasants' support—through redistribution of the big landed monopolies.

But this was merely another deliberate Kremlin-planned deception. The plots doled out were so small in most cases that their new owners could not possibly make ends meet. After a few hopeless seasons they could be much more easily coerced into putting their land and livestock into the pooled "kitty" of a collective farm. Bankruptcy—or join up! This is how the Communists "get" the small farmer.

But even after the peasant has lost his land, his stubbornly independent habits and his spirit must still be broken. In these respects the Russian peasant seems largely unbroken, after more than thirty years. Thus the Reds' relentless battle to chain and subdue Eastern European peasants has only begun. They face an inestimably tough, prolonged struggle. No less than some 55 million people, farmers and their families, are involved in six Curtain countries (excluding those in Eastern Germany). They are proving daily how right Lenin was in pronouncing the peasants to be the "most difficult" element of resistance to Communism.

Collectivizing captive Europe's peasants operates like creeping paralysis. The Stalinists fight an endless succession of village battles, remorselessly advancing after each temporary check. It was not until 1949 that collectivization gained momentum everywhere. Then the classic Soviet pressures were doubled and redoubled. By June, 1951, the Red régimes claimed 7,467 collectives in Czechoslovakia; more than 3,000 in Poland (July, 1951); 4,500 in Hungary (September, 1951); about 1,300 in Rumania. But the real meaning of these figures is more clearly indicated by percentages. By the beginning of 1952 nearly 60 per cent of Bulgaria's arable land was reported to be collectivized or state-operated; nearly 50 per cent in Czechoslovakia (with Slovakia's share 85 per cent); about 15 per cent in Hungary; perhaps 12 to 14 per cent in Rumania; no more than 6 to 8 per cent in Poland. While Bulgarian and Czech peasants are strongly collectivized, the great majority of Polish, Hungarian and Rumanian farmers remain outside the Soviet *kolkhozes*.

But inside or out, the vast majority of Eastern Europe's tillers of soil resist collectivization by every means in their power. The man with the pitchfork and the plow remains the Kremlin's most dangerous antagonist. This is the greatest battle of all— Communism versus the farmer. Why do peasants resist being collectivized with such tenacity and courage? The answer lies in the answer to another question:

What happens to farmers under a Communist régime?

They exist under non-stop, year-after-year compulsions which deprive every farm owner of the right to plan his work or to call his soul his own. There is just one thing a farmer can raise without receiving strict orders from the Red state's agrarian bureaucrats—children. (The party has many other ways of monopolizing his children.) Consider what the farmer is ordered to do. The Hungarian régime's December, 1950, decree demanding a nation-wide increase in livestock is typical.

By government decree the Hungarian farmer's hens must lay 20 more eggs apiece in 1952 than they did in 1950. His pigs must gain 40 pounds in weight for every 220 pounds of fodder fed to them, etc. How many pounds the farmer and his family lose while struggling to meet these inflexible targets does not in the least concern the official Communist planners. But the farmer has plenty of other worries. The government demands that Hungary's cattle, by January, 1953, must be increased by 370,-000 head; the nation's pig population by one million; sheep by 500,000, and poultry by 5.3 million. Every peasant gets his own precise quota. The government prescribes so many more calves for every 100 cows; so many more colts, pigs and lambs per 100. By 1953 Magyar peasants must also increase the milk yield of every cow, no matter how old or sick, by 400 quarts. Despite drought, pests or acts of God cows on state farms must yield more than 3,300 quarts in 1952; those in collectives more than 2,700 quarts; the incurably individualistic cows of independent farmers, more than 2,500 quarts.*

But it's not only what the farmer is *ordered* to produce. He is also told exactly how much of everything he cannot keep for his own family's use: *i.e.*, how much he must turn over from his yearly production to state granaries, storehouses and refrigerators, at *state-fixed prices*, far lower than those on the free market.

Take the 1951 "obligatory deliveries" of Czech farmers: More than 2,000 quarts of milk for each cow; 3,080 pounds of meat (beef and pork) for each 25 acres of land; 180 eggs for each hen; 88 pounds of geese and 88 pounds of ducks or turkeys; 660 pounds of sunflower seeds; and for every pig "allowed to be slaughtered," 15 pounds of lard and 11 pounds of other fats.

It's not surprising that peasants resist making full deliveries by every conceivable circumvention and subterfuge. For what they

* "Forms and Methods of Collectivization in Hungary," by Imre Kovacs. *Bulletin of the International Peasant Union:* February, 1951.

cannot escape delivering they take a terrific fleecing. Independent Hungarian farmers were paid only 18 forints per 220 pounds of wheat in 1951. (Its price on the black market was 800 forints.) The state sold the wheat which it bought from private farmers for 18 forints to workers on state farms for 80 forints—a profit of over 400 per cent.

A Rumanian peasant, writing to a relative in Cleveland, Ohio, reports: *"We had to give up all our wheat to the state collection silo. We were paid 560 lei for 220 pounds. What we needed for ourselves* we had to buy back *at 7,000 lei per 220 pounds.* We were left without a shred of grain from a whole year's work. . . . *History has never known a more thoroughly organized system of robbery. . . . The worthiest and hardest working people are branded as kulaks* [rich peasants]. *They must pay huge taxes of all sorts, including contributions of working days taken right when they ought to be working their own land. They must now be destroyed altogether.*

What can the farmer do? He is ordered to "contribute" so many working days on collectives. He contributes—or else. His crops and livestock are checked by "production controllers." They are checked again by "harvest commissars." His village and the delivery stations are guarded by armed militiamen. Communist decrees fix the obligatory dates for his "timely and proper" deliveries. If he falls short of his quotas? For delays of five days or less, the state takes an additional 3 per cent of his produce; 10 per cent for delays of over twenty days.

Finally, there are the satellite laws for economic crimes and sabotage. A peasant who hides some of his wheat or a few slabs of pork can be sent to slave labor for several years—which often happens. For no greater crime than concealing adequate food for an ailing wife or needy children he may possibly be sentenced to death—which also happens. If he is resentful and rebellious, a Red policeman can always "discover" a forbidden shotgun on his premises—a capital offense. No matter who or where he is the peasant faces one of three fates. He will be collectivized into a kolkhoz or a state farm—either by being duped or broken, or by having his land confiscated for failure to meet his taxes. He will be bankrupted gradually by impossible quotas—and so collectivized. Or he will be deported into slave labor—with a ten-to-one chance of being worked to death.

How are farmers "collectivized" by the Communists?

Inducements and lures: Split the farmers by sowing class hatred—this is basic. Small landholders with anywhere from one acre to six or ten are ceaselessly told that the larger, more fortunate landowners are their chief enemy; that these "kulaks" fatten on the little fellow's poverty; that the Red state is the sole champion of the poorer peasants. They are promised everything they most need or desire—at first, even that they will be exempt from making grain deliveries, if they form a kolkhoz. They will have advantages such as independent farmers never know—new machinery, less waste, more produce, a new and better life. The party salesmen have a promise for everything. Once a majority of villagers have signed up, the deliberate deceptions rapidly appear. But scores of thousands of peasants are trapped, especially at first, by lies of every kind.

Pressures and propaganda: The Communists flood the country-side with "people's educators," who urge the peasants to form collectives. Sometimes they persuade the villagers to sign petitions to this effect. Sometimes the peasants sign supposed petitions for "community plowing" and then discover that the petition was really for the establishment of a kolkhoz. Another village is in the bag.

Meanwhile mobile movie units—as many as 40 in Bulgaria alone—tour the rural regions with films showing the "efficiency and happy life" in Russia's collectives. But testimony from your own nation's farmers is still more effective. So the party selects large delegations of most susceptible peasants—anywhere from 50 to 200—and dispatches them to study "the great and successful Soviet models." They are wined and dined like heroes by the Russians; taken to well-prepared show-places. When they come home they are sent on nation-wide recruiting missions, assuring their wavering fellow peasants of the extraordinary collective blessings which are within their grasp.

Of course, not every peasant tourist becomes a convert and willing proselytizer, which explains a recent story out of Poland. Two Polish peasants from the same village participated in a typically conducted round of Russian collectives. Boleslav returned home without his friend Jan.

"Have you seen many contented, well-fed people in Russia?" the villagers asked Boleslav.

"Oh, yes. I saw lots of them."

"Are people on the Soviet kolkhozes really earning more money than they did before?"

"Of course. They all earn more money and raise more food of their own. There are even some who are millionaires."

"Do the peasants in the villages actually have radio sets? Did you see them?"

"Of course, I saw them," declared Boleslav. "I saw everything with my own eyes."

"And what about Jan?" asked one old villager.

"Oh—Jan? Well, he got arrested because he *didn't* see all those things."

Trickery and fraud: Communists have as many ways of skinning a farmer as the proverbial ways of skinning a cat. Force is expertly mixed with the double-cross. Sometimes the security police pounce on a village and confiscate the peasants' houses and furniture. Next day a party official makes the rounds. "Just join the kolkhoz," he suggests blandly, "and all your belongings will be restored." (How would a Minnesota or a Normandy farmer get around that one?)

The independent peasant is supplied with moldy seed—but he will get first-class seed if he joins up. His cows lack sufficient fodder—but they will have plenty in a kolkhoz. As an independent farmer his spring-sowing instructions are delayed; so are his materials—but if his village votes for collectivization, his troubles will be over. If he is then unavoidably late with his sowing he can be fined or jailed for "sabotage." There are scores of ways to "persuade" the hesitant; as many more to browbeat the resistant into surrender. The ranks of the "capitalist landowners" are steadily diminished.

Squeeze and squeeze again! Here the Red bureaucrats hold all the trumps. They set production quotas for independent peasants ridiculously high. That pushes them deeply in debt to the state, forces them to expend all their savings. Or the quotas are based on an alleged but grossly exaggerated "fertility rating" of the peasant's land. Top that with late delivery of inferior seed—the "independent" is squeezed bankrupt and into a collective in one or two seasons. By another strangular device farmers are forced to turn over their best acres to the kolkhoz, especially those nearest the village. Then the peasant has to travel several miles to reach his own fields; must work longer; produces less. He is worn down until he is relieved to join a collective—but he often must actually beg the authorities to permit him to continue living in his own house.

Extortionately high taxes are a favorite Red squeeze. Taxes in arrears for several years are frequently trumped up. Any farmer who does fairly well invites big increased levies the following year. In Poland taxes were boosted 150 per cent in one year, then jumped higher still the next season. Meanwhile the prices which the state paid for farm products were lowered by 50 per cent. That wrings out the juice of rugged individualism very fast. But the Communists also employ mixed and shifting tactics. They offer cash prizes for winners of "delivery competitions," sometimes two-week vacations at a state hotel. "Cooperating" farmers who meet their quotas promptly, or exceed them, may qualify for a percentage of much-needed coal or an exemption of 200 pounds of wheat for each hog supplied under contract. Those who have everything rigged against them are merely out of luck—in the wringer for collectivization. Originally they might even have been disposed to give it a try.

An old Bohemian farmer was almost talked into it by his city-employed Communist son. Then a young Czech, serving as a controller of agricultural production, came along. Being secretly anti-collective and anti-Soviet, he employed a subtle method of opening the farmer's eyes—by explaining very precisely all the supposed advantages of the collective farm.

"I would have to give my cow to a stranger to take care of? Never!" exclaimed the farmer.

"But as a good comrade, you must share the advantages of the system."

"You say my hens will be under someone else's control? The children sent to party nurseries, so their mothers can work longer in the fields? My son didn't mention this."

"But think of your grandchildren. They will grow up to be good collective farmers."

"You mean to say, I must give up all my land sooner or later?"

"Of course. How else can you have a co-operative farm?"

The old Bohemian had had enough right there, but a "people's educator" might have won him over with ease. This same controller, since escaped to the West, met another Czech peasant who had lost all his earlier illusions. When he revealed his own opinions the peasant took him inside the house and excitedly pulled out an old Communist propaganda poster.

"Here is a speech Gottwald made in 1945," he exclaimed. "Listen to what Gottwald said *then: 'Do not believe anyone who tells you that we Communists wish to collectivize the land, that we would force you into a collective farm.'* . . . The peasant gripped his visitor's arm. "You see, young man. I did believe him, and what a fool I was. When I showed this poster to our village Communist committee they kicked me out of the party. They called me a reactionary, an instigator against the régime—because I showed them Gottwald's own words!"

Peasants of this type will resist to the end. But what about those already caught through naïveté or compulsion? What does the collectivized farmer get?

The state takes the maximum—the farmer retains the barest minimum from his own labors.

In reality the collective farm is a state company for state profits. It's true that the average kolkhoz member usually retains a household plot of half an acre for vegetables. He may keep one cow, one sow, poultry and as many as five sheep or goats at times. Everything else, both land and livestock, goes into the collective. There are "work quotas" for every member of the family capable of work: the kolkhoz member's own garden comes last. The peasant himself must perform at least 80 work quotas per year in Hungary; mothers with small children must perform 40 work quotas. Most families combined cannot total more than 250 to 300 work quota credits per year. The average earnings of Hungarian collective-farm families vary between $165 and $250 per year (according to the actual free market value of the currency). For this barely subsistence-level existence the farmer's entire family must slave the year round.

When the state has purchased the crops and produce the collectivized peasants' pay-off comes last. The collective's management must first meet the following obligations: *1)* Pay its taxes to the state. *2)* Pay the machine stations for plowing, harvesting, threshing, etc. *3)* Refund yearly installments to members for their contributions in land, livestock and implements to the kolkhoz. *4)* Pay interest on credits and working capital. *5)* Pay veterinary services. *6)* Pay insurance on the collective's stock. *7)* Put a percentage into the collective's reserve fund. *8)* Set aside funds for next year's sowing, fuel, etc. After all this the remaining net profit, if any, is divided up according to each member's work-quota credits—and a Communist kolkhoz official almost invariably keeps that record. If personal grudges or party revenge influence his mathematics—well, that's not exactly an occasion for surprise.

In addition to collectives the Communists are also creating *sovkhozes*, or state farms, as rapidly as possible. These are the Kremlin's ultimate goal, not so much because they are larger and potentially more efficient under some conditions, but chiefly because peasants who are corralled in state farms can be controlled most completely. Collectives operate under their own executive committee, with a General Meeting where members may theoretically influence decisions and occasionally do, but state farms are run by a single manager with absolute authority, appointed directly by the Communist Minister of Agriculture. Members are rigidly disciplined, while kolkhoz members retain some possibility of protest. This is why the latter are scheduled, wherever practical, to be absorbed into state farms. An authority on the subject justly says: *"The fundamental policy of a Communist régime is to make each person as dependent as possible upon the government, in order more effectively to control his behavior and his allegiance."* *

State farms actually comprise some 5 to 10 per cent of arable land in captive Europe's puppet states. Their numbers increase year by year. Collective farms are merely a transitional expedient in the process of agriculture's complete sovietization. In due time most kolkhozes will be merged into sovkhozes. But meanwhile they serve as a most useful buffer—a neat device which eases the shock of wrenching the peasant from his land. In reality they also serve as schooling and pre-conditioning for the later round-up of peasants into state farms.

But the Soviets have also invented a useful "half-way station" between the village collective and the much larger state farm. This is called the "agrotown"—an experimental refinement which the Kremlin, during 1951, seemed to be considering as a possible future innovation inside the Soviet Union. Hungary's peasants are serving as guinea pigs in this new agrarian strait jacket. A group of village collectives are offered tax reductions, machinery and other inducements if they combine into the much enlarged unit of an agrotown. Once they are there, the party and police can control them far more effectively. Massed populations are duck soup for those who hold a monopoly on sub-machine guns, block "secretaries" and house-to-house canvassing.

The Hungarian agrotowns of Turkeve and Mezvetur were formed forcibly in January, 1951. More than 200 peasant families who refused to join were deported. The Red press announced that 98 per cent of the merged collectives' members joined "voluntarily." A city of 16,000—Mosonmagyarovar in western

---

* "Changing Status of the Peasant in Eastern Europe," by Irwin T. Sanders. *The Annals Of The American Academy:* September, 1950.

Hungary—became the country's fifth agrotown in September, 1951. Hatvan, which was fourth in order, has a special significance. It is the first industrial city known to have been super-collectivized, and may herald revolutionary changes ahead. Agrotowns are signposts to the future. They point to what the majority among Eastern Europe's 55 million peasants and their families—at least those who escape liquidation—must eventually expect. Under these merciless turns of the screw:

How do peasant-farmers continue to resist Red collectivization?

The boy bell-ringer of Arcus and the martyred women and children of Bovatova are merely among the more striking and tragic examples of peasant resistance. Hundreds of physical battles have been fought by outraged Eastern European farmers since the kolkhoz drives were inaugurated. But peasant resistance takes many forms. They fight back with every means provided by their peculiar and exceptional circumstances. Rather than pay exorbitant taxes they leave part of their privately owned land uncultivated—a total loss of production from scores of thousands of acres. Rather than be robbed by state-fixed prices they secretly slaughter much of their livestock. They deliberately destroy good breeding stock, overwork draft animals, get rid of excess poultry. Hatred of collectivization drives good farmers to specialize in being wasteful and sloppy farmers. Communist bureaucracy and flagrant injustices make personal initiative futile, hard and honest work a self-punishment. Whether inside or outside a kolkhoz, peasants have equally valid reasons to make a maximum of trouble for the Red bureaucrats.

This creates maddening dilemmas for party collectivizers and controllers. How to tell what and how much is sabotage? What and how much is inefficiency? Especially when the state's agrarian administrative machinery is riddled with pseudo-technicians and mismanagement. How to tell when pigs or chickens die from perversity, and when they pop off from over-encouragement?

Every spring sowing and summer harvesting on satellite collective farms brings repeated chants of Red officialdom's acute
dissatisfaction, annoyance and frustration. From Poland to
Bulgaria the party press snorts and fumes. "Less than half the
plows have been inspected and repaired. Some of the causes are
lack of spare parts, irregularities in electric power, etc. But
main reasons are lack of good organization and *lack of efforts to
overcome difficulties*." These perennial complaints flourish like
epidemics of measles. In due time they are followed by the
chicken pox of harvest-time muddles. "Threshing is lagging behind. . . . The majority of machines in the Stara Zagora district
are not properly overhauled and are out of order. . . . In
Plovdiv County only 25 per cent of threshing machines are
operating. . . . Tractor stations have overlooked many mechanical defects."

These accusations appeared day after day in Sofia's leading
party organ during July, 1951. Yet Bulgaria's farms, longest and
most thoroughly collectivized, should logically be more efficient
than elsewhere. The Communists themselves admit that great
numbers of tractor-station mechanics are extremely poor workmen—or something else. They berate their own farm managers
and bosses for negligence and third-rate performance. But many
thousands of thresher repairmen and other kolkhoz members
have their own personal reasons for compounding blunders and
confusion. Peasant shrewdness is a barbed weapon. Peasants are
in no position to stage sit-down strikes. Instead they practice a
perverse stumble-and-bungle strike. The Communists possess
huge police and militia forces. But they can never be sufficiently
numerous to scotch such tactics effectively.

Every summer "accidental fires" destroy thousands of acres of
grain. Many peasants have been hung for setting them, but there
are always more fires. Pigs and cows continue to be slaughtered
illegally, regardless of extreme punishments. Resistance in-
tensifies as collectivization spreads and its coils tighten. Among
all the elements of the captive nation's populations, the farmers
enjoy and exploit the greatest opportunity to fight back. They

do so increasingly, in a highly specialized kind of guerrilla warfare. In this mixed war of primitive cunning and explosive wrath:

*Peasant revolts continue in spite of mass deportations and
brutal executions.*

The heroism of Eastern Europe's farmers must be measured
against the harshness of Communist laws regarding village sabotage. One of these declares that "every negligence toward collective or state property, every wrecking attitude toward
machinery and livestock of a farm *is treated as treason* and as a
help to the enemy of the state." But despite frequent death
sentences, the peasants' bulldog resistance cannot be broken.
Under slave-driving quotas and cynical exploitation their pent-up
wrath erupts, again and again, with an almost incredible dis-
regard of the consequences. Inside the Curtain terms of life imprisonment and executions by hanging fail to eradicate scattered
but continuous peasant explosions.

Aside from death itself the Red régime's most terrible punishment is mass deportation. Peasant families are permanently uprooted from their cherished home soil, and sent by trainloads
into the doom of slave labor. According to underground information, 40,000 Bulgarian peasants met this fate during 1951
alone. One of Eastern Europe's most authoritative journalists in
exile, my friend Michael Padev, writes that "reliable estimates
put the total (postwar) number of Bulgarian peasant deportees
at more than 150,000 families." The number deported in other
Red-ruled countries, although not yet so great, grows steadily
larger as collectivization mounts. Deportation is Moscow's chief
weapon to beat the "last capitalists" into submission.

The independent farmer is unpardonable because he is un-
regimentable, because his fierce attachment to land ownership
and his desire to be master of his own life cannot be extirpated.
So the Communists retaliate with utmost ruthlessness. A witness
in Rumania reports: "In some villages people were locked up in
cellars with water up to their knees, and taken out two days

later more dead than alive. Some were beaten and their ribs broken. Others died. They were beaten by party members from other towns who said they wanted to see all kulaks begging for a living."

Yet other Rumanian farmers destroyed an entire crop and threshing machinery by fire in a Prahova district commune; three were killed and many wounded fighting the militia in another district; peasants of the Vlasca district killed the mayor and several militiamen; in Tulca and Dragoesti many militiamen were killed in revolts in which many farmers also lost their lives and hundreds of others were arrested. These were Rumanians— usually regarded as Eastern Europe's most compliant, easygoing and least belligerent people. A farmer's patriotism belongs and begins beneath his feet.

The farmers receive and give no quarter. Their resistance smolders and erupts like sparks blown by the winds. They number many millions. Their fight for independence has no foreseeable end. If the Stalinists succeed in jailing or destroying most of them, what then? That danger is of very personal import to every citizen in the Western democracies. For if the majority of its land-owning farmers is ever uprooted, deported and crushed, we must recognize that Eastern Europe would be very close to being permanently sovietized. The Kremlin's favorable position for waging war against the West would not only be enormously enhanced. The possibilities for future, large-scale underground resistance or guerrilla warfare against Soviet domination would be most seriously reduced. Any East-West war, if it should come, would be lengthened inestimably. This is the meaning behind:

Moscow's scheduled liquidation of millions of Eastern Europe's independent farmers, the kulaks and middle peasants.

One fact must be clearly understood. The greatest horror and most brutal destruction of human lives, by deliberate Kremlin planning, lies somewhere ahead for the Iron-Curtain countries. Millions of their independent farmers are marked for annihilation by the Kremlin. Only very drastic counter-measures by the United Nations and the free world's governments can delay or diminish the Soviets' vengeance, and only if a strong program of joint action is prepared well in advance. The Stalinists repeatedly proclaim their plans to destroy the so-called kulaks, once and for all. They are the Red version of the Nazi gas-chambers—Operation Extermination, merely by more protracted and more brutal methods. By 1953 or 1954 this operation threatens to be in full swing. Nothing less than an outbreak of general war seems likely to deter it—not unless determined intervention by the United Nations should occur as soon as widespread liquidation of the kulaks begins. The free nations' leaders can have no excuse for surprise, in any event. The Communists literally shriek their mass-deportation, mass-murder projects for the land-owning farmers.

A Bulgarian Red daily declares:

"While the capitalistic class in the cities is liquidated at its foundations, this is not yet achieved in the villages. Now the capitalistic class makes its main base in the villages, in the person of the kulaks. Our party and government are forcing the kulaks out of the country's economy. *The liquidation of the kulaks is inevitable.* . . . There is no place for them."

The deputy chief of Czechoslovakia's State Planning Office proclaims: "The kulak is the sworn enemy of the agricultural collectives and must not be allowed to belong." But who exactly is a kulak? The Stalinist theoreticians have been careful never to define precisely what makes a farm-owner a kulak, save that he has proved able to earn his own living. By common Communist practice any American, Canadian, French, Italian or other farmer owning more than about 25 acres of land would automatically be listed as a kulak; in due time dispossessed and liquidated. For by Bolshevik interpretation 25 acres is a grossly "exploitive" amount of earth for any individual to own and till.

But even a ten-acre farmer is often branded as a "sworn enemy" kulak.

A leading Prague Communist is obligingly candid: "Any peasant who has conducted himself as an enemy of the Socialist State" [meaning anyone who has resisted being collectivized] "is to be considered a kulak." Also those who have failed to meet their full quotas for crop deliveries, or who have refused to join a collective. Their land and other property is subject to confiscation. Thus "total liquidation of the kulaks" really means "total enslavement of all independent farmers." So-called middle peasants (usually possessing between 12 and 25 acres) find themselves classed as kulaks whenever they run afoul of Red quotas and other regulations. A struggling farmer's cows fall off in their milk yield; his aging sows produce smaller litters; his crops decline because of inadequate fertilizer—and any Red functionary may attribute his unavoidable misfortune to "perfidious kulak machinations." Thus almost any land-owning farmer is either a kulak by today's definition or by tomorrow's cunningly planned redefinition.

During 1951 the Stalinists launched new drives against the kulaks in all the puppet states. Such drives are always spearheaded by widespread arrests, trials and convictions on charges of alleged sabotage or of "aid to Western imperialists." Even milder sentences range from six months to two years at slave labor—but they also confiscate his land outright or impose heavy fines that he cannot pay. In this way unknown thousands of independent farmers are eliminated, month by month. Wholesale deportations accomplish the same end. By such devices Eastern Europe's land-owning peasants are scheduled to be wiped out by many hundreds of thousands, possibly by millions, over the next few years. So long as their Red rulers remain in power this program is unalterable—save through some unprecedented outside intervention.

This is definitely planned mass enslavement and mass extermination now impending. Its projected scope is indicated by official Communist statistics. In Poland 170,000 farm families were listed as kulaks in 1950; in Hungary 93,200 in 1951. Peasant families often average four children or more. But take three, to be conservative. Even counting the average family as five, including parents and children, these figures mean that—in Poland and Hungary alone—some 1,316,000 persons are listed for liquidation, for eventual death, in the case of most adults.

But there are several times as many middle peasants (possessing from 12 to 25 acres) as there are "official" kulaks in all captive countries. Sooner or later an identical fate is reserved for them. Peter Kovacs, agrarian specialist of Budapest's régime, emphasizes their menace: "The middle peasants systematically accumulate and expand their farms." To aspire to an additional acre or two is an intolerable threat to the entire Soviet agrarian program. And in Hungary alone there are 587,278 families listed by the government as middle peasants—no less than approximately 2,936,000 persons.

Matyas Rakosi, Hungary's big Red, declared in February, 1951: "The greatest obstacle to our development is the fact that with one foot we are standing on Socialist ground, and with the other foot on *several hundreds of thousands of private farms.*" Rakosi was not talking only about 93,200 kulaks. He frankly branded all Hungarian middle farmers as "sworn enemies," to be dealt with in due time. The Stalinists apply the same sweeping definition in every Curtain country.

A little simple arithmetic is in order at this point. It sometimes tells more than a thousand adjectives. Take the number of kulaks and middle farmers officially listed in Hungary. Kulak families: at least 466,000 persons; middle peasant families: some 2,936,-000 persons; combined total: more than 3.4 million men, women and children. Hungary's population: slightly above 9.5 million. Thus, approximately 33 per cent of her population is listed for forcible collectivization by confiscation, or for deportation, slave labor and complete liquidation.

A little more arithmetic is required. In Poland, Slovakia, Rumania and Bulgaria, the proportion of kulaks and middle farmers combined is nearly as large as in Hungary; less in Bohemia and possibly in Eastern Germany. It is conservative to estimate that a minimum of 20 per cent of Eastern Europe's combined populations belong in these "farm enemy" categories; perhaps considerably more. But take 20 per cent of 90 million people. That is no less than 18 million men, women and children. *The Communists plan to liquidate, economically or physically, most of 18 million farm people throughout Eastern Europe—in stages, but absolutely.*

These hardest working, most able and most democratic minded East European peasants and their families are guilty of an unpardonable crime. They exist under the wrong Red foot—under the Leninist-Stalinist foot which has no intention of leaving "hundreds of thousands of private farms" beneath it for very much longer. These are the dimensions of the immeasurable human tragedy which now looms ahead and is seemingly inescapable. But:

Why are the Communists determined to uproot, imprison or destroy the vast majority among some 18 million satellite farm-owners and their families?

First of all, because Eastern Europe's independent farmers are infinitely more dangerous—in the Kremlin's eyes—than Russia's peasants ever were. They are strikingly different from the Russian kulaks whom Moscow liquidated long ago as a menace. These East Europeans may be called peasants, but they are far from being politically inexperienced. For fifty years Polish, Czech, Hungarian, Rumanian and Bulgarian peasants have had their own organizations. Their National Peasant Parties established notable, staunchly democratic records, especially since the First World War. These same parties became the chief defenders of free and representative government, the outstanding opponents of Red totalitarianism, after World War II. Their leaders have been murdered or driven into exile. But the humble small farmer remains everywhere in Eastern Europe. He remains fiercely, inextinguishably loyal to democratic self-government and to the inalienable rights of free, independent citizens.

Here is a new and greater "man with the hoe." With callused hands, in his soiled and worn garments, he still stands unbowed and unbroken; he is the Kremlin's deadliest and most enduring foe inside captive Europe. Even in the Soviet Union itself, after some thirty years, peasants continue to resist, as and where they can. Consider the infinitely greater menace to Communist rule of these millions of land-owning farmers in Red-dominated Eastern Europe. "With them," in Michael Padev's perceptive words, "the instinct for private ownership is as strong as the instinct for life itself." Mr. Padev concludes with an accurate, authoritative warning. For the survival of their own freedom the West's free peoples must somehow understand its meaning:

"To crush the peasant opposition to collectivization in Eastern Europe *the Communists will have to organize their repressive measures on a proportionately bigger scale than in Russia. . . . Several million peasants (and their families) will first have to be ejected from their homes and their fields.*" *

Eastern Europe's modest farmers have no illusions about the perils which they endure and the savage fate which confronts them. Yet they continue to resist with heedless courage. They continue to fight for independence with an amazing tenacity and an incomparable defiance—with the strength of the good earth itself. Somehow and somewhere they will fight on as long as they live. There are no more noble or uncompromising defenders of the dignity of man anywhere in the world. Gradually the Kremlin may wipe them out. The Kremlin can never completely control them otherwise. The more the Reds squeeze them, the more stubbornly the peasants fight back. Yes, and even talk back.

As Hungary's Red puppet czar, even Matyas Rakosi is incapable of intimidating those who exist beneath the Stalinists' other foot. He was reminded rudely of their unbroken spirit

---

* "Liquidation by Deportation," by Michael Padev. *The London Daily Telegraph:* August 30, 1951.

when he spoke at Baja in September 1951, hotly denouncing the country's "land-owning reactionaries." Rakosi waxed sarcastic: "They are longing to go to America where there are 14 million unemployed," he shouted, "where the farmers feed their children with rotten fruit."

At this a peasant cut in with a roar: "It serves them right, the scoundrels! Out with them—to America!"

The peasant audience rose delightedly to the sharp innuendo. They laughed and applauded, mocking Rakosi to his face.

Of such are Eastern Europe's millions of peasant-farmers—the people who will resist communization and struggle for a free way of life so long as they breathe. Let men who are still free never forget them. Let the policy-makers of democratic governments search their consciences and arouse their imaginations. There are ways, short of war and as yet unused, by which the enslavers and destroyers of millions of human beings can be subjected to unreckoned costs and acute embarrassment. There are weapons of restricted trade and communications; weapons of unprecedented world-wide publicity; weapons within the realm of United Nations' action.

So long as its land-owning peasants survive and resist, captive Europe may hope to become liberated Europe. Despite the Red rulers' organized terror, that hope remains alive today, and with justification still, largely because the peasants remain unconquered. For how long? The answer does not lie with them. It lies in Washington, in every democratic capital, in the headquarters of the United Nations. A boy was killed for ringing a church bell in a Transylvanian village. Did he ring it only for the farmers of Arcus? The pealing of a bell could also be heard around the world.

CHAPTER EIGHT

Fifteen Million Workers in Shackles

FOR TRADE UNIONISTS TO STAGE A PROTEST under any Communist régime is an act of desperation. Despite the hopeless odds, they sometimes do, as when nearly 6,000 Polish workers rallied in a central square of Vilna on July 29, 1951, to protest a new wage system which reduced their average wage of less than $25 a week.

Security police and army units attacked the demonstrators from all sides. They were broken up into isolated groups and beaten. Several hundred were arrested. Next day firing squads executed 40 of the workmen's leaders—a Kremlin-style warning to labor. Thus the self-proclaimed "defenders of the proletariat" reverse the stirring promise and summons of the "*Internationale*" —from "Arise, ye wretched of the earth!" to "Keep down, ye prisoners of starvation!" They have indeed united Eastern Europe's 15 million industrial workers—in misery and in chains. "Justice thunders condemnation"—not from the seat of the Bolshevik Revolution, but from the free nations and the free trade unions of the outside world.

What has Communist rule brought to the worker in satellite Europe?

It has deprived him of the right of free assembly; of his right to bargain collectively; of his free vote in union elections; of the right theoretically to quit one job and seek another; of the right to strike. The Red state conscripts him and compels him to work wherever its bureaucrats decide. It fixes quotas of how much he must produce to earn a full day's pay. It forces its own wage rates on the worker. It compels him to work overtime, and frequently refuses to pay for overtime labor. It registers him with an individual "work book": with it he cannot quit without inviting severe penalties; without it he cannot get a job. The worker is also obliged frequently to work for days or hours without pay, as a so-called "voluntary contribution" to the state. These are the conditions of workingmen and women in what the Kremlin describes as "the Workers' and People's Republics" of Eastern Europe.

Take a typical specimen of the Communists' labor decrees (Hungarian version). It stipulates that "those who hamper the functioning of the company by leaving their work" are subject to as much as five years' imprisonment. The Stalinists' "labor-discipline" laws began by imposing percentage reductions in workers' pay envelopes for absences from work. They hit their high with slave-labor sentences for absenteeism. Even for minor infractions a worker may be deprived of his ration card.

While the Communists were trying to make their régimes secure, they established sickness and unemployment-insurance and pension laws—soon rendered largely meaningless by inflation. A Swedish union delegation recently visited a social-security office in Poland. One member picked up from the manager's desk a list of payments for liability compensation. "The highest benefit payment was 15 per cent monthly," she said. "I did not find a single payment, for any cause, higher than 100 zlotys ($20). They ranged chiefly from 40 to 50 zlotys. These were clearly not insurance annuities, but a parody. All the social-welfare offices we visited have a look of pretense."

How much do members of Communist labor unions earn?
How much do they get in "take-home" pay?

In Poland the average worker earned from 400 to 500 zlotys a month (from $100 to $125) in 1951. But his entire wages for one and one-half to two months would be required to buy a pair of shoes. In the same year a Czechoslovakian worker averaged

4,340 crowns or $86.80 a month, and prices for all necessities were at least as high as in Poland. The average Hungarian worker's wages were 600 forints a month, about $51. But his take-home pay averaged only 500 forints ($42)—which is enough to purchase exactly two yards of good suit or dress material—or five shirts. A Rumanian factory worker earned from 3,500 to 7,000 lei monthly ($25 to $50). To buy a man's suit—at relatively bargain ration-card prices—required his total wages for from one to two months.

Thus the Communist wage scale throughout satellite Europe ranges between $12 and $25 *per week*. But in purchasing value puppet-state wages are below the subsistence level, and are far lower than in 1938, when free markets, vast amounts of goods and relatively moderate prices existed.

But state-fixed wage rates, of themselves, have no meaning in a Communist country. The state constantly raids the worker's pay envelope before it reaches him. He is compelled to accept repeated deductions (known as "voluntary contributions") as proof that he is a staunch proletarian devoted to "the rule of the working class." For this privilege he loses as much as 10 to 15 per cent of his monthly earnings. The Red rulers do not trust or tolerate fund-raising by the notoriously oppressive, capitalistic method of free donations and independent subscriptions. They tell every union member how much he is to contribute, and he merely finds his wages docked that much, a system admittedly much more efficient than an American-style defense-bond campaign.

The Red régimes call their cash-extracting schemes "loans." In Hungary they proceeded from a "Plan Loan" to "Peace Loans." The officially announced results are rather startling. The "take" in the 1949 plan loan is said to have been 751 million forints, or approximately $55 million; for the first peace loan (1950) just over one billion forints, or about $85 million. (The official exchange rate is 1 forint equals 8.5¢). The latter figure would put the Communists' collections at the almost incredible rate of nearly $10 for each man, woman and child in Hungary.

Even with allowance made for exaggerated claims, it is certain that a very large proportion of these sums was deducted from the wages of 1.6 million Hungarian workers and from all others who are state-employed. The second peace loan for 1951 was expected even to exceed the "take" in 1950.

In considerable measure, the miserably low wages of satellite Europe are caused by the Stalinists' excessive industrialization. No foreign capital is available to underwrite this headlong expansion; therefore, as a Polish economist points out, the people's labor is the only source of capital to finance the vast economic development. What this means is very simple. The industrial laborer is not only compelled to work himself to the bone. He is likewise forced to supply the Red state with great amounts of capital out of his insufficient earnings.

In addition, satellite workers are compelled to labor without pay for many days each year. These are the trade unionists' so-called "special offerings"—in honor of Stalin's birthday, "Liberation" Day, May Day and other Red anniversaries. Speed-ups for these compulsory celebrations frequently cover one or two weeks. Communist officials ram through a union resolution, which no member can oppose without provoking severe penalties. By it the workers "pledge themselves" to exceed their quotas for so many days, possibly necessitating much unpaid overtime—as an "offering." Here are periods of "celebration by work" imposed on Hungarian industrial employees in a space of nine months:

1. Korean Week celebration: August 1 to 7, 1950.

2. "Competition" commemorating Hungary's constitution: August 14 to 28, 1950.

3. Competition for 10th anniversary of Rakosi's release from prison: first part of September, 1950.

4. Competition for Bolshevik Revolution's 33rd anniversary: September 15 to 30, 1950.

5. Competition honoring elections of local soviets: part of October, 1950.

6. To fulfill the year's plan: from October through December, 1950.

7. Competition to honor Stalin's birthday: also late December, 1950.

8. Another to honor the second congress of the Hungarian Communist Party: January and February, 1951.

9. Competition for Liberation Day, April 4th: part of March, 1951.

10. May Day competition: In April, 1951.*

Work quotas and piece-rate wages

When they were courting labor the Stalinists denounced piecework as "capitalistic exploitation," but by 1951 they were introducing it wholesale. In Hungary, following a May, 1951, decree, 56 per cent of industrial workers were put on piece-rate wages. In most plants overtime pay was also abolished.

A further method of exploitation is the use—and abuse—of the quota or norm, the amount of work that must be turned out each day by the worker and on which his wages are based. To cut the pay it is necessary only to raise the norm. For example, the Sopron State Lock Company in Hungary pays its lockmakers (on paper) 468 forints a month, but the joker is that this is for a norm of 136 locks a day, which is so far beyond what the worker can turn out that the actual wages average only 240 forints a month.

Norms are fixed according to the capacity of the 5 or 10 per cent of ablest, most skilled employees. Rumanian shipyard workers were already pushed hard by a norm of 400 rivets to be driven per eight-hour day. To justify a speed-up, the Red bosses brought in a shock-worker, Peter Banu. (Shock-workers function like demons, greatly exceed their quotas, and become party pets.) Of course, the press hailed Banu's "great achievement." It soon

* *The Right to Work in Hungary,* by Dr. Alexander C. Brunauer of the European Studies Center. National Committee for a Free Europe: November, 1951.

developed, however, that most of his record-breaking rivets were driven askew. Nevertheless, the shipyard workers' daily quota was boosted to 800 rivets. Most of them could manage barely half that number. Their wages automatically declined in proportion. Even apprentice miners, aged 16 to 20, labor against quotas in the Czech coal pits: four carloads to be filled during each shift the first year, five carloads the second year.

During 1951 many workers had their wages reduced, through increased production norms, by 20 to 25 per cent. This policy of "more work for less pay" and numerous other abuses antagonized industrial workers to such a degree that the five-year plans fell seriously below their goals, a condition the planners attempted to meet by means of:

Speed-ups through "Socialist competitions."

"Socialist competitions" are Stalinist speed-ups—nothing else. One shop department or group of workmen competes with another to exceed production quotas. The worker who smashes all individual records for output becomes a "labor hero" or Stakhanovite. He is hated by his fellow workers because he serves as a dupe—the Communists' necessary excuse to impose equally killing efforts on everyone. It requires enormous endurance, some skill and a minimum of brains to become a Stakhanovite.

Poland's first, Wincenty Pstrowski, drove himself far beyond sane limits for sixteen months. Then he contracted pernicious anemia. Despite that, the party sent him on a propaganda tour to sell the idea of workers' competitions. In Lodz workmen's wives beat him up badly. Pstrowski's tour was canceled and he died a few months later. But while they can hold the pace Stakhanovites are fêted and fawned upon and extravagant publicity is showered on them. For the speed-up champions are useful to goad and coerce their fellow-workers; they are an alibi for imposing brutal work quotas on all labor.

Throughout captive Europe *compulsory overwork* is the foundation of Communist labor policy. In Poland schools for Stakhanovites are established by the z.m.p. (Communist Youth Union), in conjunction with factory councils. A network of "speed-up" training schools is planned, with experienced shock-workers and technicians acting as instructors. A new system for training industrial workers was introduced in Hungary by an August, 1951, decree. Stakhanovite champions teach candidates for "honor and glory" how to speed themselves up toward permanent undermining of their health. Hungary's Reds have also started organizing "party groups, headed by trusted agents," in factory shifts and shop brigades. They educate workers for overfulfillment of quotas and expansion of the shock-worker system. But these ceaseless pressures cannot diminish the rank and file's resistance to speed-up exploitation. Out of three million Czechoslovakian workers, with 900,000 allegedly members of the Communist Party, only 200,000 were listed as shock-workers in 1950. Such facts as these explain:

Slow-downs and sabotage.

"Labor discipline" is an obsession of the Red slave-drivers. All satellite régimes have strongly punitive laws on this subject, providing that workers "have no right to dissolve the contract of work" and imposing deductions from wages up to 25 per cent for absenteeism. Heavy penalties still fail to prevent workers from quitting their jobs in large numbers. Their continued absenteeism remains a major problem. Eastern Europe's workers fight back as the peasants fight back, with every ruse and obstructive practice at their command. It is almost impossible for the Communist bosses to determine where slow-downs, shoddy work and similar subterfuges pass the line into outright destructive sabotage. A few examples of the weapons used by workers must suffice.

Absenteeism: At Hungary's Danube Construction Enterprise the party press admitted that 35,180 work hours were lost, and that 1,552 workmen were reported absent without adequate reason in the month of May, 1951, alone. The Communist daily *Nepszava* stated that "between 300,000 and 400,000 tons of coal are lost annually through absenteeism" (July 13, 1951). In this manner rebellious trade unionists are inflicting serious, often very large, losses on five-year plan production in all Iron-Curtain countries.

The intimidations and warnings to which the governments are driven is clearly shown by Prague's *Rudè Pràvo* (October 18, 1951): "An employee who misses one shift without good reason may not be aware to what extent he is cheating himself by doing so. Assume that he earns 22 crowns (44¢) per hour. He loses 176 crowns ($3.52) in his wages for that shift. His vacation is cut by two days, which means a further loss of 352 crowns ($7.04). He also forfeits his claim to one-sixth of his Christmas bonus, or 250 crowns ($5.00). Thus he cheats himself out of at least 778 crowns ($15.56). If he is a miner, he suffers the further loss of his loyalty bonus. . . . Finally, the shirker disqualifies himself for selection for recreation teams, participation in cultural tours, etc."

Labor Turnover: Everywhere workers resort to disruptive tactics. Labor "migration" remains extremely high, although the legal penalties are severe. So many workers change jobs—and their work is so badly needed—that the state is relatively helpless. In the third quarter of 1951 Hungary's labor turnover (admitted by the régime) was 46.2 per cent in building industries; 38 per cent in mining; 15.6 per cent in textiles—all a marked increase over the previous quarter.

Szabad Nep reported on June 15, 1951: "At [Hungary's] Danube Construction Enterprise 1,205 workmen, *i.e.*, almost one-third of the total workers, quit of their own accord in April. At the Concrete Construction Enterprise within one month 1,112 workmen left without the manager's permission. The Szuhavolgy Coal Mines lost 538 workmen in recent months. . . . Migration of workers has assumed dangerous proportions in mining, building and in numerous heavy-industry plants." While most satellite régimes avoid publishing specific figures, their denunciations of labor "migration" speak eloquently.

Sabotage: Deeply resentful overworked employees drop a

remarkable amount of sand, dirt or tools into intricate machinery. Communist dailies reiterate wrathful demands for "increased vigilance against saboteurs," denounce "damages to plants," "lack of workers' responsibility," etc. Rumanian oil wells catch fire mysteriously, or storage-tank valves are left open. Courageous villagers secretly tap oil pipelines, even though they face death sentences if caught. Factories in every satellite country report an extraordinary number of "accidents" which take insidiously untraceable forms. Trials of persons charged with sabotage, accompanied by very harsh sentences, have not stopped the rash of accidents. Who can tell how much is due to old or overstrained equipment, to bureaucratic bungling or to clumsy, unskilled personnel, and how much to shrewd manipulation?

Rejects and waste: The Red press regularly publishes items like these: Bulgaria: "Because of poor quality the output of the September 9th plant remains in warehouses as frozen capital." In Hungary: "The Men's Wear National Enterprise of Kispest manufactured several thousand suits which cannot be sold because the color of the trousers differs from that of the coats. . . . Twenty suits, size 52, were taken out of stock. Not one complied with the prescribed size. . . . Because of a serious defect 2,000 women's overcoats are useless." In Rumania: The régime was driven to issue a decree (January, 1951) that "workers responsible for rejects are not to be paid. Cases of partial rejects will bring reductions in wages."

The speed-up and poor-quality materials cause much of this. Take a report on the condition of certain new workers' apartments in Budapest, smuggled out by an occupant just two months after their completion: "40 per cent of the doors cannot be closed because their frames are loosened and cracked. The same is true of 60 per cent of the windows. 27 per cent of the latches do not work. About 25 per cent of electrical switches are broken, and as many water pipes are entirely useless. More than one-fourth of the lavatory plumbing does not function. One out of five wooden toilet seats are cracked; nearly as many toilet bowls are broken. Our elevators operate about ten days out of the month; are under repair the rest of the time."

The Russians themselves are responsible for much industrial inefficiency. The Hungarian underground reports that 32 carloads of defective Soviet-manufactured carbon and graphite electrodes have been stored in Diosgyor since 1947. The electrodes melted almost immediately when they were tested. Finally, in 1950, Budapest asked Moscow not to ship in any more Soviet electrodes. But the Russians refused to cancel the orders and kept shipping them—still of very inferior quality, and at three times the world price!

How to run railroad locomotives on half oil rations

A chief engineer from the Hungarian railroads' engine shops escaped to Yugoslavia in June, 1951. A few weeks earlier the Hungarian government had ordered rigid economy in the use of oil and lubricants. The engineer got his orders to reduce sharply the oiling of his locomotives. Since it was impossible to keep them in constant use on inadequate oil, he disregarded the planners' instructions. Then he received a curt command to cut down the oil used on his locomotives by 50 per cent. He had no choice but to comply. Soon afterward the engines were breaking down right and left. For obeying absolute orders in the face of his own warnings the engineer was promptly accused of sabotage by the Red bureaucrats. He lit out for the border that same night. He reports that the only engines which are not breaking down constantly in Hungary today are the so-called "Truman engines"—American locomotives delivered to Hungary after the war.

Russian-style "efficiency" and Communist bureaucracy are unwitting allies of the resentful, malingering workers. The Stalinists overwork machines exactly as they do men and women. Even when machinery is badly in need of repair, a Polish observer reports, "no company exists that would dare undertake repair jobs which are not provided for in the state plans. By pausing to make repairs they fear they will fail to meet the factory's norms. So machines are used until they are useless."

The Tatabanya mine disaster

The alarm lamps flickered in the Hungarian coal mines at Tatabanya one day late in December, 1950. It was a sure sign of the menacing presence of firedamp. Recognizing the danger of an explosion, the chief engineer ordered the pits evacuated and closed down operations. But local Communist officials refused to take his word that the mine was dangerous. They informed Budapest that the engineer was sabotaging production. The Ministry of Mines ordered the pit crews back to work. When they refused, more than 200 were arrested, and their vegetable plots also confiscated. The remaining miners still boycotted the contaminated pits.

But the Red régime had an answer. It ordered hundreds of young Communists, members of the D.I.S.Z. youth organization, to work the mine. The chief engineer insisted that they first sign papers stating that they assumed the risk voluntarily. The young men went down, under party orders, and for two hours nothing happened. Then a terrific explosion rent the mine. Eventually more than 400 bodies were removed from the pits. No word of this disaster appeared in the Hungarian press. It was only five months later that Radio Free Europe received, via the underground, a reliable account of the exact causes and the dimensions of this disaster.

Save for those in slave-labor camps, Eastern Europe's miners are the most brutally exploited of all workers under Stalinist domination. They are everywhere forced to work with antiquated, worn equipment under notoriously unsafe conditions. In scores of Polish, Czech and other puppet-state mines very few automatic boring machines exist. Cars are almost entirely loaded with shovels and pushed by the men—or by women. Fatal accidents are frequent; loss of legs or arms is a common occurrence. If a Polish miner fails to report for work four days in a month, 20 per cent is deducted from his wages. A fifth absence sends him to a "labor court," where sentences range from six months to one year of slave labor—the only worse living fate possible for any East European miner. In Czechoslovakia four monthly absences bring a sentence at slave labor, and miners who miss a single shift are not allowed to eat in the company canteen. Miners everywhere are worked to near exhaustion by excessively high quotas. Their daily risks are enormously increased by the importation of recruits, half-trained or untrained, from Communist youth organizations. No less than 10,000 youths were drafted to work in the mines by the Prague government in February, 1951.

Captive Europe's hundreds of thousands of miners (more than 325,000 in Poland alone) react to these intolerable conditions by sabotaging production through slow-downs, fake sickness, breaking equipment and in every other possible way. Miners are so openly hostile that Communist control officers rarely dare to go down into the pits. Yet the great majority of these same miners were originally enthusiastic Communists. Within a few years most of them—in many pits 80 to 90 per cent of them—have been permanently transformed into bitter anti-Communists.

By mid-autumn, 1951, a coal-production crisis seriously disrupted the satellite régimes' five-year plans. Not surprisingly, Hungary's Tatabanya mine, the scene of the Red-precipitated disaster, was held "responsible for almost 50 per cent of the amount with which the mining industry fell short of the set target." At an emergency conference of Red chiefs Matyas Rakosi bitterly assailed "unwarranted absenteeism" and threatened "severe action . . . against the enemy in the mines." The coal shortage forced cancellation of various trains from the winter timetables in Czechoslovakia. The leading party daily, *Rudè Pràvo*, on October 16, 1951, published unprecedented admissions: "The work of our most important coal region, the Ostrava-Karvina mines, is not at all satisfactory. . . . The number of regular workers has decreased by about 5,000 since 1947. . . . The chief cause of this shameful state of affairs are very serious shortcomings and mistakes of our economic authorities and organs of the party. . . . Above all, from the fact that the economic and party authorities paid very little attention to technical progress."

Instead of compromising, the Kremlin answered the workers' intense resistance by drastically boosting the satellites' five-year plans during 1951; those of Poland, Czechoslovakia and Hungary (the most industrialized Curtain countries) by approximately 100 per cent. Along with this, the puppet governments were ordered to accelerate their labor-recruitment drives. Moscow's programs for sweeping industrialization of its colonial puppet nations are so vast, their deadlines so extreme, that desperate expedients are unavoidable. This explains:

The gigantic labor drafts.

Warsaw's Minister of Finance, Hilary Minc, declared in 1950 that Poland must put two million new workers into industrial jobs by 1955. (Other Polish officials have since cited a minimum goal of 1.3 million.) A previous rate of 100,000 new Polish workers annually has been increased to more than 350,000 a year. In Czechoslovakia the projected average increase exceeds 100,000 a year; party leaders were aiming to corral 350,000 into industry by January, 1952—including 77,500 former state-employed white-collar citizens, now forcibly put into overalls. Under Hungary's plan 650,000 new workers must be created by 1954, the goal for 1951 being 160,000.

These figures are necessary to convey the vast scale of the Stalinists' labor-recruitment programs. Millions of peasants and housewives are slated to be drafted into factories and forced into Communist unions, where they can be regimented, coerced and controlled. Approximately one-third of all new recruits will be women. This percentage is due to be much increased as part of:

The Soviet exploitation of women.

In industry, in militarization programs, in collective farms, in Women's Unions and other activities, the Communists have already harnessed close to a majority of Eastern Europe's women. Their tragic plight should serve as a warning to women in every free land. These are samples of authentic underground information from several Iron-Curtain countries:

Poland: "At Wroclaw 1,000 women are employed as turners, machinists and blacksmiths in the state railroad repair plant. . . . 7,000 women in electrical industries . . . More than 2,000 as construction workers on the great Nowa Huta industrial project, including the first women's bricklayer brigade. . . . As engine-stokers on the railroads . . . Under instruction at the Znin professional school for female railroad workers, to become conductors, brakemen, etc."

Czechoslovakia: "Women are working as railroad conductors, signal operators and porters. . . . In coal pits as miners . . . As gas-station servicemen . . . They are replacing men as trolley conductors, in bakeries, as mailmen, also at shoe-repairing. . . . Several thousand are now carpenters, bricklayers and electricians."

Hungary: "Women are being given six-week courses as locomotive engineers, carpenters, masons, etc. . . . Ever larger assignments in heavy industry, at all kinds of jobs previously monopolized by men . . ."

Conditions in captive Europe's mines do not deter the Communist labor czars. From Poland to Bulgaria more and more young women and girls are being sent down into the pits. Bulgaria has "women's brigades" in the mines. Rumania's leading party newspaper launched a recruitment drive, in September, 1950, under the headline: "Even women can learn to become miners." Teen-age girls, as well as women, are reported digging coal or loading carts in Rumanian mines. Girls' brigades also work in Rumania's oil fields.

Why are the Stalinists putting Eastern Europe's women into men's jobs on an enormous and expanding scale? Their basic concept is perfectly sound: huge industrialization programs cannot be achieved without women. This means the all-out mobilization of captive-state women in every conceivable sphere where their strength and capacities can be used. Labor-recruitment drives center on housewives and young girls. After putting nearly 150,000 Czechoslovakian women into industrial jobs in 1950, Prague's Red leaders were still drafting women at the rate of more than 200,000 a year the following autumn. Their quota for 1953 is 250,000—33 per cent of new labor. The ratio is almost identical in Poland and Hungary, where females above 18 are urged to "cease being household slaves."

Budapest's régime sharply raised its demands for increased womanpower in production in a May 20, 1951 decree which stated: "Women should constitute a significant part of new workers (about 50 per cent) in all branches of state administration, especially in transportation and commerce. Women should participate in technical-training courses to the extent of from 30 to 50 per cent."

Moscow's method for controlling Eastern Europe's women can and would be used by Red régimes anywhere. The party abolishes all women's organizations except its own "Unions of Democratic Women." Working women and other state employees are forced to join. Many others are enticed by false promises, or seek to provide their husbands and families with political protection. Both in Poland and Rumania more than two million women had been enrolled by 1952. Including Eastern Germany, the total membership is approximately seven million.

Man hunts for workers

The Red governments' exploitation of workers is so widely known that puppet-state adults, male or female, have no desire whatever to volunteer for the new labor brigades. Ever since 1950 satellite authorities have staged what amount to nationwide man hunts and woman hunts, combing both the cities and the rural areas. In Budapest, Prague and Warsaw, party recruiters and "educators" stop people in the streets and demand their identity cards. The "Economic Division" of the secret police raids cafés and restaurants. Anyone whose papers do not indicate satisfactory working or political status is dispatched to whatever job the state and party may select.

The Stalinist planners' need for labor is so great and increasing so fast that 100,000 East Germans, mostly skilled metal workers, were shipped into Polish factories by September, 1951. They had two-year contracts, with higher wages than are paid to Poles. According to Berlin reports, at least another 150,000 East Germans are scheduled for transfer to Poland, Czechoslovakia and Hungary. Meanwhile, by July, 1951, the Soviets had imposed labor-conscription laws in satellite Germany for the first time, affecting able-bodied males between 14 and 60 and females between 15 and 51. In September new labor offices for compulsory registration were set up. The labor transfers, both carried out and planned, indicate that Eastern Germany's pool of skilled labor (most of 4.5 million workers), unique behind the Iron Curtain, will hereafter be exploited to the limit by Moscow.

The Communist régimes' endless difficulties are not only due to the fact that the great majority of labor draftees are conscripted against their will. In addition, the "greenhorns," being totally unskilled, are deeply resented by experienced workmen, who are supposed to transform them into reliable performers within a few weeks. The party press repeatedly publishes criticism and complaints such as this: "The railroad-construction companies did not provide living quarters for recruited manpower. . . . In some places new workers were kept waiting for many days. No notice whatever was taken of them. . . . The same situation occurred at the enamelware plant in Kebanya [Hungary]. The excuse was that new workers were unskilled, that they cannot be entrusted with work, and are good only for sweeping the premises." * What else might be expected of forcibly converted farmhands, government clerks or housewives? A Czech Communist roundly berates plant managers who previously complained about lack of personnel "and now they find all sorts of reasons for rejecting the offered new workers."

Whether they like it or not, several million Eastern Europeans

* *Nepszava* [Budapest newspaper], April 8, 1951.

will be forced to join the ranks of Red-unionized labor during the next few years. But already Soviet industrialization has radically changed the occupational composition of Poland and Hungary, is changing it considerably in all Curtain countries. In 1931 the percentage of Poland's population dependent directly upon agriculture was 61.4 per cent; for other occupations, 38.6 per cent. By December, 1950, the Polish census revealed only 45.7 per cent in agriculture, with 54.3 per cent in other occupations.

The over-all percentage of industrial workers and their families has risen in Hungary from 14.7 per cent in 1930 to 17.2 per cent in 1949. But another change is much more striking. The percentage of workers in manufacturing enterprises, as compared with all types of industrial workers, has increased from 35.3 per cent in 1930 to 69 per cent in January, 1951. By now, workers in Hungarian heavy industry have more than doubled their prewar numbers. And Russia's industrial-revolutionizing programs rumble heedlessly onward, irrespective of their cost in disrupted lives, in overwork, in strained resources, above all, in loss of independence for the workers themselves.

CHAPTER NINE

Economic Conquest

THE COUNTRIES OF SATELLITE EUROPE ARE bound to Soviet Russia's chariot by chains of economic dependence that cut deeper into their flesh year by year. Under the constant threat of torture and punishment they must work and produce primarily for Russia's interests, Russia's profits and Russia's power. How does this Red imperialism function?

It operates through a stupendous industrial revolution, Kremlin-planned and Kremlin-directed. Six countries, four of them predominantly agricultural for fifteen centuries or more, are being transformed into industrialized states, and are being remade in the Soviet economic image. This is an utterly ruthless, typically Stalinesque operation. Although it was only started in 1949, in the form of puppet-state five-year plans, it has already progressed amazingly far.

Never before has a great industrial revolution been foreign-conceived and foreign-imposed. Radically and irreversibly, it is changing the lives of 90 million people in a vast area almost exactly as large as Western Germany, Denmark, Holland, Belgium, Luxembourg, France and Italy.

How drastically will these historic changes alter the balance of power between the Soviet East and the free West? How seriously may they affect the lives of all citizens in the democratic countries? How may they ultimately threaten the foreign markets, and hence the employment and prosperity, of Western nations, including the United States? The puppet states' five-year plans are shrouded in statistical fog. Somewhere behind it, at present barely discernible, lie answers which must increasingly affect all persons who live in the free countries. But we can already grasp the essential meanings behind the satellites' five-year plans. They are implicit in the Kremlin's major objectives:

1) To bind the East European nations' economies to Russia so that the puppet states are integrated, *de facto*, into the Soviet system.

2) To build Russia's power by making captive Europe's production supplement and increase the Soviet Union's economic strength.

3) To increase the arms and war-purpose output of the Stalinist bloc of nations.

4) To create new armament industries close to the front of any possible East-West war, as advanced bases for weapons, supplies and repairs.

Despite formidable obstacles and much blundering, the satellites' five-year plans have achieved impressive progress toward all these objectives. Consider a few existing facts and future probabilities as authoritatively presented by Dr. Jan Wszelaki, formerly Economic Adviser to the Polish Foreign Office.*

"The 90 million satellite population produces as many basic industrial goods per capita as the 200 million or more inhabitants of Soviet Russia. Roughly speaking . . . one-half as much hard fuel and electric power, about one-third as much steel, and more than one-fifth as much oil as Russia.

"In 1950 the per-capita industrial production of Poland and Hungary is said to have exceeded that of Italy . . . Czechoslovakia's that of France.

"The total electric power supposed to be produced in 1954–55 in the entire [satellite] area may be estimated at 80 billion kilowatts—more than the war output of Germany.

"The 1950 steel output exceeded eight million tons—about one-third the steel production of the Soviet Union during the same year. The goal for 1954–55 is about 16.5 million tons—a

* "The Rise of Industrial Middle Europe." *Foreign Affairs:* October, 1951.

figure which British industry reached only in 1950 . . . and
Germany used less than 16 million tons of steel in direct and
indirect preparation for World War II.

"Nearly all steel produced in the satellites will be used in
building factories, making machines and perhaps weapons of war,
or else will go to Russia and be used there for the same purposes."

Russia seizes economic control of Eastern Europe.

When the Kremlin barred both Soviet and satellite participation in the Marshall Plan it denounced that project as an instrument of "American imperialism," designed for "the economic
enslavement of Europe." Then Moscow proceeded, as usual, to
practice precisely what it denounced most violently. In January,
1949, it brought the satellite régimes into a Council of Mutual
Economic Aid, called "Comecon," but better known as the
Molotov Plan. This provided the central vehicle for the puppet-
state five-year plans (six-year for Poland), which were immediately launched. In Stalinese "mutual aid" means economic
exploitation by and for Russia. Comecon's five-year plans were
to force the industrialization of all the East European countries,
and in so doing to make them dependent upon Soviet raw materials and on Soviet markets for export. The satellite governments and peoples had no choice; Moscow drafted the main
features of their supposedly national plans. The puppet régimes
were simply ordered to put them into effect.

The Soviets' "mutual aid" programs make Marshall Plan
"exploitation" seem like 2-per cent beer. To begin to compare
with them Washington would, for example, have had to force
Britain's Labor Government to turn all of its nationalized industries back to private ownership before extending a dollar of E.C.A.
aid. Through the five-year plans and Comecon trade agreements,
Russia tells its European vassals what their economic system
must be; how fast they must build new industries; where they
must build them; how much they must increase production each
year. It also tells them what they must buy from the U.S.S.R.;

how much they must sell to Russia—and in both cases the Soviets dictate the prices. Moscow calls this absolute control of other nations' economies "building Socialism." The Kremlin's Red emperor makes prewar "Western imperialism" look like the original one-horse shay.

How the satellites' five-year plans build Russia's military and economic power

Moscow's exported, sovietized industrial revolution is not intended to produce consumers' goods for the puppet states' threadbare and hungry populations. Its immediate purpose is to create heavy industry for arms production. Hundreds of new satellite projects are chiefly concerned with production of fuel and electric power, steel, machinery, cement and chemicals—the vital war industries.

At least seven massive new steel combines are being built. Their capacity of eight million tons will double Eastern Europe's 1950 production by 1954–55. These Kremlin-ordered Pittsburghs are mushrooming at Czestochowa and Nowa Huta (near Cracow) in Poland; at Nova Ostrava and near Kosice in Slovakia; in Bradenburg and Furstenburg-am-Oder in Eastern Germany; at Dunapentele in Hungary. Nova Ostrava includes three blast furnaces, machine plants, a large power plant and more than 40 other structures. More than 30,000 workers were reported occupied on construction there early in 1951. Poland's gigantic Nowa Huta combine alone entails the creation of a city of 100,000.

Moscow conceives of the new Polish-Czechoslovakian steel regions as the "Eastern Ruhr." They will use Ukrainian iron ore and Polish coke. Actually the Bohemian-Silesian coal deposits total approximately 67 billion tons, compared with 55 billion tons in German's Ruhr. The Ukraine's iron-ore deposits are about 1.5 billion tons.*

* "Behind the Czech Purge," by Robert Dall. *The Reporter Magazine:* July 10, 1951.

After 1955 the Soviets contemplate another group of big steel plants in Poland and Saxony. Thus the five-year plans appear capable of creating an industrial complex which may finally surpass the mighty Ruhr in production. Already the satellite East has registered tremendous gains. The rapid tempo of industrialization is indicated by the 296 new major projects in Poland alone. Several hundred more are being pushed fanatically toward completion in the other puppet states.

We must not be misled by the fact that the five-year plans consistently fall short of their fixed goals in many categories. In part this is caused by inadequate coal output due to miners' obstructionism, by workers' sabotage and by bad management. But the plans also fail to meet their quotas because Moscow boosts their requirements so extravagantly. Its unreasonableness is illustrated by the virtual doubling of heavy-industry goals in the Polish, Czech and Hungarian 1951 plans. Some satellites are well ahead of their original plan schedules in certain lines. A 90 or even an 80 per cent achievement—instead of 100 per cent—still constitutes a big gain. By all past standards, Eastern Europe's industrialization, literally through blood, sweat and tears, is progressing phenomenally.

The puppet states pour billions of dollars into construction of heavy industry, dams, power plant and related projects. Poland's 1951 plan provides 19 billion zlotys (or $4,750,000,000) for heavy industry and increased coal output. Satellite heavy industrial plants already in operation are engaged predominantly in war production: small arms, armor, ammunition, grenades, tank parts, airplane engines, plane parts, railroad stock, etc. At least 30 East German factories were making parts for Soviet-type tanks, especially the T-34, as early as 1950. Czechoslovakia's great armaments plants have been operating on three shifts per day for a long time. Many of Poland's, Hungary's and Rumania's largest factories have been converted to military production.* Sections of scores of plants are sealed off for "security"

---

* The extensiveness of satellite arms production is indicated by a partial sampling of underground reports from Hungary. Even though Hungary has much less industry than Poland or Czechoslovakia, its war plants in 1951

purposes. New arms factories are so crudely disguised by name that workers joke about working in a "chocolate" or a "soap" factory.

What is behind Russia's build-up of heavy industries in satellite Europe?

This question is compelling because Moscow has completely reversed its earlier postwar policy of stripping the puppet states of mechanical installations. When the Russians shifted to a program of industrializing the satellites in 1949 the Kremlin obviously determined to integrate all of captive Europe into the Soviet system. Russia has already built up a far greater monopoly of trade with Eastern Europe than Nazi Germany established through Dr. Schacht's barter deals between 1933 and 1939. Czech exports to Russia from 50 leading factories and mines were increased from 30 per cent to 45 per cent or considerably higher in the first two years of Prague's plan. In 1951 more than 50 per cent of Rumania's steel went to the Soviet Union, as well as much larger amounts of oil and lumber. More than 50 per cent of Poland's trade was diverted to the Soviet during 1951, and it is expected to reach 75 per cent in 1955; Russia's trade monopoly is scheduled to be further increased in regard to every satellite.

The Russians are driving toward a new strategic objective. In the event of war Russia's armies once would have been dependent on Soviet-produced arms and equipment delivered from distant Leningrad, Moscow or the Ukraine, transportable only over a very few railroad lines which are extremely vulnerable to Western bombing. The only means to reduce this "target ex-

included the following: The large Csepel Island plants near Budapest—reported making airplanes, arms and ammunition; the big Budapest Ganz Works—naval engines and equipment; the large Meinl plants in Budapest—operated entirely under Russian control (nature of products not established); a highly secret plant near Budapest, employing 6,000 (nature of weapons unknown); a large new arms plant at Törökbalint; at Diosgyör—spare parts for tanks and planes, also munitions; at Mason-Magyarovar—also munitions; in underground factories near Bobbagyi—airplane engines and munitions.

posure" was by the creation of heavy industries in the Curtain countries. The five-year plans, if they succeed, assure Soviet armies of great amounts of weapons, munitions and spare parts much nearer any combat front in Europe than Russian factories. In the advanced forward area of satellite Europe such supplies are now being produced, distributed and stockpiled.

Another vital feature of this gigantic industrialization concerns Moscow's assignment of specialized roles to each puppet state. Dr. Wszelaki shows graphically how this operates: *

"Czechoslovakia is intended to become the principal steelmaker . . . to supply heavy machinery . . . also precision tools. Eastern Germany's long tradition of specialization in electrical, optical and electronic equipment gives it first place in this field . . . also for heavy machinery, ship-building, synthetic oil and rubber. Hungary is slated to produce aluminum, rolling stock and much machinery. Poland . . . will become the principal producer of chemicals, as well as a large manufacturer of medium machinery. Rumania is to concentrate on the output of oil and gas . . . to develop new industries. Bulgaria's industrial role is inconsequential for the time being."

Poland's director of economic planning, Hilary Minc, reveals the Stalinists' strategy without circumlocution: "Thus the development of economic relations between the u.s.s.r. and the people's democracies leads to a planned tie-up of their economies. Every country builds those branches of industry, especially of heavy industry . . . of which there is the greatest need in other friendly countries." **

How a five-year plan is applied under a Communist government

The system is virtually identical in structure wherever a Stalinist régime exists. At the top is the big Red boss—the Office of State Planning. Next come the federal ministries which direct

* The Rise of Industrial Middle Europe." *Foreign Affairs:* October, 1951.
** *Pravda,* September 25, 1951.

and administer the plan—one for each type of industry. Since each ministry required some kind of organization to see that its directives were carried out, satellite régimes originally established regional or field directorates under the ministry concerned. These directorates have recently been abandoned in Czechoslovakia and some other puppet states. The nationalized industries are really split up into regional groupings of steel, automotive, chemical, electrical and all other types of plants. These regional groups of related industries are called "National Enterprises." And all the individual plants, National Enterprises and federal ministries are bound hand and foot by the directives of the five-year plan.

The first five-year plans came from Moscow. The original experts in "Communist building" had to show their disciples exactly how it was done. But once the Soviet pattern was imposed—the vast skeleton of state control established—executives of the individual National Enterprise were permitted to try to figure out how much their combined plants could produce during the coming year. So each plant works out its own draft plan and submits it to the manager of the National Enterprise to which it belongs—say N.E. #147. Since N.E. #147 is composed of eight plants, its management gets eight separate tentative plans. The planning department of N.E. #147 and its top executives meet and revise the eight production plans into a proposed plan for N.E. #147 as a whole—say for 1953. Finally this plan for a single National Enterprise goes up the ladder to its particular ministry in Warsaw or Prague.

The plan proposed by N.E. #147 is based on what its own officials are convinced its units can produce. Nevertheless it ultimately reaches the capital's Office of State Planning along with hundreds of other Enterprise Plans. Then the big Red planners put all these individual plans under the microscope, shuffle and revise them—almost invariably upward—according to what the top Communists demand—really according to what Moscow says must be produced. When the big Red planners have worked out their own sets of quotas for each segment of industry, that plan is delivered to its respective ministry—as an absolute order. The ministry has to see to it that its plan is fulfilled. The over-all regional plans are sent down the chain of control and the bad news of "how you are to accomplish the almost impossible" is delivered to National Enterprise #147, in the shape of its (normally) upward-revised plan. Ditto for all other enterprises.

Everything is ordered from the top of the Communist economic pyramid. What happens in the individual plant and to its executives is of no consequence to the Red bosses, so long as their demands are met. But the system's weaknesses and contradictions are most apparent when you examine:

How a nationalized enterprise is organized and managed.

As a typical and important example, take the world-famous Skoda Works in Czechoslovakia. I am indebted to Dr. J. F. Charvat, formerly general manager of the Czechoslovak Ceramics Works, for the following authoritative summary. Dr. Charvat emphasizes the fact that Skoda's plant management operates exactly as all other National Enterprises operate in satellite Europe. Its administration is divided as follows:

1) At the top a general manager or director, appointed by the government or by the specific ministry concerned, or with their approval.

2) A board of directors, purely advisory, which meets once a month and whose recommendations are not binding on the manager.

3) A general secretary.

4) Separate departments: for planning, purchasing, technical matters, labor and social security, bookkeeping and "plant security."

"The only fields where Skoda's general manager and his heads of department have an opportunity for some initiative and independent thinking," Dr. Charvat reports, "are in the planning and technical departments. It's true that the manager presents his suggestions while preparing for a new five-year plan. But his recommendations are bound to fail if they are based on purely economic considerations. The manager must give most rigid attention to the Communist Party's general policy. The people's and the country's economic interests are completely irrelevant. Party interests always win. *In the Communists' view the national economy is an obedient servant of party policy.*

"At the outset of a five-year period the Ministry of Heavy Engineering hands the Skoda Works its particular Enterprise plan in detail. It specifies the exact quantity of goods to be produced over the next five years; the estimated quantities of coal, power and raw materials Skoda factories will require to fill their quotas; the number of new workers and salaried personnel that must be taken on. On this basis the management apportions separate quotas for each of its plants, for every week of the year. The more detailed the Enterprise plan, the more restricted is its manager's initiative.

"But even within these limits the management is subject to further restrictions. A National Enterprise's management has no authority over the sale of the products which it makes, nor over its profits. In any communized industry there are two entirely independent organizations concerned with sales: one in charge of distributing goods inside the country under the supervision of the Ministry of Internal Trade; the other handling exports under the Ministry of Foreign Trade.

"Like all National Enterprises, Skoda has to sell its products to one or the other of these trade organizations. But Skoda's management cannot determine the prices at which its products are sold. Another Red state agency, the Price Office, fixes prices for all products, and they are usually frozen for the duration of the five-year plan. The Enterprise management has no more say about the materials it needs. It must purchase coal, power, machinery and raw materials exactly as and where the plan stipulates.

"Of course there is no such thing as a free market for labor.

Skoda, like all other Enterprises, must apply to the Government
Employment Office, wait for its royal decision, regardless of
emergency needs—and take whatever it sends. Perhaps the
norms are impossibly high and the plan's specified amount of
new labor entirely inadequate. Production is falling badly behind. The state planners themselves may be solely responsible
in fact. But the general manager and his staff are held responsible.
The State Employment Office has no extra labor available in the
frame of the specific Enterprise plan. So if a labor shortage becomes acute, then it's the turn of the secret police to solve the
problem. The pattern is always the same. They set up a slave-
labor camp near the factories concerned. The police have no
difficulty in providing prisoner-workmen in any amount."

Dr. Charvat adds that "in a Communist economy the plant's
management is reduced strictly to an administrative function.
It is snowed under by inconceivable masses of paperwork. No
time remains for personal initiative or development of new ideas.
Even if there were time and ability, it would be too dangerous.
Failure means several years in a labor camp—where large numbers of former managers and heads of departments already are
confined throughout captive Europe. Specialists in the plants'
technical department are immersed in endless conferences and
paperwork. In addition they must wrack their brains ceaselessly
over thousands of "suggestions" which the party compels the
workers to submit as demonstrations of their devotion to the
great god production. The technicians are always on the spot.
They must carry out plan provisions which are often forced
upon them against their considered judgment. Yet they are held
responsible for the plan's fulfillment, by quotas and by dates.
In any sovietized Enterprise life is an uninterrupted nightmare of 'musts' and 'don'ts'—for every executive, of whatever
rank."

Theoretically workers participate in the management of the
National Enterprises through the Communist trade unions and
Works Councils. In practice the workers' alleged representatives
are merely Communist officials of the unions, following party

orders regardless of the workers' interests. The workers' share in management is largely or wholly fictitious. Actually it is the Communist Party which exercises a double control: over the workers by party members inside the unions and by the secret police; over management by Communist union delegates below and big Reds in upper state plan echelons above—plus "security units" inside the plants.

Factory managers' nightmares are exacerbated by critical shortages which vastly complicate or prevent plan fulfillments in all the satellites. The mad pace of industrial expansion seriously outstrips available resources. No puppet state possesses anything like the amounts of electric power, scrap iron, oil, machinery or coal-production facilities required—least of all when Russia takes huge quantities of many strategic materials. These mounting shortages provoked a general plan crisis in mid-1950 which has persisted ever since. Rather than lower the extreme demands of five-year plans, the Stalinists imposed most cruel restrictions upon their captive populations.

Tens of millions of East Europeans have been forced to go through two winters almost without coal or wood. The consequent suffering and sickness far exceeded anything experienced during World War II. Beginning in October, 1951, electric current for heating homes in Czechoslovakia was provided only from 9 P.M. to 6 A.M., no heat or hot water during the rest of the day. In restaurants, cafés, bars, movies and theaters electricity consumption was reduced 50 per cent. In Rumania all Enterprises and government offices were closed by 5:30 P.M. to save heat and light. The use of electric heaters in homes is prohibited. Such conditions are universal in all puppet states, with gasoline also rationed most drastically—even in oil-rich Rumania.

Even so, shortages in the most critical categories interpose harsh brakes on expanded production: shortages of coal, of modern oil-field equipment, of deep-drilling apparatus, of key machine tools—shortages even of screws or needles. A new plant in Craiova, Rumania, advertises for urgently needed items—among them eight slide rules! Bottlenecks beset the five-year plans in fiendish varieties and numbers. But the plans are equally confounded by:

A maze of red tape in a jungle of Red bureaucracy.

Communist state planning spawns ever increasing swarms of big and little bureaucrats. Because the plans require compulsion, from top to bottom, they necessitate a stupendous system for supervising, checking, counter-checking and watching every aspect of operations—in every line of production, in every National Enterprise. Special cadres and "security" agencies keep close tabs on everyone, ferret around for inefficiencies, search for deviations from fixed blueprints, make incessant reports, look for sabotage and evidence of "class enemy" activities. Political reliability is enormously more important than professional ability. Hence the system is full of boot-lickers and opportunists; there is much personal favoritism as well as personal vengeance. Whenever anything goes wrong scapegoats must be found and spies in every office and shop can always pin it on someone—or one department on another.

Most of all, the five-year plans present a spectacle of thousands upon thousands of bureaucrats pushing, jumping and squirming in squirrel cages of contradictions and frustration. The Red régimes' party publications are my direct authorities for this statement. Prague's *Rudè Pràvo* is plain-spoken: "The main defect in our economy is . . . insufficient individual responsibility. . . . A certain division of work is necessary. . . . However, it must never happen that instead of one Enterprise director there are, in fact, several Enterprise directors . . . that the manager, if he needs something, is referred to a number of places. . . . Frequently it occurs that orders given by the Minister either do not reach the Enterprise with their original contents, or do not reach it at all." *

Bulgaria's National Conference of Construction reached these official conclusions in April, 1951: 1) An "absurd situation"

* September 16, 1951.

has arisen in which "numerous construction projects were started before plans for them had been studied, causing a loss to the State of millions of levas"; 2) "Contradictory orders are given by each of numerous administrations . . . geologists draw their plans without taking account of technical possibilities"; 3) "There is an absence of any co-ordination in the decisions of the ministries concerned, their administrations and the engineering teams."

The Soviet control bureau for Rumania's economy scathingly blamed the country's 1950 plan failure upon "the chaos and incapacity of the bureaucracy of various nationalized Enterprises." Gross errors of planning were cited by the Russians in Rumania's petroleum and heavy industries; the incompetence of technicians (hostile toward Socialist methods of production!) was also denounced. The Soviet report demanded a radical housecleaning of economic bureaucrats—who must inevitably be replaced by more bureaucrats.

By their own confessions, the master-creators of red tape stumble around, blindly and interminably, in twisting tangles of more red tape. Hungary's Reds find a long list of reasons for their plan's serious shortcomings, but include notably among them "lack of individual responsibility, constant and unnecessary reorganization of enterprises." They cite "whole branches of industry which did not fulfill their quotas . . . [in] machine tools, diesel engines, large electrical turbines . . . [in] iron, steel and coal." Yet "individual responsibility" is precisely what the vast, state-planned bureaucracy most distrusts and is afraid to permit.

Bulgaria's State Control Commission comes up with more aggravating facts. "By allowing clerical staffs to be increased beyond authorized limits, tens of millions of levas were spent unlawfully on salaries. . . . 2.4 million levas were paid to officials who never did a day's work. . . . In 21 Enterprises 2,287,-000 levas were given unlawfully to the staff as advances against wages." *

* *Rabotnichesko Delo* [Sofia newspaper], July 17, 1951.

Bookkeeping troubles harass Hungary's régime in other ways.
Minister of Economy Gerö explains: "We pointed out the importance of the chief bookkeeper and his place in various concerns. The role of the head engineer was only defined later on."
(A curious oversight.) "So many believe the chief bookkeeper
is second in rank to the general manager. This is definitely
wrong. The manager's first deputy is the head engineer." Perhaps such confusions are not surprising. The Hungarian Reds
originally established a so-called "Factory Triangle" system in
their plants. The triangle consisted of a party secretary, the
chairman of the trade union's Factory Council and the Enterprise's manager—only three conflicting bosses for each plant.
In 1950 the triangle was ostensibly reduced to a single manager,
with party supervisors peering over his shoulders. But no reforms in the satellites have even slightly diminished:

Fantastic runarounds between the Red bureaucracies.

Poland's Ministry of Foreign Trade supplies an enlightening
example. It seems that Warsaw, faced with a steady decline in
coal production, ordered three million dollars worth of modern
mining equipment from France in 1948. By 1951 the Foreign
Trade Ministry had paid for half of this machinery in exports,
but had not yet received a single French machine. After investigating (for how many months?) the Ministry finally exploded
with extreme indiscretion: "In fact, the French factory has not
even started to work on the order because its specifications for the
work have not yet been accepted by what is described as obsti-
nate party bureaucrats." Warsaw's chief planners, after three
years, were still arguing among themselves.

Here is what happened to an order for a type of workers' caps
which was prepared in October, 1950, by c.k.d., a big Czech
machine-making plant:

December 4: Order is placed with Technomat National
Enterprise in Prague.

December 11: Technomat replies they cannot fill the order, but caps are available at N.E. Chemodroga.

December 17: Chemodroga also replies in the negative, but says N.E. Factories for Bands and Laces in Brno has the caps.

January 3: The Brno National Enterprise advises: "We are not distributors of caps, but write to N.E. Obchodni in Prague."

January 10: C.K.D. appeals in writing to a national technical magazine.

January 19: It answers: "Caps are available at the Co-operative Clothes Store in Prague." So the order is sent there.

February 6: The Co-operative Clothes Store replies: "Try and place your order with Technomat National Enterprise, 9 Rybma Street, Prague."—where the request was first made!

What C.K.D.'s procurement department officials did then was not included in this report, which is based upon C.K.D.'s files.

The Red bureaucrats' "runarounds" supply almost the only comic relief in Iron-Curtain countries. A Brno citizen needed an oil lamp. First he went to N.E. Kovomat where he got a lamp stand and a tank. Then he had to go to a branch of N.E. Technomat to get a wick; then to a glass Enterprise in a nearby town to buy the chimney. So far, so good. After a whole day of shopping around the persistent man hurried home to put his lamp together. But a screw to move the wick up and down was still missing. Next day he combed the city for a lamp screw. He was finally assured that this particular kind of screw "is not manufactured in Czechoslovakia."

The little Red bureaucrats are driven to subterfuges of every kind in attempts to escape responsibility for blunders and bottlenecks. Regarding one of the Matyas Rakosi Works' factories, an employee writes: "The warehouses are full of motor bicycles, as if everything were in perfect order. But they cannot be delivered because a certain part is still missing. The plant puts the blame on the workshop that manufactures the missing part, accusing them of delivering only 40 per cent of those required. The workshop admits this, but blames the steel foundry which

never sends the required material on time. The steel foundry
in turn puts the blame on the Material and Trade Division. That
is the way it goes throughout the factory—always someone else
is made responsible for the shortcomings." Passing the buck is
an immediate defensive reaction created by fear of discharge
or sentences at forced labor.

The lack of industrial technicians

All the puppet states suffer from grave shortages of technical
personnel, from qualified planners and engineers to specialists
of every kind, down to chief mechanics and foremen of key
departments. This is an important cause of persistent muddles
and failures in the five-year plans. Eastern Europe simply
does not possess more than a small fraction of the technological
army which is required by such huge and accelerated industrialization.

Yet Communist policies tremendously increase this deficiency.
Thousands of the captive nations' best qualified engineers and
other experts have been imprisoned as "class enemies," even
though they are irreplaceable. Then the party makes confusion
more confounding by putting communized workers into administrative posts far beyond their limited education and
capacities.

Under Hungary's plan apprentices in manufacturing industries
should be increased from 31,600 in 1949 to 85,000 in 1954; the
number of university students should be more than doubled;
science graduates tripled; technical-school students quintupled.
More than 25 per cent of the technical pupils will be women.
By March 1951, the party claimed to have 80,000 technical
apprentices, with 49 training schools in Budapest alone.

The Stalinists are driven by desperate urgency, chasing their
five-year plans as racing dogs chase mechanical rabbits, so they
are producing thousands of so-called technicians after only a few
months of spotty, high-speed training, with political reliability
placed always above technical ability. The result is something

utterly new in technological education: the creation of "technicians" with complex specialties by party-line specifications. It's not surprising that *Scanteia*, a leading party organ, deplores the Rumanian industrial managers' "lack of interest in the new technical cadres" and reports that "attendance at the four Bucharest training schools is extremely low. . . . The party strongly condemns . . . those who ignore or belittle the role of the technical cadres." Radio Bucharest describes new schools set up in factories, mines and oil refineries which are expected to turn out skilled mechanics in six months' time. Satellite universities clamor for students in engineering, chemistry and other sciences—but party interference has everywhere reduced academic standards to unprecedented lows. A good many years will be required before captive Europe's shortage of technicians can be notably decreased. Under the Reds' system it is certain that the quality of technicians can never rival the standards which are common in Western democracies. But the system does produce something else.

Red bureaucracy breeds more and bigger bureaucracy.

A striking demonstration was provided by the serious breakdown of Czechoslovakia's 1951 plan. Prime Minister Zapotocky publicly confessed before Prague's parliament that the plan had fallen badly short, especially in coal, ore, electric power, oil and heavy industry.* Significantly, this happened in the most industrialized satellite nation. Czech industry, under Red-state operation, was patently in a serious mess. Prague had just taken drastic action. The régime announced a sweeping reorganization of the entire industrial set-up on September 7, 1951. "Too many bosses! Excessive personnel!" was the reformers' cry. Administrative authority was to be centralized. As a streamlining measure, 21 general or central directorates of major industries were abolished; also ten area directorates in Slovakia.

---

* October 13, 1951. Informed Czech economists in exile estimate that these key industries actually fell from 20 to 30 per cent below their fixed quotas, far lower than was officially admitted.

These included the directorates for heavy engineering, fuel and power, chemicals, and mines. Their functions were ordered taken over by their respective ministries. It was stated that the industries' administrative staffs would be reduced by an unheard of 39 per cent. Dr. Dolansky, chairman of the State Planning Office, told the Red world that industrial enterprises had "always had to deal with a multitude of directives . . . from different superior organs, and such directives were often opposed to each other. Now a unified management of the industries concerned will be secured. Everywhere, on various levels of production management, the principle of the responsibility of one single person will be consistently applied." *

Were the Red bureaucrats themselves staging an anti-bureaucratic revolution?

When the details were examined the spots were still all over the leopard. *Five* new ministries were carved out of the Ministry of Heavy Industry: fuel and power; foundries and ore mines; chemicals; heavy engineering and general engineering; and forests and timbers. Finally, a new "Ministry of State Control" was established. Where would the heads and staffs of the "abolished" directorates go? You could safely bet that most of them would be found cozily installed in the new ministries. A lot of ambitious party "specialists" would also be looking for cushy jobs and new authority.

But the big joker was the new Ministry of State Control. The governmental decrees gave away the whole streamlining farce by declaring specifically that its sphere of activity "shall extend to all sectors of our economy; *i.e.*, to all state, co-operative and other economic and administrative organs, and also to individuals who control means of production." So the Ministry of State Control will supply another layer of bureaucrats to keep a close, suspicious eye on every branch of Czechoslovakia's production.

The Czech régime's Ministry of State Control emerges in reality as an economic M.V.D. The government's decree declares that it must wage "a systematic struggle against all shortcomings

* *Rudè Pràvo*, September 8–9, 1951.

and deficiencies in our economic and administrative machinery. The cause of these deficiencies is lack of economy in management, red tape, lack of personal responsibility—in many cases, even direct diversionism on the part of the class enemy. It is therefore essential to build up an effective system of state control which would decidedly . . . reveal the causes of shortcomings and hit those who are indeed responsible." The Czech Communists' great streamlining reform was merely a round of musical chairs.

But for all their red tape and runarounds, shortages and waste, rigidities and stupidities and flagrant exploitation of the population, the five-year plans continue to register important gains. The Kremlin-imposed industrial revolution lumbers painfully from quota to quota, from plan to plan. Like a three-legged alligator hitching itself over rocky terrain, industrialization crawls convulsively, slipping and sliding. But it cannot retreat because it is prodded savagely, without respite, by the pitchforks of slave-labor terrorists. So it keeps crawling. As long as Soviet Russia rules captive Europe this gigantic, floundering creature will keep going.

And if the frenzied Red compulsion should be removed? Whenever that may occur and in whatever fashion, a very considerable part of Eastern Europe's new industrial foundations will remain. Certainly, a new, industrialized way of life will be deeply embedded, together with new habits and new ambitions. What will happen eventually and in one way or another to much of Asia has already happened to the peoples of captive Europe. How it happened is acutely paradoxical. They have been driven into a twentieth-century economy by medievally brutal and reactionary imperialists. Nevertheless their countries have been industrialized, though at a fearful and inestimable price, much of it unnecessary. Yet the long-term gain is ineradicable. Whatever their future political systems may be, Eastern Europe's peoples can never go back.

CHAPTER TEN

Slave Labor

IN HUNDREDS OF RED PRISONS AND FORCED-labor camps throughout Eastern Europe, as in thousands of other prisons and camps throughout the Soviet Union, starvation is universal, torture a commonplace. Whole volumes could be devoted to the personal testimony of those who have miraculously survived and escaped from captive Europe. What remains truly extraordinary is the scale on which the Kremlin has exported its system of terror and torture into Eastern Europe, largely unnoticed by the press and public of the Western democracies. The free peoples remain largely ignorant of the true dimensions of Red terror in the puppet-ruled nations. The Communist inquisitors' crimes, like the Nazis', are so inhuman that our imaginations can scarcely grasp their enormity. But testimony by numbers of escaped prisoners has confirmed the procedures established in many widely separated Red prisons and camps. Their evidence demonstrates conclusively that identical refinements of torture, based on incomparable Soviet experience, are used by Communist interrogators in all captive countries. The Kremlin has simply extended into all of Eastern Europe its highly perfected police-torture systems, the result of thirty years' experience in the Soviet Union.

The expansion of Communist concentration camps far exceeds that of their prisons. At least dozens—possibly scores—of new slave-labor camps are being built every year throughout captive Europe. Some of the latest are reported to be designed to confine from 20,000 to 45,000 persons. Underground reports clearly indicate that new camps, some now nearing completion, are definitely on a larger scale than earlier ones.

How many men and women are locked up in them? Up to this writing I have never seen a single newspaper survey giving a factual report on prisons and slave-labor camps in all of Eastern Europe. The true dimensions of one of history's greatest crimes cannot be perceived by scattered, occasional news items about this or that slave camp, nor by disconnected snatches of testimony from escaped victims. But by pooling testimony from many sources it is evident that:

More than one million people are now confined in the prisons and slave camps of Eastern Europe.

This total is certainly conservative. As of May, 1951, Czech exiles in Europe and the United States had already identified 42 slave-labor camps, with approximately 200,000 occupants, in their native land. By late summer Czech underground sources placed the total at about 70 such camps, with about 30 in the region of the Jachymov uranium mines.* Major Czech prisons are also jammed to capacity. They must account for another 50,000 to 100,000 victims.

Polish authorities in exile had identified more than 50 major camps and prisons (as of September, 1951) in which were slave laborers totaling between 400,000 and 500,000. In Rumania more than 40 slave camps are known to exist, indicating a minimum of from 300,000 to 400,000 prisoners. Between 20 and 30 major camps have been identified in both Hungary and Bulgaria, to which more than 100 prisons must be added.

In Eastern Germany the Russians and local Communists continue to operate many of the most notorious death camps founded by the Nazis. Early in 1951 a Pole was finally released from Buchenwald—the same Buchenwald whose barbarities, it

---

* Among the prominent Jachymov slave camps are those known as Bratrstvi I, Svornost, Marianka, Elias I and II, Svatopluk, Prokop, Loznice, Krasno, Barbora or Vrsky, Nikola, Ostrov and Vikanov. Slave camps for Czech women include those at Plzen, Stod, Jaroslavice, Ceske Budejovice and near Pardubice.

was fervently hoped, would end forever with World War II. After five years of imprisonment and slave labor, the Pole reported that 10,000 persons, nearly 3,000 of them women, were still held there. "Until the end I never knew why I was kept a prisoner," the Pole added.

From these facts it appears probable that the total number of East Europeans in slave camps and prisons may actually approach one million, as of 1952. For all of Red-ruled Europe, including Eastern Germany, at least one out of every 90 persons is locked up either in a Communist prison or a forced-labor camp. To be more accurate, however, the ratio should be based on those citizens who are twenty years of age or older. This means that *one out of every 70 adult East Europeans is imprisoned by the Reds*. The number of jailed and slave-labor citizens is being further increased month by month.

How the Russian system works

Production and construction by forced labor is one of Soviet Russia's biggest businesses—a cartel for human exploitation. It is the greatest slave system ever imposed on humanity. This has been demonstrated irrefutably by masses of evidence submitted to the United Nations Economic and Social Council by its Commission of Inquiry into Forced Labor. Over a period of many years it is certain that the number of slave laborers in the Soviet Union has varied between a minimum of about eight million persons and a possible maximum of 20 million.*

The Soviets have now exported this system into all the countries they rule. It is one of the main features of Communism. It is also an indispensable instrument of Soviet conquest, since it is an important means of getting rid of opposition. As Communism expands slave labor must—and does—expand. To understand this clearly one needs merely to examine how the system began and how it functions in the Soviet Union.

"Compulsory labor" was provided for in the very first labor

* Albert Konrad Herling, *op. cit.*

code adopted by the Soviets in December, 1918. Its first article declared that all Soviet citizens, except for those under 16 and over 50, and those physically unfit, "shall be subject to compulsory labor." In 1922 the Soviet Criminal Code frankly introduced "forced labor" as a penalty for those whose "actions are *not proved* to have been counterrevolutionary." Thus the Bolsheviks have enslaved suspected opponents of their régime without trials since their first years in power.

It appears that originally "re-education through labor" was not intended to introduce a vast slave system, but it was soon brutalized by the Bolsheviks' new "state within the state," the G.P.U. (later renamed M.V.D.). How the Soviets' compulsory labor evolved into the gigantic and barbarous Gulag system is told with rare clarity by Edward Crankshaw.* The urgency demanded by the first five-year plan coincided at the end of the 1920's with the liquidation of the kulaks, and the deportation of nearly five million peasants and their families. In 1930 the Kremlin ordered planning commissions "to incorporate the work performed by those deprived of liberty into the planned economy of the Five-Year Plan." With that the G.P.U. established a new organization called Gulag to exploit prison labor to the utmost. Slave labor has played a major role in the Soviet economic system ever since.

By 1933 it had reached enormous dimensions, and the Soviets' Corrective Labor Codex then replaced the term "forced labor" with the much less revealing phrase "corrective labor work." But even the Soviet Encyclopedia of 1940 stated: *"Forced labor is one of the basic measures of Soviet Socialist criminal law."*

Russia's M.V.D. police are directly in charge of the entire slave-labor system. The M.V.D. not only operates thousands of camps, it also supplies prison labor by contract to a great variety of state industries, collectives and other enterprises. Among these are gold mining, timber cutting, fish-packing plants, railroad and highway construction, oil production and much else. An

* *Cracks in the Kremlin Wall*. New York: The Viking Press, 1951. Pp. 207–223.

escaped former employee of the Soviet planning agency for the five-year plans has testified that, in 1939–40, the M.V.D. slave-labor agencies provided 14 per cent of all capital construction in the U.S.S.R.—more than the quota for any other ministry. The M.V.D. has separate organizations for railroad building and high-way maintenance by slave labor. Gulag is the agency that administers the so-called "corrective" camps where millions of prisoners are literally worked to death. Albert Konrad Herling, research director for the U.N.'s Commission of Inquiry into Forced Labor, reports authoritatively no less than 160 Gulag mining camps, 75 lumber camps, 41 factories and scores of other M.V.D. enterprises.

Soon after the end of World War II this system was extended into Eastern Europe. The Communists began by creating concentration camps, ostensibly for pro-Nazi elements and traitors. Titled aristocrats, big landowners, wealthy industrialists, judges and generals in the Iron-Curtain countries were soon added to the category of "people's enemies." Soon afterward came the turn of leaders of the democratic opposition parties; finally, members of the hated bourgeoisie; then anyone who aroused suspicion or envy. What to do with these increasing multitudes of "class enemies"? As in Russia, they were put to work producing for the Communist state.

The Communists turn foreign peoples into slaves.

As early as 1945 Bulgaria's régime created, by decree, "Communities for Educational Labor." Similar forced-labor laws were introduced gradually in each Red-ruled country. The Czechoslovakian government's Forced Labor Camps Act of October, 1948, is typical. Under Section II any person between the ages of 18 and 60 can be branded "a threat to the building of the people's democratic order or the economic life" by a ruling of a three-man, all-Communist commission. Without a hearing of any kind, such persons are sent into slave labor for periods ranging between three months and two years. The law's professed aim is "to educate citizens for work as a duty to their country."

Russia's Gulag system has thus become an integral part of the sovietization of all Eastern Europe. Puppet-state prisoners are confined in camps identical to those in Soviet Russia—heavily guarded, encircled by barbed- and electric-wire obstacles, surrounded by watch towers with searchlights blazing all night. Hunger is used to compel prisoners to work to the limits of their endurance. Death rates are extremely high. Under M.V.D. controls hundred of thousands of East Europeans now construct five-year-plan projects designed to increase the military power of Russia.

Several recent decrees indicate the growth of the slave system. In January, 1951, a "Central Labor Office" for all satellite states was established in Prague. Each Red puppet government was instructed to report to this office the total number of persons it had available for forced labor. A Soviet representative said that various East European states might be obliged to send their quotas of prisoners to work on major projects, such as the Danube–Black Sea Canal. This launches an all-satellite slave-labor pool, controlled by Moscow.

The Communists camouflage their slave-labor system with titles intended to conceal their true purpose. A "Construction Company of the Ministry of Interior" was set up in Rumania in March, 1951, concerned with the exploitation of prison labor. A May decree reorganized this company under the even more innocuous title of "General Management of Workers' Reserves" (the D.G.R.M.). According to this decree the D.G.R.M. "can dispose of reserve workers, skilled and unskilled, from cities as well as the countryside, as it sees fit . . . in accordance with the needs of the national economy." But who are these suddenly discovered "reserve workers" in a country where a notorious labor shortage exists? The "reserve workers" are taken from lists of jailed or suspected persons, or by seizing citizens in categories marked for liquidation. The D.G.R.M., in fact, is a direct counterpart of the Soviets' Gulag—the provider of slave labor to state and military projects. Such labor is now building:

Hundreds of military and industrial projects
throughout captive Europe.

For the immediate future the five-year plans of the puppet régimes are, above all, military programs. Slave workers have already built army barracks, bases and airfields; coastal fortifications along the Baltic and the Black Sea; underground depots for arms, food and fuel and much else.

Each Communist country has large-scale projects which need slave labor for their execution. Hungary's gigantic ironworks at Dunapentele requires many thousands. An industrial complex comparable to Pittsburgh's is being created there from the ground up. One now being built at Kosice in Eastern Slovakia is scheduled to be even larger. Another is located in Czechoslovakia's Ostrava region, matched by several others in Poland; camps for political prisoners supply workers for all these projects.

More than 7,000 slave prisoners work in Bulgaria's Pernick coal mines; 3,000 more from the Cherno More camp in other coal mines. Another 2,000 are completing a dam on the Tundzha River; about 1,000 more are building the Rositza dam. At least another dozen big construction or mining operations that use slave labor could be cited in Bulgaria alone. The Danube–Black Sea Canal, designed to create a 60-mile short cut through the Danubian delta, is perhaps the largest slave-labor project in Eastern Europe. More than 40,000 prisoners are said to work there under the harshest conditions.

A reported 10,000 to 20,000 Rumanian prisoners are slaving on the big Bistritza Valley hydroelectric project. Another 3,500 work on the Argesh Canal project. Notable slave-construction programs also include Bulgaria's Christo Botev line fortifications, the Tulcea and Sozopol submarine bases, and the Budapest subway. Probably the greatest armies of slave laborers are mobilized in the many Czech and Polish uranium mines, where as many as 150,000 have been reported by some underground sources.

This far from complete summary suffices to show how the Soviets have already built satellite slave labor into big state business. But the Kremlin's plans envisage much greater exploitation of the Gulag system. The Soviets' all-satellite program requires:

*Bigger slave camps—for more and more
East European slaves.*

In every captive country Communist five-year plans include construction programs with excessively difficult deadlines in the face of acute labor shortages. This partially explains the steady building of more and larger slave camps. Through its D.G.R.M. it is estimated that Bucharest's Red régime alone may make nearly 500,000 additional prisoners available for slave-labor enterprises within another two or three years.

What the free world must somehow comprehend is this: In Eastern Europe the Communists hold in their power *several million candidates for slavery*. The better-off independent farmers and middle-class citizens listed as "suspect" for various reasons run into millions. Hundreds of thousands of workers, increasingly resentful of brutal work quotas and intolerable conditions, may eventually be accused of sabotage and deported for "re-education." * Until vast numbers of these unreconstructible

---

* These same "irresistible pressures" are cogently summarized by Edward Crankshaw in *Cracks in the Kremlin Wall*, (p. 220). "The counterrevolutionary opposition had to be coralled off and set to work. . . ." (His reference throughout is to the original slave system's development in Soviet Russia.) "The apathetic . . . land-seeking masses had to be terrorized and coerced; industrialization had to be forced through at a breakneck pace . . . everyone who stood in the way . . . above all, the peasants resisting collectivization, had to be removed . . . the obvious organization to carry out these projects was the G.P.U., which thus developed a vested interest in prison labor. . . . Add to these pressures the insecurity of an unpopular régime."

All of these pressures now impel the Kremlin to expand the slave-labor system in Eastern Europe. At the time he wrote, Mr. Crankshaw was apparently not informed of the suprising growth of slave camps in the puppet states. He added that "With the Russification of the Baltic States the M.V.D. exhausted its last major source of slave labor." Actually, as evidence emerging since then demonstrates, the M.V.D. has taken over a far greater source of slave labor in the populous Iron-Curtain countries.

people have been put behind barbed wire the men in the Kremlin will fear that Communist control of the "colonial" states remains inadequate. Eastern Europe can only be rendered "secure," by Soviet definition, through expansion of the slave-labor system. It is therefore conceivable that the Reds' slaves in captive Europe may total two or three million persons by 1954. The Stalinists are already using these countries as a new slave-labor pool for Soviet Russia itself. This is being accomplished through:

The slave-train route into Russia and Siberia.

Tens of thousands of East European political prisoners are now being sent to Soviet slave camps on a regular schedule. At the end of World War II the Soviets shipped several hundreds of thousands of persons into Russia from concentration camps in the "liberated" countries. They were Germans, Russians, Ukrainians, Balts, Poles and also satellite citizens of German descent. These war-vengeance deportations seemed to conclude Moscow's Gulag-recruitment program in the Iron-Curtain regions until 1950. Then the Russians secretly inaugurated "transfers" of East European political prisoners into the U.S.S.R.—a new device to reduce the Soviet Union's labor shortage. Thanks to the changing of the Trans-Carpathian railroad lines to Russian broad-gauge, the operation was greatly simplified. A regular Soviet slave-train route has now functioned through the Carpathians since early 1951, if not before then.

Approximately 50,000 Hungarian prisoners were shipped off to Soviet slave camps during 1950, along with unknown thousands from the other puppet-ruled nations. These "transfers" continue to operate on a fixed Red timetable. Every week one or two trainloads of satellite prisoners are dispatched from Uzhorod in western Trans-Carpathia. Their occupants are destined for Soviet Gulag camps, which the great majority cannot survive. A few thousand Rumanian soldiers, held as war prisoners in the Soviet Union since 1945, were at last returned home —more skeletons than men—in the late summer of 1951. They stated that between 80 and 90 per cent of their fellow-prisoners—more than 200,000 Rumanians—had died in Russian camps. Death is the true destination of the Soviets' new slave trains.

Uzhorod (formerly Ungvar), an important rail junction just east of the Hungarian border, with direct connections to Poland, Czechoslovakia and Rumania, serves as the chief collection point for satellite deportees. The Reds' secret police select for shipment those prisoners with longer sentences, those regarded as most untrustworthy, or those who are particularly hated. Deportation is thus a means of vengeance; it also removes persons who might be capable of leadership. In the single month of March, 1951, some 17,000 Hungarians were gathered in Uzhorod for deportation to Russia.

How does the slave-train route to Russia operate?

The prisoners have no possible escape except death. The once Polish, now Russian city of Lwow constitutes the point of no return. In fact, I have learned of only a single prisoner who reached Lwow, yet somehow managed to be released. He got back to Hungary and finally escaped to Western Europe with a unique account of what the Soviet death-camp trains are like.

"We were transferred by night to the main Budapest prison, which is entirely run by Russian M.V.D. officials. They also brought in several hundred prisoners from Austria. We were all given Russian prison uniforms. In that way we would always be taken for Russians by anyone who might see us entraining or en route. Then they jammed us into freight cars—as many as could be forced inside standing up—and the cars were sealed. All the time we were in the cars they gave us no food or water. By the day we reached Uzhorod we were half-crazed from thirst. The air inside the cars was almost unbreathable. In two days and nights the mixed odors of vomit, defecation and urine under such conditions cannot be imagined. Even the misery and hunger of the Uzhorod camp was a relief.

"Two long trains of prisoners leave Uzhorod each week—but for what destination we did not know. The M.V.D. packed the cars with Hungarians, Czechs, Poles or Rumanians. After a week my turn came. Again we were locked up in unheated, sealed cars. It was mid-winter and frightfully cold. This time the journey was indescribable. It was much longer. The trains crawled and then stopped for long periods. But they never let us out. Some prisoners went mad from thirst. Whenever the train stopped shrieks and cries burst out on all sides: 'Water! Water! In God's name, water! . . . We are dying! . . . Mercy!' The guards pounded the sides of the cars with their rifle butts and threatened to shoot. Or they paid no attention.

"When we reached Lwow at last we fell out of the doors. Few of us could stand. We were beaten and pulled to our feet. I saw the guards drag several corpses from the freight cars. We had been pressed so tightly together that men gasped their last breath, but they were kept erect by their neighbors, who did not even realize they were dead. Their bodies froze in these cramped, erect positions. Many prisoners emerged raving like madmen, and some never recovered their senses. Others were so ill that they died during the next few days.

"Lwow is the big collecting point for all East Europeans who are being sent into Russia for slave labor. A steady stream of shipments goes east, but there are always 10,000 or more in this camp. The conditions were almost as terrible as on the trains. In the coldest days of winter we were pushed into damp cellars, without heat, with almost no coverings. They gave us only thin soup and bread of the worst quality. Nearly everyone suffered from scurvy and dysentery. Lice and bedbugs spread disease everywhere. But there were no doctors—not even for the dying.

"On the slightest excuse the Russian guards beat prisoners brutally. The camp's only law is the law of the fist and rifle butt. People were dying, day and night. The death rate was very high. But the Russians were sending an average of 2,000 prisoners each week. At that time they were all being sent to the infamous Gulag camps in the Komsomolskjaer region. Some of the Lwow camp employees admitted that 15 to 20 per cent of the prisoners died en route. That means between 300 and 400 out of each 2,000 dispatched eastward from Lwow by train.

"When a prisoner reaches Lwow he has no hope of ever being free again; no real hope even of remaining alive. I was ill and I had also lost all hope. Then something happened like an intervention by God. I can't tell how it happened, and how it finally enabled me to return to Hungary. Someone else may possibly be saved through the same kind of miraculous accident. But until now I have never heard of anyone else who has come back."

During 1951 more than 100,000 men, women and children were evicted from Yugoslav border regions in Bulgaria, Rumania and Hungary, and also from major Hungarian, Czech and Polish cities. Great numbers of these evacuees disappeared completely, many of them undoubtedly into Russia. Does Moscow plan to maintain and increase its "importations" of slave labor from the Iron-Curtain countries? It would be logical to expect this. The Gulag system literally devours its victims. Its slave-labor enterprises multiply. Its corpses also multiply. The Red state can never get enough slaves to supply the mounting needs of the five-year plans in the puppet states as well as in the Soviet Union.

The "class-enemy" and "political-reliability" motives for enslavement are even more compelling than the economic. Actually all three compulsions are inherent in the Soviet system. The Communist state cannot avoid wholesale enslavement because it *is* enslavement, *per se*. The Kremlin itself is exactly what its frowning, barricaded exterior indicates—a citadel of fear. In all of captive Europe Stalin and his Politburo fear vast proportions of the population with an intense, irremediable fear—because they are profoundly, unalterably anti-Communist. Thus, slave labor is not only an indispensable Soviet means of production; it is an equally irreplaceable means of reducing so-called "class enemies" either to skeletonized human wrecks—or to corpses. The world's greatest numerical assemblage of armed manpower —unprecedented in magnitude in all history—is still not enough to provide the fear-haunted men in the Kremlin with "security." They still endeavor to build security on mass enslavement and human bones.

In reality the establishment of a vast Communist slave-labor system throughout Eastern Europe is a warning to every citizen in the free world, most of all in the Atlantic community of nations. By this policy the Kremlin has proved that the Soviet-style state, the Red system, must create and expand slavery wherever Communism wins power. Without forcing large proportions of any country's population into slave labor the Communists cannot hold power. Under a Red régime every person becomes some category of a slave—including the master-slaves who are members of the party. Only the Great Slave-Driver remains relatively or temporarily immune. But suspected people and potential rallying points of resistance must be beaten down into the lowest human denominator—the absolute slaves. These are the slave laborers—millions today and millions more tomorrow. Nowhere in the world are there so many candidates for future Communist slave camps as in the advanced, predominantly middle-class populations of the Western democracies. That is a fact which it might be realistic to keep in mind. The chances are roughly fifty thousand to one that you belong on the Reds' lists of these "assured future candidates." Eastern Europe is only a first step, the prelude.

It is one thing, of course, to recognize that the average Western citizen is the perfect candidate for labor slavery under a Communist régime. But how far would the Stalinists dare to go? They are already answering that question in every Red-ruled nation in Eastern Europe. They are preparing to make the answer more devastatingly emphatic with each passing year. The Great Slave-Maker himself has given the most cynically frank answer which it is possible to imagine.

In the early postwar period Stalin once spoke glowingly to Stanislaw Mikolajczyk, then a leader in the Polish government, about a great Slav empire stretching from the Pacific shores of Siberia through Russia up to the mid-European fringes of the Iron Curtain. Mr. Mikolajczyk pointed out that the Hungarians, after all, are not Slavs. The Hungarians, he said, would resist being swallowed up in this fashion by every means in their power.

Stalin replied with calm, arctic assurance: *"The Hungarian problem is only a matter of box-cars."*

When the rulers of the Kremlin are prepared to deport the majority of 9.5 million Hungarians in sealed box-cars, why should we imagine that Communists would hesitate to treat several times that number of Western Europeans, Britishers, Americans and other capitalistic peoples in similar fashion? In its first stage Stalin's "box-car" solution for Hungary is already under way. It is also under way in five other East European countries. The methods become amazingly efficient as the Red slave empire expands.

CHAPTER ELEVEN

Conquest of the Churches

BETWEEN THE SPRING OF 1950 AND SEPTEM-
ber, 1951, the Communists won control of
the great Roman Catholic hierarchies in Eastern Europe, cut
them off from the Vatican and eliminated Moscow's last organized ideological opponent inside the Iron Curtain. No Soviet conquest has been executed with more astuteness. Its implications
are ominous for freedom of worship for all sects in every free
nation.

The Kremlin's victory was startling in its rapidity and dev-
astating in its "Trojan Horse" technique. In less than eighteen
months the Stalinists usurped the centuries-old church power in
the great Catholic strongholds of Hungary, Czechoslovakia and
Poland. These revolutionary reversals were of infinitely greater
historical significance than the trial of an archbishop or a cardinal.
But they were managed so as to attract far less attention abroad.
To this day few Americans comprehend the true dimensions and
meaning of the Red régimes' subjugation of the Catholic hierarchies. The Kremlin has inflicted upon the Vatican its most
crushing defeats in many generations. But, outside of ecclesiastical circles, amazingly few Western citizens are aware of what
the Soviets have accomplished—least of all, of *how* it was done.*

The Communists have demonstrated their ability to dominate
every church, of whatever denomination, in any country where

* In a resolution adopted by the Roman Catholic bishops of the United
States on November 18, 1951, they were understandably prompted to declare:
"We are . . . appalled by the apparent inability of the free secular press to
inform the public of the true facts of the persecution."

a Red régime is established. No organized church—Christian, Jewish, Moslem or any other—can hope to escape being reduced to an instrument of Kremlin policy. No believers, however devoted and loyal, can escape the subversion of their religious organizations to Communist designs.

This has already happened to the Greek Orthodox Churches in Rumania and Bulgaria, to the small and impotent Protestant sects everywhere inside the Curtain and to the Jewish congregations. Because their church was by far the most powerful—numerically, organizationally and, originally, in financial resources—it happened last of all to the Roman Catholics. But today *all* organized churches in captive Europe are not only isolated from the outside world; they are occupied—by servitors of the Politburo.

Moscow launched its offensive against the Hungarian, Czechoslovakian and Polish hierarchies in February–March, 1950. In less than eighteen months the Red régimes had split Catholic leadership in all three countries; had installed "fellow-traveling" prelates in key bishoprics, dioceses and religious publications; had seized control of Catholic policy-making and administrative offices. The great majority of bishops and priests, and millions of laymen remained staunchly loyal—but utterly helpless. The three great traditional bastions of the faith, where Catholicism had been unchallenged and unchallengeable since the Middle Ages, were progressively undermined, infiltrated and captured. Since then the Red régimes have moved into the final phase: consolidation of their cunningly maneuvered Trojan conquest. But already they have revealed impressively:

/ How the Communists divide and dominate organized churches.

1) They destroy their financial strength by confiscating church properties and sources of income.

2) They suppress religious education or render what survives entirely dependent upon the Red state.

3) They enlist the services of weak, politically ambitious or

corrupt priests or pastors—so-called "patriotic priests"—as champions of co-operation with the Communist régime.

4) They use these "patriotic" clergymen to found Moscow-style "Peace Movements" which all adherents of whatever faith are urged to support—to prove their opposition to war.

5) The collaborationist clergy (in reality, separatists) split their church leadership wide open. They champion acceptance of harshly oppressive state-church agreements.

6) The Communists put their "peace priests" into key bishoprics and control posts, and take over church publications and organizations, such as Catholic Action.

7) The Red state appropriates the right to appoint all future bishops and canons. Those in office who resist are deposed or arrested and replaced by clerical renegades.

8) When diocesan chapters stand firm, the Stalinists appoint an "advisory committee" of "patriotic clergymen," who then name one of their own collaborators as vicar or titular head.

9) Loyal laymen are deliberately confused by publication of false statements attributed to church leaders and by numerous tricks which spread bafflement and disruption.

10) Both force and cynical pressures are employed against the clergy and laymen alike.

In their ruses and tactics the Reds stoop to anything. Budapest Catholics rallied for a Good Friday procession in 1951. They found their entire route cluttered by great sewage-cleaning operations; in some places the streets were blocked entirely by city sanitation trucks and equipment. The religious pilgrims had to march through nauseating stench and ankle-deep, filthy water.

When Prague organized a "National Peace Congress" in September, 1951, many priests refused to attend. The district commissioner for religious affairs called on them personally. He warned they would be arrested unless they accompanied him at once: "Why risk your liberty for a mere formality?" Some priests yielded rather than be permanently isolated from their congregations. In Rumania the Reds operate a school which graduates alleged priests, actually ardent Communists trained to supplant loyal clergymen. If a priest or pastor knows he will be replaced by a Moscow tool or a Communist masqerading in the cloth, should he invite arrest? Or should he strive to remain with his flock?

The position of Hungary's Catholic hierarchy and Church had proved unassailable for centuries. The devotion of its millions of followers was uncontestable. Its spiritual authority was notably enhanced by its exceptional material possessions and its uninterrupted political influence. But the early postwar agrarian reforms had shattered the church's vast economic and financial power in a single blow. In August, 1946, Jozsef, Cardinal Mindszenty, enumerated the seriousness of these losses to me in the archbishop's palace at Esztergom.

As the nation's largest landowner, the church and its religious orders had possessed more than 1.4 million acres of land.* Of these Cardinal Mindszenty stated that 1.2 million acres had been expropriated by the state. More than half were in forests; the remainder in extensive farms, vineyards, orchards and coal mines. Actually about one-seventh of all land expropriated by the Communists in Hungary belonged to the church. Part of the large annual incomes thus produced had helped to finance Catholic schools and colleges, including more than half of the country's secondary schools, which were operated by church orders.

But the very extent of the church's landed holdings and its large income from agricultural and other enterprises had played directly into the hands of the Communists, who demanded that the great feudal landlords' estates be broken up for the benefit of several hundreds of thousands of landless peasants. The anti-Communist Smallholders Party strongly supported this reform. "I am a good Catholic and I think it is sad that the church lands had to be taken," one Hungarian layman said. "But I believe the church performs a greater service where it is poor. France is a good example of this. Here our church could have done much more. But its leaders always had one eye on their

* Official Hungarian government statistics placed Catholic-owned lands at one million cadastral yokes in 1935, one yoke equaling 1.422 acres.

property. As a result they often failed to take a strong stand on behalf of the common people."

Cardinal Mindszenty told me how Catholic educational institutions had suddenly been pauperized. Where Catholic organizations had previously published no less than 17 daily newspapers and more than 40 weekly or monthly organs, they were reduced to two weeklies. There remained, nevertheless, approximately six million communicants, led by prelates of exceptional ability, for few Catholic hierarchies in the world benefited by such closely knit, long established organizations. For all these reasons it is particularly important to examine:

How the Communists split Hungary's Catholic hierarchy and won decisive control of church affairs.

First they nullified the Primate's indomitable leadership by sentencing Cardinal Mindszenty to life imprisonment in February, 1949. Day and night, for many weeks, he had been subjected to the m.v.d.'s most intensive mental and nervous breakdown treatment, including persistent undernourishment and prevention to sleep. Thus the Cardinal's so-called "confession" was as meaningless as the many similar products of the Red inquisitors' "invisible" torture methods. Years before his arrest some of his fellow churchmen had felt that Cardinal Mindszenty was too inflexible about defending every aspect of church authority and property rights, perhaps too obdurate about making some unavoidable compromises before it was too late. But not even his bitterest enemies could question the Hungarian Primate's extraordinary courage, his devotion to his faith, or his personal integrity. Red vengeance had simply demanded the public humiliation, as well as the martyrdom, of an opponent of such caliber.

For about a year afterward the Communists applied their pressure with relative discretion. Then they launched a carefully plotted terrorist campaign in the spring of 1950. The police arrested and jailed nuns and monks, taking over their convents and monasteries. More than 1,000 nuns were also ejected from hospitals, without warning, and without being given other quarters. Intimidation of the clergy mounted everywhere. In April a "Priests' Peace Committee" was formed. It soon proved to be Moscow's chief weapon for seizing control of Hungary's church.

Simultaneously the party press bitterly attacked the Catholic Church as "an enemy of peace," and a frontal assault was launched on its religious orders. During the nights of June 11th and 17th more than 3,000 monks and nuns were arrested and locked up. This accomplished its intended purpose. The Bench of Bishops was forced to begin negotiations for a state-church agreement. They opened on June 28th with the Communist régime's promise to cease deporting members of the religious orders, but within a few weeks another wave of wholesale arrests broke out. With approximately 9,000 monks and nuns in custody, the Reds circulated rumors that these hostages would shortly be deported to Siberia. This, too, had its intended effect.

The "negotiations" were entirely one-sided. Rakosi and other Hungarian Communists refused to admit a single grievance of the church. They shouted down the protests of the clerical delegates and dictated the Kremlin's terms. Their life-or-death power over the 9,000 they had arrested was used as blackmail. In this cruel dilemma Archbishop Jozsef Groesz finally saw no choice but to sign a document which dissolved all but four of Hungary's once-powerful Catholic orders and ended the church's long established supremacy in Hungarian education.

Under the state-church agreement a date was fixed when federal aid to church institutions would cease and all convents and monasteries would be taken over by the state. Although several thousand monks and nuns were released, they were deprived of the right to wear their robes. Ejected from their ancient homes, they were forced to live with relatives or to seek jobs. Large numbers were also deported to unknown places. From inside Hungary one church authority reported: "By terror and diplomacy the government has succeeded in eliminating the religious orders. If any former monk now disappears, no one notices it, for he no longer belongs to an organization. He is hardly in contact with his brethren."

It might have seemed that the Kremlin's major objectives were already attained. But the Soviets' final onslaught was just being mobilized. It was delivered by:

The "Peace Priests' Movement" and its capture of the Catholic hierarchy.

Only three renegade priests were needed by the Communists to undermine and break the solidarity of Catholic leadership in Hungary. The Hungarian priests who betrayed their faith and church for the Kremlin's "mess of pottage" have since been decorated with the Red régime's Order of Merit. Fathers Istvan Balogh, Richard Horvath and Miklos Beresztoczy, formerly Canon of Esztergom, constitute this triumvirate. As an under-secretary of state in 1945–46, Father Balogh was already deeply involved in political intrigue and the accumulation of personal wealth, rare paintings and attractive young women. It now seems regrettable that his eventual excommunication did not come at that time. Father Beresztoczy also held a political office in the Ministry of Education until finally dismissed in a Red purge during 1948. Horvath, primarily a teacher, was virtually unknown.

How the Communists made tools of Beresztoczy and Balogh is revealing. The former was arrested and cruelly tortured during the Mindszenty trial. When released he seemed a broken man. The Red police are said to have rigged up a damaging file, accusing Beresztoczy of affairs with women, and thus blackmailed him into serving Moscow. By arresting a church-approved incumbent, and promising to arrest any other choice the bishops might make, the government forced them to accept Beresztoczy as Canon of Esztergom. Thus he became a member of the Bench of Bishops, and a champion of the Peace Priest Movement; the Kremlin had an influential collaborator in the hierarchy's inner council. When the bishops finally forced Beresztoczy's resignation irreparable damage had already been done.

There were no extenuating circumstances in Father Balogh's case. This huge-bellied *bon vivant* and libertine had long since abandoned any pretense of religious or personal integrity. The Communist press reportedly published a few of the more notorious details of his personal life. But it seems unlikely that this was necessary. Balogh had mysteriously acquired a large private fortune. His fleshly proclivities and appetites seemed almost insatiable—and the Red rulers had much more of the same to offer. A thoroughly cynical opportunist, Balogh had tasted power for too long, in too many ways—and power corrupts.

Through the services of these three renegades the Communists slowly built up the Peace Priests' Movement. By August, 1950, the first large meeting of about 300 clergymen was convened. Some boldly demanded that the church be given a "fair deal." But other priests, with influential names—some of them sincerely concerned about another war—were seduced into joining. The party employed their names and reputations to create the impression that serious church leaders supported its "peace campaign."

The "peace priests" remained a small and unimpressive minority into early 1951. But the renegades attacked unceasingly. At a February meeting Beresztoczy declared that "priests must fight against reactionaries hidden in the clergy; against those who try to thwart the great Peace Movement." Horvath demanded adoption of a resolution bidding "every member of the Catholic Church to proclaim their loyalty to the People's Congress . . . and to condemn the criminal policy of the Vatican." Thus the clerical traitors unmasked their peace propaganda as a separatist maneuver directed against Rome. Out of 70 attending priests, only 17 voted for Horvath's resolution. This initial steadfastness must have greatly heartened the embattled church hierarchy—but events were soon disheartening.

At this point Soviet officials appeared in Budapest to investigate the Hungarian party's "ecclesiastical policy." They roundly denounced Rakosi's Reds for having "virtually abandoned liquidation of church power in Hungary." The Cominform gave drastic orders. Within a few days Jozsef Revai, Minister of Culture, told the second Communist congress on March 2, 1951, that "the clerical ideology is the only remaining hostile ideology still opposing Communism in Hungary. . . . The lower clergy must be mobilized for the fight against clerical reaction and war-mongers."

In the same month Canon Beresztoczy announced the slogan "Not one priest must be left out of the Peace Movement!"; he also claimed, probably falsely, that 1,000 priests already had joined the committee. Meanwhile the Reds' Ministry of Interior dropped broad hints that hundreds of priests and nuns, still under arrest, would be released—provided the bishops approved the "movement of progressive Catholics." Again the jailed members of religious orders were used for blackmail. The hierarchy stood firm.

Through the spring pro-Soviet clergymen energetically organized clerical peace committees throughout the provinces. Priests who refused to sign Moscow's peace referendum were denounced as "enemies of the people" or arrested. The Communists' tone became increasingly menacing. They accused the Bench of Bishops of violating the state-church agreement. The party press bitterly attacked as "allies of the war-plotting American imperialists" such courageous prelates as Archbishop Jozsef Groesz, Bishops Endre Hamvas and Jozsef Petery, and Canon Jozsef Csintalan—all of whom had refused to sign the Reds' "Peace Appeal." In a moving pastoral message Bishop Petery proclaimed: "God does not depend upon earthly powers. Men are mortal, while God has existed in all times and will exist forever. It is still God, and God alone, Who directs the history of mankind."

But inevitably there were a few prelates of weaker fiber. When Rakosi, as top Communist, attended a centennial mass in Debrecen, Bishop Revesz actually asked for a special blessing for "Hungary's wise leader." On the following Sunday, as the bishop ascended his pulpit, the entire congregation walked out. Not a communicant remained. The bishop forthwith resigned.

Everywhere the overwhelming majority of Hungarian Catholics stood unshakably loyal to their faith.

Nevertheless the "patriotic priests," backed by terrorist pressures, continued to win many waverers among the lower clergy. And the Red régime could employ still more powerful weapons of coercion. In May came a report that two of the most devoted and heroic Catholic prelates, Bishop Endre Hamvas of Csanad and Archbishop Gyula Czapik of Eger, had signed the "Peace Appeal." If so, they had surely been subjected to extreme threats gravely affecting the church's welfare. No mention was made regarding nine others on the Bench of Bishops. Simultaneously the régime created a new State Office for Church Affairs and appointed as its head Istvan Kossa, a Moscow-trained Communist and former streetcar employee.

On July 3, 1951, came the Stalinists' knockout blow. Budapest issued a decree by which all higher-ranking church prelates "may be appointed only with the previous approval of the Presidium of the People's Republic." This applies to the appointment of archbishops, titular archbishops, bishops, assistant bishops, abbots and generals of religious orders. It was also made retroactive, covering "all appointments that have been made to any of the above-mentioned church positions since January 1, 1946."

This decree destroyed the hierarchy's administrative control of their own church. Collaborationist priests could hereafter be placed in the highest positions: the most loyal Roman prelates would be compelled to endorse Moscow's double-talk "Peace Movement," or would be removed from all contact with their fellow clergy and communicants. The Bench of Bishops became the prey of the Politburo. A deep split in Hungary's clergy was inevitable. The Kremlin-organized anti-Vatican separatist movement had scored a decisive triumph—somehow scarcely noticed in the Western press, even though this event exceeded the trial of Cardinal Mindszenty in historical significance.

The most humiliating scene of Roman Catholic annals of all Eastern Europe occurred on July 21st. The church's capitulation to Communist dictation was carried out with ceremony in the

Hungarian Parliament's magnificent Gothic chamber, where cardinals and archbishops had only appeared in roles of respect and honor since Hungary first became a kingdom. Archbishop Czapik of Eger led the eight bishops still at liberty, the auxiliary bishops and four provincials of the drastically reduced but still tolerated religious orders. They marched into the hall in full ecclesiastical robes. Their physical masters, Rakosi and his fellow Stalinists, listened as the archbishop read the Bench of Bishops' declaration of loyalty to the "people's republic." After two years of courageous resistance, the hierarchy's support of the so-called "Peace Movement" was publicly avowed. Seldom, if ever, had the princes of a once mighty church been so publicly humbled. As a prelude to this fateful turning point, the bishops were obliged to "pay their respects" to the Communist chief of the State Office for Church Affairs, the ex-streetcar man Istvan Kossa.

Thus the long rule of Hungary's Catholic hierarchy was usurped by the Kremlin's henchmen. In six years a Vatican citadel of nearly twice as many centuries had been shattered and occupied. The Stalinists had captured the bishops and prelates; had split the clergy; had isolated all Catholics from the Vatican. Millions of the faithful must hereafter exist in a spiritual underground, doomed to years of persecution.

Suppose the church had broken up its huge feudal estates and redistributed its lands among the peasants in the 1920's or 1930's? Would this have made any appreciable difference in the church's present fate? That will remain a moot question. But in at least one respect the lack of a much needed land reform before World War II seems to have had a considerable effect. It permitted the Communists to deceive several hundreds of thousands of Catholic peasants, and to lure them under rigid Red controls into collectives and state farms. The peasants had not had time to dig themselves in on the first small parcels of earth they had ever owned. So the Stalinists more quickly and easily coerced vast numbers of them into collective strait jackets. What could have been the church's strongest ally had been infiltrated, confused and seriously weakened—notably for lack of a comprehensive prewar land reform.

In any event the lessons to be derived from this must apply to any church which has inherited close involvement with a feudal land system which inevitably renders landless peasants wide open to Kremlin enticements. But the lessons must equally apply to churches of every denomination; to the leaders and followers of every faith. If there is no immunity from possible Communist conquest, neither can there exist in the twentieth century any immunity from recognition of the urgent need for social reforms where they have been overdue for generations.

Flushed with victory, the renegade, Dr. Horvath, proclaimed in October, 1951: "There is no separate Christian peace and a separate Communist peace." But this obvious catch-phrase represented merely a follow-through in the Kremlin's "Peace Priest" offensive. It had already achieved an equally startling success in:

The Communists' conquest of the Catholic hierarchy in Czechoslovakia.

This was particularly surprising because the Czech Catholics had long been recognized as among the most progressive and social-minded of their faith anywhere in the world. For this reason it seemed that they were better placed to resist Communist domination, even though the church was much less powerful and wealthy than in Hungary and Poland. Ivo Duchecek, a parliamentary deputy and editor of the Catholic weekly *Obsory*, told me about Czech Catholicism in Prague in October, 1946.

"You must understand that we are different from most Catholic parties in Europe," he said in regard to the Catholic People's Party. "Our party is not a church party, but a party of Catholic laymen. We do not believe that a cardinal or an archbishop should mix in politics. Prelates do not direct the party or hold political office. These things make the big difference between Czech Catholics and the church in Hungary or Spain.

"As laymen," Mr. Duchecek continued, "we try to fit our

Christian philosophy into political action. There are no high churchmen telling us what we should do. We take our religious inspiration and guidance from the Vatican. But politically our party stands on solid Czech grounds. We have always been a liberal party, a party of the proletariat, because we are based on the common people and our church has never been rich. By defending the working people's welfare, we are convinced that we render a greater service to our church."

The liberal and staunchly democratic record of Czech Catholics might possibly have been expected to offer exceptional obstacles to Prague's Communist régime. Or their very progressive traditions and habits might render them all the more dangerous in the Soviets' eyes. The latter proved to be the case. A strongly liberal church, backed by staunchly democratic laymen organized in a notably effective political party, constituted a most dangerous menace. As a consequence the Red régime struck hard, fast and mercilessly.

It encountered considerably less resistance in the clergy than in Hungary. By January, 1951, the Peace Priests Movement had progressed ominously far. A good many Czechoslovakian bishops, canons and priests were enlisted. Bishop Jan Dechet reiterated that "the task of the Catholic priest is the protection of peace." Father Hlbina, the Slovak poet, declared: "Socialist peace is the only peace for which a Christian should fight." Canon Stefan Zareczky voiced unalterable opposition to the Vatican. The secretary of the Communist-infiltrated Catholic Action insisted that "the moral principles on which Socialism is based are in complete harmony with Christian principles." Many other clergymen or laymen of influence had already been won over to pro-Soviet collaboration. Then came the Red steamroller.

The régime had installed an obscure priest, Antonin Stehlik, as Vicar Capitular. On February 13th he attended as four "patriotic priests" were elevated as canons of Olomouc diocese. The next day the Capitular and General Vicars of most Catholic dioceses met in Prague. In a telegram to Communist President

Gottwald they pledged their continued service "against all insti-gators of a new war." With this, the hierarchy's defenses, in a country almost 80 per cent Catholic, were clearly shattered. The Red régime proceeded to "pack" the church's key posts at this headlong tempo:

February 28, 1951: A new Vicar General and three "patriotic" canons were installed in Brno's cathedral in the absence of the bishop. On the same day seven new canons were installed in Kosice cathedral in Eastern Slovakia.

March 3: Four collaborationist canons were appointed to the Prague Metropolitan chapter "with the consent of the state."

March 7: Dr. Joseph Beran, archbishop of Prague and chief leader of the hierarchy's resistance, was placed under house ar-rest outside his diocese, and fined for his "negative attitude" toward state-church laws.

March 8: The forced "resignation" of Vicar General Opatrny of St. Vitus' Cathedral was announced. He was replaced by collaborationist Vicar Capitular Stehlik.

March 12: Having removed the incorruptible Archbishop Beran, four bishops and other prominent prelates took the oath of loyalty to the "People's Republic."

March 15: Three new "patriotic" canons were installed at Ceske Budejovice.

Easter: The bishops complied with the Red régime's order and issued pastoral letters urging their communicants to pray and work for "peace."

March 27: Installation of eight new "peace" canons at Brati-slava by Bishop Lazik.

April 14: A conference of Slovak bishops and ordinaries was presided over by the notorious Red quisling, Zdenek Fierlinger, as chief of the State Office for Ecclesiastical Affairs. It expressed "deep gratitude" to Gottwald "for the happy solution of the relationship between the Roman Catholic Church and the state."

After taking the March 12th oath of loyalty, Bishop Jozef Carsky of Kosice declared, in the name of all church dignitaries present: "We shall no longer recognize church punishments and shall not punish priests and believers if these punishments are given for political reasons. We want to support by all means the building efforts . . . of our People's Democracy, because we know this effort . . . is in full harmony with the ethical demands of our Holy Church."

The Communists' infiltration of Czechoslovakia's hierarchy had become more than a tragic rout; it was, in large measure, a moral disintegration. By September 27, 1951, a "National Peace Congress" brought 1,700 clerical delegates to Prague and another telegram assured Gottwald that the "overwhelming majority" of priests would co-operate with the régime in its "fight for peace." Many had been subjected to severe pressures. But what the Stalinists meant by "peace" was clearly indicated by the hymns of hate in their party press. Prague's *Mlada Fronta* was typical: "With the Americans you cannot use human argumentation. . . . You have to use the guns of the People's Army in Korea and the fists of Chinese volunteers . . . the language of power. . . . We will present our bill for all their bestialities. It will be a frightful settling of accounts, just and merciless."

The profound tragedy of Czechoslovakia's hierarchy and church cannot be exaggerated. Prelates of notable distinction have been swept aside or have crumbled before a savage assault. Once again the faithful were isolated, their organizations completely in the enemy's hands. Could it be that no church—whether liberal or conservative or even "feudal-minded"—could withstand the Reds once they were in power? Could it be that all churches in free countries can only hope to survive by keeping Communism from political ascendancy?

The Stalinists' capture of Poland's Catholic Church

The Russians have repeatedly betrayed an utter lack of comprehension of foreign peoples' psychology, but in their handling of the Czechoslovakians and the Poles, both Slavic peoples, they have shown a remarkable degree of psychological finesse. While pursuing identical ends in both countries, the Russians usually employ diametrically opposite tactics. Where they strike with savage directness at the Czechs (as in their original coup d'état) the Stalinists rather consistently treat the Poles with dilatory methods.

The Reds knew that 25 million fanatically patriotic, intensely Catholic Poles were not to be taken by storm. This is why they have gone much more slowly in their efforts to collectivize the peasants in Poland than in any other Curtain country. Their moves against the Polish Church were equally cautious.

The record shows Moscow carefully applying "on again, off again" pressures against the Polish hierarchy. First the seizure of control of "Caritas," the great Catholic charitable organization, in January 1950. Then a period of marking time. In February Cardinal Sapieha and Primate Wyszynski addressed a letter to President Bierut. They protested most courageously against state restrictions on religious education and suppression of Catholic publications and declared: "The war against the church, against religion, against God, in Poland is obvious to all."

The Communists actually made some concessions which enabled the signing of a state-church agreement in April. It included, however, an admission by the hierarchy which eventually precipitated fatal consequences. The Episcopate recognized that the "recovered territories" (the western regions formerly German) "belong forever to Poland," and agreed to ask the Vatican to give church administrative offices in these areas permanent status. Thus the hierarchy was maneuvered both into endorsing a Polish nationalist claim sponsored by Moscow, and into a position of potentially strong disagreement with the Vatican. The Polish people's fierce insistence on permanent possession of traditionally German regions had trapped their church leaders. Of course the Kremlin's shrewd design was to get the right for Warsaw's Red régime to control appointments of Catholic prelates in the disputed districts.

By the April agreement the Episcopate was also maneuvered

into pledging that it would "support all endeavors toward a permanent peace." That was the Communists' classic opening wedge. Nevertheless Cardinal Sapieha and the bishops steadfastly refused in June to sign the Comintern's false-front "Peace Appeal." But with that the venom specialists of Moscow's press went into an orgy of calumny, charging the Polish prelates with breaking the state-church agreement.

Through this barrage of rage and menace the Kremlin scored a most damaging point. On June 22, 1950, Bishop Choromanski, as Episcopal Secretary, was forced to register a major retreat which amounted to capitulation. His official announcement stated: "The Episcopate takes a positive stand in regard to the Stockholm [peace] appeal . . . and will support the present peace action by collecting signatures for the appeal." The hierarchy probably felt compelled to save such religious safeguards as existed by avoiding a repudiation of the state-church agreement by the régime. But the Reds' "peace campaign" stiletto had again pierced the church's armor.

Meanwhile Warsaw's Communists enlisted a group of so-called "patriotic" priests, many being more easily seducible because of their extreme nationalism. They became ardent champions of Poland's sacred right to the "recovered territories." In September their leader, Father Antoni Lemparty, attacked both the Vatican and the Polish hierarchy for failure to appoint permanent bishops in these regions. Then the régime delivered a flat ultimatum to the Episcopate in October, 1950: "The government will no longer tolerate the provisional nature of church organizations in the Western Territories . . . and calls upon the church to liquidate [them]." In January, 1951, it was followed by a decree abolishing the temporary status of church offices in the West.

The church was still better off than it was in Hungary or Czechoslovakia. For there existed in Poland some 2,000 monasteries and convents (as remains true up to this writing). The Stalinists had carefully refrained from wholesale suppression of

Poland's religious orders; had imprisoned fewer of their members than elsewhere. The church still operated 600 primary schools; Lublin's Catholic University still functioned; convents were conducting more than 300 kindergartens. These were unique concessions.

Instead the Russians struck where Polish character was exceptionally vulnerable—its nationalist fixation. The Poles' fierce attachment to the former German regions was an understandable obsession. A Polish hierarchy could not oppose a permanent status for Catholic organizations in the "recovered territories." If it did, the church would be condemned by the whole Polish people. Thus the Kremlin trapped the Polish hierarchy and isolated it from the Vatican. Warsaw's régime removed from office those priests acting as apostolic administrators in the western territories and appointed collaborationist clergymen as their successors. These victories assured the Red conquest of Poland's church administration. The hierarchy was at the mercy of the Stalinists and admitted this on May 13, 1951. Episcopal Secretary Bishop Choromanski declared, in an official message to the Polish clergy, that they "should stand strongly on the principles of Catholic teaching regarding collaboration of church and state. . . . Priests will therefore shun all activities of a political nature. . . . Priests will also keep away from all activities which would aim in any manner at State or political authorities, at the structure and economy of the State."

The "Peace Priests' " activities were obviously of a "political nature"—but the church had been forced to endorse the Reds' "Peace Appeal." Actually Bishop Choromanski's message urged at least a neutral co-existence with the Communist régime: "the clergy will keep away from all anti-state conspiracy." Despite its vast power and its communicants' devotion, Polish Catholicism was reduced to a resigned tolerance toward its anti-religious enemies in order to exist at all. As catastrophe had smitten the Hungarian and Czechoslovakian churches, so it had smitten Poland's—but by more adroit and insidious means.

Red capture of the Orthodox, Protestant, Jewish and other churches in Eastern Europe

The story of the Communists' domination of churches of all creeds in Rumania and Bulgaria is tragically repetitious. Because these two countries were nearer and more helpless, Moscow chose to attack there much earlier, with a ruthless brutality which assured a swift decision. The Red régimes employed naked terrorism to a degree only approached or equaled in Hungary, later on.

Thousands of Orthodox, Protestant, Jewish or Catholic clergy were put into jails or slave-labor camps. Scores of Rumanian and Bulgarian bishops met the same fate, many dying in prison. Large numbers of clergymen who refused to betray their faiths were tortured. Vasil Ziapkov, leader of the Bulgarian Congregationalists, was tortured for sixty-three days before signing a "confession." Nikola Mihailov, head of Bulgaria's Baptist Church, suffered similar martyrdom. But there were always some who bowed to the Communist government and became its docile instruments.

One of these was Patriarch Justinian Marina, leader of Rumania's powerful Greek Orthodox Church. The Communists later rewarded him by forcibly dissolving the Greek Catholic Church and requiring its "return" to the Orthodox faith. Exarch Stephan of the Bulgarian Orthodox Church vainly tried to ride the storm, as priests were arrested and killed, church buildings closed, seminaries and religious publications shut down. In 1948 he was deposed. The terror intensified; Bishop Boris, Metropolitan of Nevrokop, was assassinated. Soon both Bulgaria's and Rumania's great Orthodox Churches were in the hands of collaborationists. Russia's Orthodox Church and its servile Patriarch exercised an immense influence, although persecution was also required. Moscow held all the trumps. The next step was merely the setting up of more clerical "Peace Movements."

The Kremlin, in fact, neatly demonstrated the *universality* of its methods in Rumania. Its National Peace Committee included Patriarch Marina of the Orthodox Church, bishops of the Reformed and Unitarian Churches, the Grand Rabbi, the chiefs of the Moslem and Lipovan faiths and a Catholic priest. (All Catholic bishops had already been deposed or arrested.)

The scattered Protestant congregations in satellite Europe were small and bereft of any common organization so that they presented little difficulty. While some leaders resisted, many others were snared by the "peace" lure. Bishop Lazlo Dezsery, Hungary's Lutheran bishop, stated in an Easter message: "Today's most deadly sin is that committed in the countries of imperialism by those who are preparing a new World War." Certain outright Communists or professed atheists infiltrated the lay organization of Hungary's Presbyterian Church. In Czechoslovakia a "peace pastor," Jan Chabada, was named bishop general of the Slovak Lutheran Church. Disunited Protestantism, despite the heroism of some clergymen, became a swift and absolute conquest for collaboration. Large numbers of faithful parishioners thereafter boycotted churches in which renegades or "patriotic pastors" were installed.

After the terrible toll of Nazi persecution and extermination, the surviving Jews in Eastern Europe were in a most tragic and defenseless situation. Everywhere the Red régimes "reorganized' Jewish institutions, outrightly suppressing the Zionists. Of Poland's Jews, reduced to a mere 80,000, half were registered for emigration by 1951. Europe's largest remaining Jewish population, outside of Russia, consisted of approximately 300,000 in Rumania. A few thousand per month were again permitted to emigrate during 1951. But the Bucharest régime imposed brutal discriminations upon the overwhelming majority of Rumania's Jews. They were robbed of their small enterprises; denied the possibility of earning even a modest livelihood; progressively pauperized; progressively deprived of their communal organizations. In Hungary only a single Jewish organization survived by February, 1950. In Poland all Jewish cultural, social and welfare organizations were merged in non-Jewish bodies—leaving only a Central Committee of Jews, completely controlled by Stalinists.

"Separatist" or nationalized churches—the final step in Communist domination

Throughout captive Europe the Soviets have successfully split the church administrations and leadership of every denomination; have filled their key positions with collaborationist clergy; are using every organized religious body for the Kremlin's political ends. Moscow needs to take but one more action, which is almost a formality. All the largest churches, of whatever creed, must be nationalized and made permanently subservient to Moscow. The once powerful Roman Catholic Churches in Hungary, Czechoslovakia and Poland must be utterly divorced from Vatican authority and influence.

The Soviets have already set the pattern precisely where this revolutionary separation could be most easily imposed. The Catholic Church in Albania, smallest of all Red puppet states, was unobtrusively nationalized in August, 1951. Through a "new statute" all of its organizational, political and economic links with the Vatican were severed. The Communist government assumed control of all future church relations with any foreign or non-Albanian church. All new priests must now be trained only in Communist-administered seminaries. It is a legal offense for any Albanian Catholic priest to communicate with another Catholic priest outside the country, save through governmental channels. Separation from the Holy See is absolute.*

Unquestionably the same "separatist solution" is envisaged for the Catholic Church in Poland, Czechoslovakia, Hungary and Rumania. It must be expected that its imposition will depend purely on expediency—whenever circumstances are most practical or most urgent. In the timing of religious con-

* *The New York Times*, September 23, 1951.

quests the Communists' record to date has approached split-second perfection.

Above the fate of any particular church or creed, however, stands the Stalinists' determination to render all organized religions utterly subservient to Kremlin policies, propaganda, purposes and power. Above the fate of all those churches now subjugated throughout Red-ruled Europe stands one further fact: that no church's freedom of worship and of conscience can conceivably escape destruction wherever Soviet Communism seizes power.

CHAPTER TWELVE

Youth Communized

UNDER A COMMUNIST GOVERNMENT WHAT happens to your children and to everyone else's children?

They are literally kidnapped by the Red state. But no amount of gold can restore the children to their parents' free guidance. The Stalinists' ransom is the child's mind and soul. Sooner or later that price is exacted—unless your children are so heroic as to choose martyrdom or a tormented existence as social outcasts. Far more likely, they will insist on doing "what the other children do." Then what?

The answer to that came to a good Hungarian father in this fashion. The A.V.O. secret police beat him so terribly that he was sent home on a stretcher in October, 1950. For the third time they had arrested him for listening to Western broadcasts. But he had taken extreme precautions: how could they have found out? Beside his wife, no one had shared the secret but his 12-year-old son. Bandaged and crippled, the father asked the boy the awful question.

"You are an enemy of the people's democracy if you listen to the imperialists' radio," his son replied coldly. "Of course I reported you. If you listen any more, I will report you again." As soon as he was able to walk the father went out and obtained a revolver. That night he killed his son, then his wife—and committed suicide.

A Rumanian mother started to box her small boy's ears when he was arrogantly disobedient. "You'd better not touch a

Pioneer Guide," he shouted threateningly. "I'll tell our leader you are profiteering with food. We Pioneers are Stalin's children. We don't need any other parents. Stalin is my father. If you punish me, I'll run away to Russia."

"Father" Stalin celebrated the twentieth century's most gigantic Father's Day (by proxy) in East Berlin on August 12, 1951. From 8 A.M. until nearly 4 P.M. hundreds upon hundreds of thousands of boys and girls from Eastern Germany and other satellite countries poured in a vast, ceaseless flood through the great Marx-Engels Platz. They were led by an army of white-shirted children between the ages of six and 14—a section of the Communists' Young Pioneers. Wave after wave and hour after hour they came. Wave after wave, multitudes of shrill, frenzied, juvenile voices cried, "Long live Stalin! Long live the Soviet Union! Long live the Communist Party!"

On these same Berlin pavements Adolph Hitler himself had never won an identical adulation. For never once had massed legions of *foreign* youths demonstrated such delirious devotion to Hitler and Nazism, least of all the representatives of seven foreign nationalities from half of continental Europe, mobilized in a capital far removed from the demigod's home. Beside this youth demonstration the Hitler Jugend had been a crudely nationalistic, strictly Teutonic manifestation. This was "Father" Stalin's greatest triumph on non-Soviet soil. Nothing that has happened since the Bolshevik Revolution is so ominous.

In the course of two weeks two million adolescents and children from every section of Eastern Europe participated tumultuously in East Berlin's "World Festival of Youth and Students for Peace." Day after day they marched behind blaring bands, sang the hymns of Red Revolution, roared their chants of "Long live Stalin!" They carried hundreds of portraits of the Great Red Father. They flaunted huge banners with fiery slogans, many reading "Death to the Anglo-American War Criminals and German Imperialists!" Never in living memory has there occurred such a terrifying "peace" demonstration as this. The faces of boys and girls in peasant costumes from Poland, Bohemia and Slovakia, from Hungary, Rumania and Bulgaria, were flushed with exaltation. Parades and pageantry; music and dancing; speeches and fireworks; glory and delirium—while the citizens of democratic nations everywhere continued walking in their sleep.

The Stalinists have already kidnapped an alarmingly large segment of Eastern Europe's youth. Quite probably they have now converted at least one-quarter of its 20 million young people below the age of 21. But how do they seize them? And with what do they lure them? What made possible the mammoth "peace festival" in East Berlin? Nothing more—but nothing less—than the Communist's enormous capacity to *organize*. Not to organize shops or tractor stations. To organize human beings —first and above all, to organize children.

The Reds' secret of organizing youth

To perpetuate Red power the Communists must win the minds of adolescents and children. Throughout captive Europe they have already demonstrated how effectively this can be done. The Kremlin's orders are written in its policy of these postwar years:

1) "Force the satellites' youngest generation into Soviet-type youth organizations!"

2) "Indoctrinate and communize the youth incessantly; in school and out!"

3) "Isolate all children from their parents and from religious controls! Alienate them from both to a maximum!"

4) "Instil in youth the concepts and practice of class warfare!"

5) "Teach youth to worship Stalin and Soviet Russia!"

6) "Saturate the youth with hatred of Western democracies and of 'decadent bourgeois idealism'!"

7) "Exploit the natural rebelliousness of youth!"

8) "Appeal to youthful idealism, ambitions and sense of adventure!"

A Bulgarian Communist leader wraps much of this up with

these incisive demands: "Teach the children allegiance to the Communist Party, to the Soviet Union and to the great leader of nations, the great Stalin. Teach them to hate with all their hearts the instigators of a new war, the Anglo-American imperialists and their agents. Teach them to be ready to defend their country, to carry on an irreconcilable struggle against bourgeois ideology."

All these things, and more, are being done through steadily growing Communist Youth Unions and Young Pioneer organizations, directly copied from Soviet models. Their combined memberships were known to exceed seven million by early 1952—fully one-third of all boys and girls in the Iron Curtain countries.* The Young Pioneers encompass children of both sexes from six to 14; the Youth Unions' memberships are adolescents from 15 to 21 or slightly older. The youngster who yearns to "belong" can only belong to these. Boy Scouts, Girl Scouts and all other youth groups are abolished. The Red state holds an absolute monopoly on every form of organized youthful activity. It takes an almost fantastic parental authority to hold a finger in the dyke against simply enormous governmental and party pressures.

A majority of satellite elementary-school children belong to the Pioneers. They alone enjoy the group games, excursions and free movies, and can win and wear attractive badges. These things are even more appealing than a TV set in your parlor. How can you persuade your young son or daughter to go without them, year after year? Your Jack and Suzie are admittedly excellent students, but they regularly receive shockingly low marks in high school, even though they do their homework scrupulously. "But it's your fault, Mother. They only give good marks to those who belong to the Youth Union. We are out of everything. If you and Dad would just let us join. . . ." How long could you hope to hold the lines in this battle inside your own family in a Red-ruled America, France or any other country?

* See chart giving 1951 totals in Chapter IV, page 58.

Or perhaps your boy has gone into a factory precisely because he "refused to join" in senior high school. Undoubtedly there were a good many like that among the young workers in Polish Silesia. But all of them in 402 industrial plants were ordered to join the Union of Polish Youth (z.m.p.)—or lose their jobs. Polands' students were members of a national university federation which was merged into the z.m.p.: now, to be a student, one must belong. The Bulgarian régime demands that all youths from 14 to 21 affiliate with the Dimitrov Union of Working Youth (d.s.n.m.), but so far has encountered a great many stubborn youthful boycotters.

The Stalinists' youth program is a non-stop Red round-up. The Kremlin's ideological cowboys swing their lariats, day in and day out. While they roped a mere 130,000 Rumanian children during the Young Pioneers' first year (1949), they had packed 600,000 into the corral by 1951. Recruitment drives for Communist youth organizations operate under full steam the year round. Moscow's *Pravda* placed the Soviet Union's Pioneers at an all-time high of 19 million children—a tremendous recent increase—in 1951. That was roughly one-tenth of the u.s.s.r.'s total population. It indicates what extraordinary numbers the Kremlin is aiming at in the Curtain countries. Already more than one million Young Pioneers have been enlisted in Poland and Czechoslovakia. Such facts compel serious consideration of:

How the Communists "get them while they're young."

When you control all the armed, police, lawmaking and governing powers in any country it's frightfully simple. Children are taught Stalinist "double-think" in school—then the party steals virtually all their free time outside of school. After-school activities are a nation-wide specialty: "learning circles" for more political indoctrination; group readings of Communist publications; hiking and singing; assignments to Young Pioneers to distribute "Peace Movement" tracts or to "patrol" their neighbors' homes for the anti-waste campaign. Older girls belonging to the "Waybreakers" practice shooting rifles and throwing grenades. Red group leaders have alluring tasks or pastimes for everyone, designed to make those who "don't belong" feel sadly out of things, but designed, above everything else, to keep children away from home until supper time every day. On Sunday mornings there are "free occupation" periods. It's a party order. That keeps your child from attending church. The Communists publish daily newspapers exclusively for young people, and magazines as well. Those in Poland, with circulations of 850,000 in 1951, undoubtedly reach five times as many young readers.

Child seduction is a master art of the Stalinists and no expense is spared. They opened a fabulous "Children's Palace" in Warsaw late in 1950. How many youngsters can resist having a palace of their own? This one is a strikingly modern, lavishly equipped building which accommodates 2,000 children daily. To children who live in shabby, ill-heated rooms or crude structures salvaged from bombings the appeal of this place of extraordinary delights must be almost irresistible. Polish Youth Union leaders supervise every activity and spread propaganda at the same time. There are workshops for the mechanically minded, separate departments for radio, aviation, chemistry, astronomy, photography and stamp collecting—even a tiny tots' dream place called the Fairy Tales Room.

Under the Red régimes all orphans become outright state property. Where they were previously in the care of religious orders as a rule, orphans are now housed and instructed in "State Education Institutes" up to their fifteenth year. Red kindergartens and day nurseries, for small children whose mothers work in factories, are increasing by hundreds every year. These are also direct copies of the Soviet Russian system. In Czechoslovakia annual funds for establishment of kindergartens were increased by 25,527,000 crowns in 1951, or $510,000. The deputy Minister of Education, Anna Karlovska, declared: "We have to learn from Soviet teachers. Like careful gardeners they bring up the new Soviet man from his earliest youth. They

instruct children in collective habits . . . to work with enthu-
siasm for the cause of Socialism."

The "careful gardeners" plant their seeds with skill. Take the
Young Pioneers' oath. Under impressively solemn circumstances
a Hungarian boy or girl swears "in the presence of all my
comrades, to fulfill all my duties . . . to fight with body and
soul the battle of our people against the American imperialist
assassins; and declare myself ready to defend, with my life if
necessary, my happy Socialist homeland." Puppet-state children
are offered knighthood in a new crusading order. How can any
mother, prattling about "bourgeois" virtues and home duties,
compete with this? How, especially, with only one or two hours
of opportunity out of each twenty-four?

The methods of Communist youth indoctrination

Hungary's Reds obligingly publish the main objectives of
what they call "the ethical education of youth" in school discussions or "learning circles." These are: 1) "To help pupils to
distinguish clearly between what is considered moral and what
immoral from the Communist point of view"; 2) "To teach
pupils to examine every phase of their activities from the point of
view of whether it is in line with Communist requirements";
3) "To instil in pupils the correct Communist behavior outside of
school. . . . Junior high school pupils are to be made aware of
the meaning of the Pioneer greeting, 'Be ready to fight! For
Lenin's and Stalin's cause!' . . . Pedagogues are to teach
pupils to examine every cause . . . from an ideological and
party point of view."

Communist Youth Unions provide special courses in political
organization and "culture." Instructions in Soviet training
methods are given by "political officer" comrades. In the words
of the president of Bulgaria's D.S.N.M., the "Youth Union
educates youth in an implacable hatred toward the class enemy.
. . . Special attention should be paid to the training of young
propagandists." A circular of Hungary's Pioneers specifies that

youth must be taught "always to pursue those bourgeois elements which might dare bring into our schools moods and nostalgia for the old bourgeois world." They must also be taught "readiness to act quickly, even with denunciations to the police, against those who . . . condemn or criticize the superior orders of our association, such as laws of the state or orders of the party."

Thus nearly one-third of Eastern Europe's boys and girls are not only being indoctrinated with Lenist-Stalinist ideology; they are being saturated with class hatred, with readiness to fight against the free, democratic nations at a word from the Kremlin, with scorn for their parents' standards and "old-fashioned morality," with anti-religious sentiments, and with skillfully promoted convictions that they are nobly patriotic when they serve as spies and informers—against their parents and teachers, against resisting workers and farmers, against anyone whom the party may designate.

Along with all this (as reported in Chapter IV), millions of captive Europe's school children and teen-age workers are being given regular and intensive military training in a wide variety of specialized fields. Military instruction receives greatest emphasis of all, save for political indoctrination. But the Red state, in Barbara Ward's discerning phrase, also "fulfills while it perverts some of the best yearnings of youth."

The Communists give young people real jobs and flattering responsibilities.

An impressive series of "youth shops" has been operated exclusively by members of Poland's Youth Union (z.m.p.) in Bydgoszcz since 1950. Zealous teen-agers manage and staff 14 food co-operatives, several bakery and clothing shops and the city's largest confectionery store. Their sense of importance is deliberately inflated by lavish praise in the party press. "Experience has shown," one Red daily states, "that young people work much more efficiently in shops managed by themselves, rather than in mixed shops. Efficiency and cleanliness in shops run by z.m.p. members has been on a very high level." In scores of activities and occupations the Reds assign youngsters of both sexes to hard work. Adolescent egos are played up to adroitly. Youths are given a rare and heady sense of participation, and praised for contributing to great, nation-wide programs.

Nowhere in the democracies are very young people handed so many and such adult responsibilities. Official posts in trade unions and Workers' Councils go to a surprising number of young members. In Polish mining unions 25 per cent of the "trustees" are from the z.m.p.; in the textile industry 10 per cent—but party organs denounce this as "too small." Young Communists are also pushed into executive jobs in municipal soviets; as group leaders, "educators" and propagandists; as junior bosses of tractor stations and much else. Even the Central Committee of Hungary's party announces proudly that more than one-third of its 65 top Reds are below the age of 35. Boys and girls between the ages of 15 and 21 are much less critical of Marxist innovations; much less concerned about obstacles, more scornful of old ways of doing things, more blindly obedient —above all, enthusiastic.

"Cops and robbers" is a wonderfully enticing game for the young of every race and clime, and the police state's masters exploit these susceptibilities to the utmost. What could be more thrilling than to become a real spy in the service of the government and party? What could be more acceptable, when even grade-school children are taught "what is considered moral . . . from the Communist point of view"? So puppet-state Pioneers and Youth Union members are constantly mobilized as informers. First, against parents and teachers. But bands of youngsters are dispatched annually to search peasants' homes for hidden produce. A local unit of Czechoslovakia's c.s.m. describes its "fight against the village rich." The party's junior snoopers "patrol" and act as crop guards; ransack peasant homes in thousands of rural centers in every Curtain country, vastly excited by their unprecedented authority. Acting as agents of

Red terrorism is perverted into a notable "patriotic service."

Nevertheless the majority of farm-bred youth remains antagonistic to Communism, and these children of peasant orgin far outnumber all others in the puppet-state nations. In addition, the hold of strongly religious families and independent-minded middle-class parents cannot be broken down swiftly or uniformly, especially in regard to older children.

These resistances account for the Red régimes' drives to recruit and organize the youngest generation, and for recurring purges of their Youth Union memberships. During a clean-up campaign in the spring of 1951 the Czech Communists admitted that investigations had revealed "hostile supporting elements" in the ranks of the C.S.M. Bulgaria's Youth Union (D.S.N.M.) vigorously conducted a "purification drive against members of bourgeois origin." Its press also railed against "the isolation of the Union from rural youth"; about weakness in political education, and cited "many cases where not one member has paid his dues."

At a meeting of Rumania's Union of Working Youth (U.M.T.) in February, 1951, the head of its university section reported that 55,000 students "had been found guilty of hostility and indifference." In Hungary a new daily newspaper, *Free Youth*, was selling only about 40,000 copies in September to a D.I.S.Z. membership of more than 600,000. The difficulties encountered with Poland's strongly Catholic youth are indicated by a pair of facts: The government's Statistical News placed those in the country's ten-to-19 age bracket at more than 4.8 million; but by late 1951 Warsaw's Reds could not claim more than approximately 1.7 million in their youth organizations.

These facts indicate an extraordinarily courageous resistance among the teen-age portion of Eastern Europe's youth. Nevertheless it remains true that more than seven million of captive Europe's 20 million young people are already in the Red Youth Unions and Pioneers. It seems conceivable that nearly five million of these have either been thoroughly communized or are far advanced toward that Kremlin objective. One is compelled to estimate that the Stalinists have already captured, or seem assured of capturing, about 25 per cent of all young people in the Iron-Curtain countries, a formidable percentage of tomorrow's ruling generation.

Inside the Youth Unions the Communist Party decides all vital aspects of its members' existence. Its officials decide what schools they will attend; what members may enter high schools or proceed to universities; what jobs boys and girls may take, and when; what members are sufficiently communized to be trusted with a professional career or a chance at an army commission.

Youth Union leaders decide what members will benefit by state scholarships; what members will be honored by being sent to Russia for special training in the Komsomols, as students or as specialists. In the phrase of Poland's z.m.p. spokesman: "It is the leaders of the younger generation who have to be organized in the patriotic and international spirit, and in fighting alliance with the Soviet Union." Once corralled inside the Reds' Youth Unions, every teen-ager loses all freedom of choice and decision. Those who remain outside are relegated to a permanently inferior status. Youth's only opportunity lies in becoming an enthusiastic conformist and party-line automaton. It is not disputable that the Soviets' greatest secret weapon is the corruption and conversion of youth.

The Kremlin's goal for youth

Suppose the Stalinists are able to transform from 12 million to 16 million young people now below the age of 20 into convinced Communists during the next decade. Then, short of an East-West war, Soviet Russia would be in a position to dominate all of Iron-Curtain Europe for at least another generation, perhaps indefinitely. The Politburo's strategists recognize this as their supreme opportunity. Their struggle for children's minds may well decide Eastern Europe's fate for this century. But it is by no means certain that the Red kidnappers can succeed in corrupting a decisive majority of their hostages; that depends on how much time they have at their disposal.

Satellite Communists cannot count on converting the older children who were influenced by their families and by religion during their formative years before the Red régimes gained power, not even on the great numbers already inside their Youth Unions. Referring to these older teen-agers, Poland's Z.M.P. monthly confesses frankly: "We can only rely on half of the youth as being indoctrinated. The others are joking." A report to the Polish prime minister states: "It is impossible to change most youths above the age of 12 and 14 years. We must concentrate on those who are 14 or under 14."

Eastern Europe's young school children, then, are the first generation the Kremlin can hope to capture completely. The Communists are concentrating on them particularly. These children will be in their late teens or early twenties by the 1960's; they are indeed tomorrow's ruling generation.

As he watched the Young Pioneers, mere children of six and eight, swept by an ecstatic frenzy in East Berlin, a Western observer remarked: "They have only had these youngsters for five or six years. Many of these little girls were probably born at the end of the war, or just afterwards. What will it be like in another ten years? Makes you think a bit, doesn't it?"

Here Barbara Ward asks the question which all of us who take freedom largely for granted must ask: "What if Eastern Europe's new generation has learned to love its chains?" *

Beyond doubt this is the Kremlin's aim. It hopes to implant a blind attachment to slavery in the youngest generation by that "hyper-indoctrination process" presumptuously described as education—in short, sovietized education.

* "The Crucial Battle for the World's Youth," *The New York Times Sunday Magazine:* November 18, 1951.

CHAPTER THIRTEEN

Education Perverted

SUPPOSE YOU HAVE FOUR CHILDREN AND YOU live in any Iron-Curtain country. What happens to them at school?

You have no more school worries about John, aged 18. Despite his above-average marks he has been barred from entering college because of his "class-enemy" background—his father once owned a modestly successful radio business and voted in 1946 for a non-Communist party. So they put John into a Workers' Brigade for "re-education"—until the army and its political commissars take him over.

Mary, at 15, is in high school; and 11-year-old Vera is in the seventh grade. They both belong to the Communist Youth organizations, over your protests, because "all the children belong." Ever since they joined, they've been increasingly enthusiastic, especially about after-school activities. You rarely see them except at supper time, and then they come out with the strangest flat statements—such as, "Only Russia and the people's democracies want peace." If you remonstrate, they argue back heatedly, Vera in particular. It merely makes them more stubborn and rebellious. Your ideas are usually brushed aside.

Peter, who is only six, is your chief comfort now that John is away from home. He still listens to his mother and father, and he frequently comes home right after school. He brings his first-grade primer with him. When you try to help him with his reading exercises you find Peter earnestly reciting: "Lenin loved children. He wanted all children of workers and peasants to have

an easy life. All who work love and remember Lenin." Peter is
surprised when his mother gasps. "But I can read it very well,
Mama!" he says.

That first night you read the primer all the way through.
Some of its passages made you utterly sick inside, such as:
"Joseph Stalin is the great leader of the Soviet Union. . . . All
those who work love him with untold love. Joseph Stalin is the
best friend of children." But you couldn't tell Peter not to learn
his lessons—and there's only one kind of school he can attend.
Just the other day he came home with a poem which his class had
learned by heart:

> "By his mighty arm so hard
> Stand the peoples, all on guard;
> Masses singing, young and old,
> Following our Stalin bold."

You know what Peter will be like in another few years. You
can see it already in Mary and Vera—only Peter will be more so.
They are robbing you of your three younger children, and you
can no more prevent it than you can make the sun stand still.
Beyond a doubt they will let Peter go to college. . . . But
what kind of a Peter?

They have already taken most of the Vera you once had. She
is a bright girl. She learns so fast that it frightens you. If Vera
were only rather stupid! (You never imagined you could really
wish that all your children were quite dumb.) But she always
gets excellent marks, as she did Thursday answering these
questions in a test:

"Why is bourgeois democracy a false democracy?"

"Show why the highest form of democracy is the Soviet
democracy."

"From what facts known to you can we see that the Soviet
Union treats us as an equal?"

"Why is the Soviet Union in the forefront of the struggle for
peace?"

"For what reason does the Soviet Union *not* pursue the subjugation and exploitation of any people, as do the imperialist states?" (These questions come from seventh-grade manuals in Rumanian schools.)

Vera proudly showed you her paper; one of the best in her class, she said. What could you say? What could any parent say? Vera also learns in her textbooks that "former owners, implacable enemies of the régime, still plot against the people." And of course, Vera's father is a former owner. "Under whatever mask they may hide," the textbook continues, "let us discover them and strike them down." You know what has happened to other parents who could not conceal their deepest convictions. Today it is mothers and fathers who should be seen but not heard.

Both Mary and Vera are in their third year of Russian; are beginning to speak many simpler phrases. Mary is also permitted to continue her French, but she finds her French textbook rather puzzling. Quite naturally, it starts out with the Communist "*Internationale*" in French. After that come reading selections from such renowned French masters as Stalin, Lenin and Marx. Mary has heard you mention Flaubert, Baudelaire, Voltaire and Pascal as famous French writers, so she wonders why none of them are mentioned—"probably they were reactionaries," Mary remarks. "Isn't it strange how few Frenchmen ever became writers?" When you insist that a great many did, Mary flares back: "Well, they must have been imperialists, like the Americans." As parents you can't really convince your children that you know the truth about anything; first because you were born and brought up in the "bourgeois-prejudiced" middle class; also because:

All satellite textbooks are either translations
or close copies of Soviet models.

What Mary, Vera and Peter get in school are strictly Communist versions, interpretations and distortions of every subject they study. In fact, thousands of direct translations from Russian textbooks are now used in the puppet states' elementary and high schools. Out of 150 new Hungarian textbooks used in universities during 1950, 79 were translated from Russian. The percentage in lower satellite schools is very large.

The Communist Party regularly issues directives to authors of new textbooks. Prospective Czech authors recently received these admonitions: "The new spelling book must be based on the best experience of the Soviets"; Russian language manuals "must stress particularly the unshatterable friendship of our people toward the Soviet people and our immeasurable love for the great Stalin." Selection of pictures in geography books "must be made more carefully" and show "the oppression and misery of the working population" in capitalist countries.

"It is absolutely necessary" that textbook writers present more impressively the Bolshevik Revolution in their history books. They must reveal clearly "the anti-democratic, anti-Soviet policy of former [Czech] governments, and show up the reactionary picture of Masaryk and Benes" [otherwise the two greatest democratic leaders Czechoslovakia has ever known]. "The glorious fight of the Czech Communist Party for the downfall of capitalism must be highly extolled." Textbook writers are also denounced for "failure to unmask the decadence of mathematics and physics" in the United States, Britain and other Western nations.

Mary and Vera, of course, are learning this kind of history and science—this kind of everything. Their teachers are compelled to apply "new methods of tuition . . . guided by the experience gained in the Soviet Union." The truth is that your children may think they are of any particular East European nationality, but their education is 100 per cent Soviet Russian to the extent that their native land's Washingtons and Lincolns, its greatest writers and heroes, are either denounced as traitors or fantastically caricatured and falsified by misrepresentations given in the classroom. All the truly great men are presented as Russians; all the great ideas, great inventions and foremost contributions to social and world progress are equally Russian—

most of all Soviet Russian. Vera, in particular, knows that these
are facts. After all, she has had a Communist education from the
first grade to the seventh. Vera knows.

Besides, schoolwork has a lot of exciting variations in a
"people's democracy." It's not just routine stuff. There's always Stalin's birthday and other great occasions. Just now Mary,
Vera and little Peter are all being mobilized to celebrate the
birthday of "our genial and glorious leader, Stalin." The Ministry of Education has issued a Circular Order. (Believe it or not,
the order's actual number in Rumania is #199,656. Communist
education requires an awful lot of orders.) It lays down an amazingly elaborate program for every classroom in the country, from
first grade through high school. Classroom manifestations "will
be organized under the slogan—'J. V. Stalin, the great genius of
the workers' world!' " It will begin six weeks before his actual
birthday. Millions of school children in six and one-half satellite
countries will participate in similar exercises and hero-worship
simultaneously—for six full weeks!

Here is how it takes off and crashes through to the grand
finale. Pupils of all ages have reading lessons about Stalin's life
and victories; writing lessons about "Comrade Stalin, the
father," "Comrade Stalin, teacher of the Pioneers," etc., etc.
Mary and Vera will participate in classroom discussions on
"Comrade Stalin and the struggle for peace"; on "Comrade
Stalin, mainstay of science" and literally a dozen kindred subjects. Order #199,656 likewise commands that "poster newspapers will publish verses, compositions and drawings made by
pupils on this occasion." Children will prepare albums with
pictures of Stalin's life, and "to show their love for Comrade
Stalin pupils may compose and address letters to him personally."
Then, finally, comes the great day. In every satellite grade school
and high school a gala program, dictated by the party long in
advance, will be staged . . . red flags, marching, hymns and
speeches to Stalin. Who ever had such a birthday? Consider
what it does to millions of impressionable young minds.

Just possibly, there might somewhere be an isolated case like that mentioned in one underground item. "Who is your father?" a Communist teacher asked an unusually bright little girl. "Stalin is my father," she piped up promptly. "And who is your mother?" Just as quickly—"Comrade Stalin." "You are an excellent pupil," the teacher declared. "Tell me, Anna. What do you want to be when you grow up?" Without a second's hesitation Anna replied, "An orphan." But of course, this is merely one of the jokes which are current in captive Europe. In reality it's a terribly sad joke: what several millions of puppet-state parents wish *could* happen, and know is far beyond the realm of probability.

Heresy toward Kremlin ideology and propaganda is virtually impossible in satellite schools, because teaching is absolutely party-controlled. Moscow's methods cannot be contravened.

To sovietize education—communize the teachers!

Through the Red régimes' ministries of education, executives, faculties, principals and teaching staffs of all universities and public schools have been purged repeatedly. Today the schools are completely party-occupied. Any secretly anti-Communist professors and teachers who remain must perform like enthusiastic collaborators or lose their jobs. Lukewarm attitudes are highly suspect, and party-appointed pupil-spies render even slyly subversive classroom comments almost impossible. Nevertheless, large numbers of "bourgeois unreliables" still retain positions, especially in elementary and high schools, simply because the Red ministries of education cannot manufacture teachers as fast as they manufacture propaganda and lying textbooks.

The Communists' chief problem is to produce new cadres of indoctrinated pedagogues fast enough to fill the gaps; gradually to obtain sovietized teaching staffs from top to bottom. They are working feverishly to this end. Party school inspectors and pedagogical bureaus meanwhile maintain a "service of guidance and control" over thousands of prewar teachers who are still needed. Most of these hold-overs are required to go to school for "re-education" courses, conducted in "guidance centers." As early as 1949 more than 80,000 Rumanian teachers (about 80 per cent of that nation's total) had reportedly taken such courses.

This party-enforced reconversion continues everywhere under high pressure, particularly in summer schools for teachers. Dubious elements are rigidly eliminated, but not yet to anything like Moscow's and the M.V.D.'s satisfaction. The Red rulers demand more and more teachers' training schools. They also keep packing the school staffs with party-approved persons, alleged to possess professional qualifications—meaning blind adherence to party doctrines. In Czechoslovakia, Poland and elsewhere many able career teachers, rated as politically suspect, have been sent into industrial jobs, some even into the coal mines. They are replaced by graduates of "workers' pedagogical courses." The worker candidate's aptitudes and intelligence are entirely secondary. If he parrots Stalinese and party-line jargon glibly, he is assured of a teaching diploma.

Hungary began its scholastic year in September, 1951, by making its Communist school directors "individually responsible" as heads of schools. The governmental decree declares: "Their task is to constantly educate school educators"—for the "political and ideological guidance of pupils and educators alike." They must also lead "parents' work groups"—which constitute another extremely cunning party device. Vast numbers of parents are strongly anti-Communist. They are coerced into joining "parents' work groups" where party representatives can get at them and bring their propaganda pressures to bear. One of these nights Mary or Vera will come home saying: "Mother, you and Dad *must* join our parents' work group. You know what they will say about us, if you don't belong!" Then you will have merely one more unsolvable dilemma. After the Reds get the teachers thoroughly trapped, they bait another trap for the parents.

You were lucky, at any rate, that you managed to keep Peter out of kindergarten, for it's becoming increasingly difficult every year. Little Red kindergartens and day nurseries may still be merely in their infancy, but they are growing by hundreds in all puppet states with each annual budget. During Czechoslovakia's 1950–51 academic year 256,300 tiny tots attended 5,865 nursery schools. That figure may be tripled by 1955. When the Communists hold monopoly influence over 750,000 Czechoslovakian toddlers they will be far on the way toward producing a blindly Red generation.

What do the Red red school-houses produce?

A Hungarian educator, now jobless and barely able to keep alive, describes the results of the Soviets' systematic perversion of education: "There is not one subject at school where politics do not play a decisive role. All spheres of human knowledge are filled with Communist ideology. Russian ideas and ideals, Russian thinking and Russian culture are pushed without interruption into the minds of Hungarian youth to turn them into enthusiastic Russophiles. Their national consciousness is being deliberately killed. Their heroes are Lenin, not Louis Kossuth; Stalin, not Szechenyi. The most dangerous result is this—Hungary's youth are being educated to be enthusiastic Russians."

That is the ultimate aim for 16 million or more East Europeans of school and college age. But for all who finish high school:

Political and class discrimination decides who can go to college.

Your Mary is definitely one who wants to go, and because she is active in the Communist Youth Union she may be permitted to do so. She might even be given a Red state (party) scholarship. A very large proportion of "reliable" students get them nowadays. But they are chiefly from the so-called "new type" students, former workers who receive high-school diplomas by attending special courses for a few months. They act as party propagandists, agitators and informers, so they never have to worry about their exams. In fact, they are often told in advance what questions they will be asked. Decidedly Mary hasn't the "new type" background, and she suffers from being better at her studies than at political work—which is exactly the wrong way round.

So how would Mary qualify for enrollment at a university? She must first be considered "fully reliable," which, alas, she seems certain to be in another three years. Then she must pass an entrance examination. After that she must still present herself for an "admission interview" at the university, which is much more important than any examination. The Communist interview official probes the student candidate's past like an M.V.D. agent questioning a suspected saboteur. He asks questions like this: "Do you go to church often? Do your parents talk religion at home? Does your father still have capitalist ideas?" And in certain cases: "Do you agree that your father was rightfully arrested?" * Unless both her parents somehow remain mum as oysters for three more years, Mary won't have a chance of getting into college.

Actually satellite universities are being packed with "new type" graduates from workers' courses. In Czechoslovakia they represented nearly 45 per cent of all students during the 1951–52 matriculation, virtually all with state-party scholarships of 2,000 crowns ($40) per month. Czech workers'-course graduates had presumably acquired the equivalent of four years of high school in courses lasting ten months. (For those of proletarian origin the Stalinist system makes education—of a sort—extraordinarily easy.) But regular high-school graduates must be recommended by a loyalty board of teachers and pupils in their high school, and after that pass the "admission interview." In Czechoslovakia the student applicant must answer questions on these subjects:

1) Parents' source of income.

2) Parents' political affiliation—in 1938, in 1948 and at present.

3) Did the applicant win a badge of physical proficiency, and if so, when?

* These questions were asked in an "admission interview" of a student entering Bratislava University, who escaped to Austria in August, 1951.

4) Does the applicant hold the Fucik Badge, attesting a high degree of political indoctrination?

5) Is the applicant a member of the Czechoslovak Youth League? If so, since when?

6) Finally and least important—what was the applicant's scholastic record in school?

Mary's middle-class background and her parents' past voting record constitute an almost insurmountable obstacle. In all satellites the majority of children of "class-enemy" parentage are barred from higher education, and those who manage to enter college are subjected to extreme financial handicaps. At Prague's University of Social and Political Sciences, in 1951–52, 67 per cent of 1,700 state scholarships were earmarked for graduates of workers' courses. In Hungary in 1949 57.7 per cent of college freshmen were reported "of peasant origin"; since then the university has increased the percentage of *all* students "from working-class and peasant families" to 55.9 per cent.

Rumania's régime now divides school children into four categories:

Category a: children of industrial workers, members of collective and state farms, and party members.

Category b: children of state officials, of employees of cooperatives with incomes of less than 100,000 lei per year, of members of the armed forces and small tradesmen.

Category c: children of members of liberal professions, and those of tradesmen and mechanics with incomes of less than 300,000 lei per year.

Category d: children of former bankers, industrialists and property owners, of purged officials, of kulaks, of war criminals, and those convicted of crimes against state security.

Children in Category d are grossly discriminated against because of their parents' previous economic status or alleged political sins. Under Rumania's class-preference system "50 per cent of available places are reserved for children of workers, of poor peasants and of public and private office workers belonging to unions."

Poland's educational laws have the announced purpose of "acceleration of the process of developing a people's intelligentsia among working class, small and medium-sized farm youth." High-school students must belong to z.m.p., the Communist Youth Union, or they will not be accepted by a university—as is apparently true in all puppet states.

The resultant undermining of youth's intellectual and moral integrity is obvious. A Polish student, now in exile, asks bitterly: "Can you, who have never known it, understand what it means to live in a state of permanent opposition? We, the young people of Poland, have had to live in this negative, frustrating condition for eleven years now—first under the Nazis, now under the Communists. Under such conditions it is better to compromise; to pretend that you believe in Communism. At least you have a chance to get some kind of education. You often envy those who are able to accept Communism."

From Hungary another student writes: "The Communist Party decides everything from a student's admission until he passes his final exams. Of course the party decides on the basis of political considerations; on how 'reliable' the student is. . . . Our colleges are regularly purged of children of the former middle class, intellectuals, etc. This program is being carried out continuously and systematically, regardless of the results— which already are deplorable.

"As yet lecture standards haven't deteriorated so much, but the level of examinations has sunk unprecedentedly low. The pre-selected and reliable proletarian students have to be passed, no matter how little they know. For those sponsored by the party, the university's exams are a mere formality. The only really important examinations are the political ones."

Soviet professors are also useful for export.

There are now scores and hundreds of Soviet specialists in "advanced learning" occupying chairs and professorships in captive Europe's universities. Visiting lectureships are constantly established for Russian authorities. In addition, each Curtain country has a satellite-Soviet Institute with a full and most influential Russian faculty. Its members keep a sharp, corrective eye on the colonial state's university education.

"The chair of surgery at our university is held by Professor Peter Petrovsky of Leningrad," a Budapest student reports. "He is no doubt a man of great abilities, but not greater than many of our Hungarian surgeons. But it takes at least twice as long for him to teach anything. He knows only Russian. So he lectures with an official interpreter. We wait, half asleep, for the translation; then we get an idea of what he is talking about.

"We are constantly told that our only pattern to follow is Russian medicine; that scientists in the West are 'money slaves.' It's impossible to get even one textbook by a Western authority. But our shelves are bursting with ideological literature. Works of Lenin and Stalin are published in fantastic numbers. We are flooded with Russian novels. The heroes are paper dolls cut out in the strictly Marxist pattern."

By another Red device, first introduced in Poland in 1950, the régime creates a "Consultative Commission" to control public education. When appointed, all the Polish Commission's members proved to be Russian. That placed Poland's entire educational system under direct control of the Kremlin. While the Communists boast about creating a new élite and a "people's intelligentsia," they are merely casting the younger generation's minds into a Kremlin mold. Captive Europe's splendid national literatures are debased and bastardized. Even mathematics, biology and other sciences are strait-jacketed in fantastic Stalinist interpretations. And in all the puppet-states:

The Soviets demonstrate how to rewrite history.

Soviet Academician B. D. Grekov is an authority on this Kremlin invention. He explained how it is done to a large audience of Bulgaria's "new era educators" on September 16, 1950, in Sofia. Moscow's so-called Institute of Russian and Slavic

History, of which he is chairman, is the machine-shop for this wholesale production of falsification.

"The main task of our Institute," proclaimed Professor Grekov, "is to write the proper history of all the Slav nations and peoples. We have started on the histories of Czechoslovakia and Poland. Bulgaria is next on our list. We believe that the full history of the Bulgarian people should be ready by the end of the year. It will be produced and controlled by Soviet and Bulgarian scientists."

Delegations of satellite academicians are frequently sent to Russia to learn the Stalinists' indispensable "new methods." Their guiding principle is that "history should be of advantage to the [Communist] state." But even as late as 1951 some Hungarian historians still had not caught on. A Budapest party organ warned the Hungarian Historical Society that "Hungary's past had been investigated from the wrong viewpoint. . . . Our new historians will now rewrite our history, pointing out the rule of the people." Editors of the Society's periodical had already made a bold start by "compiling 500 pages according to the modern trend." "Bourgeois falsifiers"—i.e., Hungary's most noted historians—have been purged from libraries everywhere.

For nearly two thousand years the Rumanians have been under the impression that they are a predominantly Latin race, descended from the Roman legionaries. But by a providential discovery made in Moscow, the nation's school children now know better. Rumanians, they learn, were first mentioned by a Russian chronicler. They are taught that "before our era there was a common civilization on today's territory of Soviet Russia and Rumania. We can say without exaggeration that the Rumanian people did not exist before its intermingling with the Slavs."

This is curious, because anyone who understands French, Italian or Spanish (all Latin languages) can understand a Rumanian newspaper without great difficulty, whereas a Russian, without knowledge of a Latin language, cannot understand Rumanian at all. Nevertheless the Rumanian Academy, on Moscow's orders, is rewriting the dictionary and replacing words of Latin origin with Slavic synonyms.

The equally non-Slavic Magyars are also having their language Russianized and de-Westernized, beginning with the alphabet. In 1950 Hungary's Literary Academy began studying methods to eliminate all traces of Western linguistic influence. For a beginning, some Soviet savant announced that the letter Y must be replaced by the letter J, its common equivalent in Slavic languages.

The role of "party schools"

All of Eastern Europe is now pockmarked by hundreds of special institutions for the training of party officials. The Communist Party's own educational system has schools for secret police, for judges, for army commissars, for agitators, for teachers, for rural "educators," for propagandists. Hundreds of thousands of party members have taken these specialized courses in recent years. But an all-satellite drive to increase the number of participants was launched during 1951. The Kremlin, to ensure the political reliability of all East European Communists, is giving them intensive ideological indoctrination to prepare them for a variety of party assignments and activities. In effect, they are being trained to serve as a permanent governing élite, to hold their countries in subjection to sovietism, perhaps to serve one day as colonizers in countries now beyond Russia's sphere of influence.

One maxim of Communist action is that "they're never too young to be put to work for the party." The Warsaw régime decreed on June 23, 1951, a unified system of professional training for three types of schools, including a category for boys and girls who have finished the seventh grade. By August more than 80 per cent of Polish children graduated from the seventh grade were said to have applied—undoubtedly meaning, ordered to apply—for these two-year courses. A second type of professional school was established for boys and girls from 16 to 19, with graduates prepared for "work which demands mass labor." The third category is a new variety of technical school.

Exactly what are these professional schools supposed to do? The Warsaw decree declares "the main purpose . . . will be to educate Polish youth to follow Socialist ethics, to strengthen them in their Socialist attitude toward labor, to train an army of young experts."

A Bulgarian daily reports that 6,323 party schools were in operation early in 1951 with 95,000 party members attending them. Studies dealt with the Communist party's statutes, the Communist Constitution, its state organization and economic structure. But "discipline, attendance and quality of work in these schools are of a lower standard than those of the evening and political schools."

In Hungary the régime claimed to have enrolled 300,000 members, or about one-third of its membership, in party schools during 1950. It announced a goal of a 40 to 45 per cent enrollment for 1951–52. This indicates clearly the enormous importance which Moscow attaches to the satellite parties' mass education. The thoroughness of organization is shown by a few major subdivisions of the Hungarian party-school program, as summarized by *Szabad Nep* on May 25, 1951:

1) Political youth circles: For 70,000 D.I.S.Z. and Pioneer members from 12 to 15 in age. A nine-month course which includes study of Stalin's and Rakosi's biographies, the five-year plan and the Communist Youth Union's statutes.

2) A medium-grade political school: For 80,000 party pupils between 14 and 17. A two-year course, with discussion of the Communist Party's internal and external policies; also "fundamental principles and problems of the Socialist build-up." In the second year of this course 130,000 young Hungarians are expected to be enrolled.

3) A special party political academy (opened in September, 1951): For adults and graduates from the basic political school. Two-year courses stressing "practical questions of Socialism,"

in which it is aimed to enroll 100,000 Communists in the first year.

4) Other special party schools: These include a five-month advanced propaganda course, three-month county schools, one-month cadre-training schools in villages and one-year evening courses for 2,000 party secretaries.

5) Private study courses: For advanced party members, under national and district Communist leaders.

6) Special Educational Centers: For party members or students who have "a bourgeois, reactionary background." Approximately 50,000 were said to have participated in these "cure for middle-class prejudice" courses during 1951.

The Communists' party schools are organized with as great exactitude as any public educational system and they receive extraordinary financial support from the parties' funds, as well as the best possible facilities provided by the Red state.

What indeed can you do—what could any parents do—about Mary, Vera and Peter in these circumstances? They are the Red régime's hostages as long as it endures. In every minute of their school life they are held for ransom. They must be Russianized, along with as many of their elders as possible: Russianized through their love for the theater and movies, through music and dancing, through literature and art and everything which once constituted their own nation's cultural heritage. It is being attempted on a scale and with techniques never before witnessed outside of the Soviet Union's non-Russian republics.

CHAPTER FOURTEEN

The "Russianizing" of Foreign Peoples and Cultures

"I HAVE HOLES IN MY SHOES, BUT I DON'T mind going barefoot," wrote an aspiring young Hungarian poet. "It doesn't matter if I catch cold, because I know that my country has a wonderful future." But the Budapest party dailies promptly told him in biting terms what does matter. Such shriveled poetic license as still survives in a "people's democracy" does not permit even a rhapsodic admission that citizens have holes in their shoes.

Jaroslav Seifert, a budding Czech poet, seemed to be on safer ground by letting his imagination soar skyward. "I envy the birds for the freedom of their songs," he lyricized. "I envy the birds their wings which enable them to fly and leave the earth." Alas, for poor Jaroslav. The watchdogs of Stalinist literary orthodoxy tore him, feather by feather. He had expressed "a mood of bankruptcy and petty-bourgeois fear." He was even stripped of his "honorary title of poet."

Under any Communist régime lion-taming is a sedate and riskless profession compared to wooing the muse. To drive this realization home the Czech Writers' Union reviewed at length the unpardonable metrical crimes committed by V. Sosyura in his poem, "I Love The Ukraine." How could a poet sing exclusively about a region's physical beauty? His verse expressed "neither angry condemnation of the [former] oppressive order, nor a clear picture of the new Socialistic life of the Ukrainian people." And Sosyura was guilty of a much greater iniquity, for "the Ukraine stands isolated without any link with other

nations of the Soviet Union. This sounds decidedly nationalistic.
. . . The remnants of capitalism conceal themselves in a nationalistic robe." (The Kremlin speaking by proxy.)

Having lived all his life in the u.s.s.r. poet Sosyura promptly
informed Moscow's *Pravda* that its criticism was a bitter but
deserved lesson. "Dear comrades, I am deeply convinced that
only thanks to the leadership of our party and beloved Comrade
Stalin has the Ukraine become what she is now." (If Sosyura
intended those last four words—"what she is now"—as a
double-edged, subdued peep, he covered up fast.) "In the future
I will dedicate all my strength only to the service of my people
and my party, which has brought me up." *

But the inordinate security risk of every poet's professional
existence in Stalinized Europe is no isolated phenomenon. All
those who are active in the creative arts, in journalism and teaching and in the fields of entertainment are equally exposed to the
slashing blows of the Communists' propagandistic and "cultural"
hatchet-men. Every theatrical performance, every musical concert or dance festival, every picture painted, every book or
pamphlet, every motion picture or radio program—all must serve
the Kremlin's purpose. Nothing in the realm of ideas or of culture
is overlooked or exempted from exploitation.

The Stalinists have already imposed physical enslavement,
political conformism, legalistic chains and economic servitude
upon Eastern Europe. What more do they want? Today they
want Poles and Eastern Germans, Czechs and Slovakians,
Hungarians and Rumanians, Bulgarians and Albanians to be
second-class Russians. The traditional instruments and forms of
imperialist rule are not enough; they are only the initial phases of
Red conquest. If Western Europe's nations were seized these
phases would come first. But in due time, if the Kremlin's ex-
pectations are realized, all continental Europeans must be Russianized. To hold the body, the absolute conqueror must also
possess the mind and the soul.

To understand the scope and cumulative effect of Russia-

* *Lidovè Noviny,* July 27, 1951.

worship, one must try to imagine that the entire population of his own country is being deluged with utterly incredible statements —a literal *salade Russe* of lies, fabrications and extravagant historical distortions—day after day and year after year. That almost nothing uniquely French or Italian, British or American (or of whatever nationality he happens to be) any longer receives either official or public homage. That only whatever is Russian or of Russian origin (real or fake) is acclaimed or treated with respect. One must imagine these protestations of a foreign nation's superiority being endlessly repeated in every newspaper and book, from every radio station, in every classroom, in every theater, at almost every type of public function. One must imagine every high governing official—aped precisely all the way down the line to the lowest underlings in the smallest communities—proclaiming such nonsense as this:

"Without the great humanistic Soviet culture our people could not visualize a dignified cultural life." (A top Czech Communist is speaking.) "The entire character of our citizen is changing quickly. He is getting rid of the heritage of our past."

"Our cultural revolution would be inconceivable without the contribution of Soviet painters, writers, composers and ballet managers," declares a Budapest daily, *Magyar Nemzet* (December 19, 1950). "Through their works we become acquainted with the most exquisite human types of the twentieth century, whom we are to follow as examples."

"Soviet culture is not only our paragon," says Hungary's Minister of People's Culture, Jozsef Revai. "It is becoming more and more an integral part of our culture."

Rumania's Academicians assure Stalin in a telegram (March, 1951) that their general science session "expresses its fervent love and pays its respects to you, our great master, our leader in science, J. V. Stalin. . . . Your work is a guide of limitless value, a never-drying spring of science to the people who drink from it and know that only by doing this can our nation progress." Meanwhile Prague's *Lidovè Noviny* soberly asserts: "Stalin himself assisted in the artistic development of this mighty artistic body (the Alexandrov chorus). They come as . . . the first enchanting moments of experience in Soviet culture. . . . Now, too, the Soviet scientists bring us joy and happiness from the great country of Socialism." One phonograph record of orgiastic adulation uninterruptedly follows another. In regard to Stalin, that "incomparable genius" in every field of human endeavor, all of the most flattering and servile adjectives in the dictionary are played over and over, sometimes dozens of times in a single issue of a single newspaper—and in every capital and corner of captive Europe.

"From my very first contact with Soviet science," writes Professor C. Balmus of Bucharest University, in his book, *What Soviet Science Has Taught Me*, "I understood that everything I had learned in bourgeois schools, in my country and abroad, was but a collection of falsehoods and errors . . . that Soviet science is the most advanced in the world." And Professor Savulescu, president of Rumania's Academy, says, "The brilliant ideas of Comrade Stalin . . . are opening new horizons not only to linguistic students but also to philosophers, economists, literary critics and scientists."

How the Kremlin Russianizes foreign peoples

As the chief instrument for Russifying foreign countries, every satellite nation has a large, fanatically active Association for Soviet Friendship. These associations send "cultural battalions" into action in every conceivable field where national heritages, loyalties and talents might find expression. In the name of "Soviet Friendship" every medium of information, entertainment and artistic expression is filled with Russian ideas and adulation of Russia.

These associations were launched on a large scale in 1949–50. Poland's branch claimed 4,250,000 members by early 1951; Czechoslovakia's 1.8 million; Rumania's more than two million. Their extraordinary reach as Russifying agencies cannot be doubted; they have already enrolled something like one-twelfth to one-tenth of the populations in the various puppet states. But their activities are so many and so shrewdly planned that they blanket much larger proportions of each country's inhabitants.

Even though Communist statistics must usually be suspect and subject to deflation, consider the types of organized cultural penetration described in the following party statements. The Polish-Soviet Friendship Society reported that it conducted 38,-177 public rallies and meetings in 13,000 villages during 1950; 124,000 lectures in 44,000 villages; and 32,400 movie showings with a claimed attendance of 11 million.

Rumania's friendship organization, called Arlus, reported 185,-000 meetings and demonstrations and the establishment of 20,000 Arlus circles. In all other satellites the "Soviet Friendship" campaign is as comprehensive, blanketing towns, villages and hamlets as well as cities. The aim is to denationalize whole countries and Russify them.

Consider the long-term effect in your own land of a Russian-prepared, Russia-glorifying program, imposed by a one-party dictatorship, and reaching into every corner of the country, not only by radio and television, but also by traveling movie theaters, by itinerant theatrical troupes, by roadshow dance teams, by mobile libraries and by "cultural show cases." In the more important cities "Culture Houses," identical with those in captive Europe, would be established. Free lectures would be given on such subjects as "The New Communist Man." Russian-language study circles would be created by thousands. Special traveling exhibits would portray "the prosperous, happy life of the Soviet peoples." All this and much more has been going on in every Iron-Curtain country since 1949.

But the Soviet Russians always have to have a spectacular, super-saturating device. The one for cultural infiltration is called "Soviet Friendship Month." Every Red satellite must celebrate Moscow's friendship for one month out of twelve. It begins for Bulgaria in mid-September, then is taken up by Rumania, Hungary and the others in succession. This is an example of the Russians' efficiency as organizers. The Kremlin sends impressive "cultural delegations" to each puppet state for its great propagandistic festival. Thus Russian culture peddlers can play the entire satellite circuit, one country after another.

When "Soviet Friendship Month" hit Czechoslovakia during November, 1951, Prague and major Czech cities were invaded by a procession of Russian delegations—scientists, historians, writers, sportsmen and whatnot. Lecturers galore, Soviet choruses and dancers, "festive performances of Soviet films, plays, concerts and other artistic evenings"—Russian culture poured on by the bucket. After a full month of this, even village halfwits are presumably conditioned to recognize the incontestable superiority of Russian civilization. Those who are still rebellious will receive another thirty-day treatment in exactly eleven months.

Russianization operates on the principle that the more molasses you pour, the more flies you catch. But it tops the treacle with such remarkably fine honey as the Alexandrov Chorus, the Russian State Choir, Georgian folk dancers, whirling Cossacks and Moscow's Bolshoi Theater ballet, with its incomparable ballerinas. This assortment of superb artistic attractions would be difficult for any single Western nation to match. When presented in synchronized relays, their propaganda impact can scarcely be measured. In foreign lands the idea is widespread that America's civilization is largely mechanical and "dollarchasing." Consider how this concept would be changed if some of the finest American symphonies, ballets and concert artists gave annual performances in all major cities from Western Europe to India, Indonesia and Japan. Today the Russians are using their most distinguished artists as political weapons.

But Soviet Friendship Months are merely grand salvos in the Kremlin's cultural-infiltration offensive. If satellite citizens are to be Russianized, they must be made absorbable. Hence Moscow's command:

"Force the subject peoples to learn Russian!"

The Kremlin's goal is to produce millions of Russian-reading or Russian-speaking citizens in the puppet states in the shortest possible time and to produce a majority among the younger generation who understand Russian very well. In this way all Stalinist propaganda could reach an increasingly large proportion of the population directly. Their thinking and attitudes would be enormously Russianized, and great numbers of them could be used in the same jobs as Russians anywhere in the Soviet empire.

Russian is a compulsory subject in lower and upper schools and in most universities. There are Russian courses for puppet-state workers and popular courses for adults. Even if they were, in reality, only half as large, figures published by party organs indicate an astonishing progress since 1949. Here are typical claims:

Czechoslovakia: "This autumn another 300,000 citizens will take part in the third year of the popular Russian courses [1951]. Last year 126,621 participants passed the courses . . . Hundreds of thousands of textbooks have been sold." * In Czechoslovakian schools Russian is compulsory from the third grade on, through junior high school and senior high school. This program has been in effect since the Basic School Act was adopted in April, 1948. The deputy chairman of the Czech-Soviet Friendship League declared in August, 1951, that Russian courses would be organized in every village's agricultural co-operative as well.

Hungary: In the autumn of 1949 Russian was made compulsory in the upper four grades of elementary schools. "Last year [1950] 305,706 children learned Russian in the elementary schools; 52,354 in the high schools; 10,900 in the universities" **—or about one-third of all college students. By October, 1951, another party organ † stated that approximately 500,000 Hungarians were studying Russian.

Rumania: More than two million school children were reported learning Russian in 1951. "4,500 courses have been insti-

---

* *Lidove Noviny*, September 8 and 13, 1951.
** *Magyar Nemzet*, July 23, 1950.
† *Kis Ujsag*, October 21, 1951.

tuted in the country with nearly 98,000 [adult] students," functioning under Arlus auspices.*

Poland: Under the slogan "A Polish-Soviet Friendship circle in every village" this association was organizing 14,000 Russian courses during 1951. Its campaign offers a striking example of the interlocking co-ordination of various Communist organizations. Enrollment in Russian study courses was pushed by the main Polish Youth Union (z.m.p.); by the Polish Teachers Association (z.n.p.); by another Polish youth group (s.p.); by the Peasant Self-Help Association (z.s.c.h.), and the Polish Women's League. Taken with the Polish-Soviet Friendship Association itself, six different Communist organizations were actively enlisted. Although over-all totals on the number of Poles learning Russian are not available, they must certainly be considerably larger than in Rumania.

In addition, the domestic Communist Parties are sending several thousand satellite students to Russian universities each year, through special scholarships. More than 300 Hungarian students received such scholarships in 1950 and again in 1951—each for five-year periods. These students will have been completely Russianized by the time they return.

Popularizing the Russian language throughout the Curtain countries is still in its infancy. But the growth already achieved demonstrates what extraordinary results may be expected. Several millions of captive Europe's school children were in their third or fourth year of Russian early in 1952. Several hundred thousand adults were reportedly in their second or third year. At this rate at least 8 to 12 per cent of the puppet states' populations may be Russian-speaking by the early 1960's; possibly nearly 25 per cent in another ten years. No such linguistic conquest as this can be found in all history. It can only be described as Russianization by saturation. And the saturation possibilities are inestimably increased by ever rising:

* *Agerpress* [Bucharest newspaper], May 15, 1951.

Floods of Russian newspapers and books.

In Bulgaria young Red zealots go from door to door in the villages offering as "bargain books" the works of Lenin and Stalin—at a 20 per cent discount. Some peasants may imprudently refuse this unique opportunity. They are reported to the Committee for Science, Art and Culture, whose central office—very conveniently—is located in the secret police headquarters in Sofia.

The all-satellite circulation of Soviet newspapers and periodicals is remarkably large—and growing steadily with the Russian courses. More than 800,000 Poles (nearly one-twelfth of the adult population) subscribe to Soviet publications. Even in 1949 Moscow's *Pravda* was said to have distributed 200,000 copies in non-Slavic Hungary.* Russian libraries exist in most major satellite cities, and all public libraries are compelled to buy a certain percentage of Russian books. The total distribution of Russian books in Poland was reported at about two million copies during 1951. According to Arlus, 1,870 Russian books have been translated into Rumanian since 1945, with a seemingly incredible distribution of 30 million copies—roughly two per capita for the entire country. Under its five-year quota, Casa Scanteia, the Rumanian party's publishing house, proposes to produce more than 93 million books by 1955.

Meanwhile the Stalinists continue to purge the finest, most cherished literature of the captive countries. In Hungary alone their list of banned titles exceeds 6,700. Of course, this includes the products of "Western imperialist, war-mongering literature"; among them Milne's *Winnie the Pooh*, Disney's *Three Little Pigs*, Grimm's *Fairy Tales* and Alcott's *Little Women*. Other notoriously subversive and "decadent" writers include Arnold Bennett, Somerset Maugham, Sinclair Lewis, Edgar Wallace, Michael Arlen—almost everyone except Howard Fast.

Love is also a subject which disturbs the Stalinists' literary

* *Magyar Nemzet*, January 8, 1950.

bloodhounds. They blame their own writers' "romantic approach to the love question" on Western influence. A Budapest Red organ declares "the love question" must hereafter be treated in a "sober and super-revolutionary way"—which seemingly would make the treatment pretty hot, indeed. In fact, romantic tendencies "smell of bourgeois idealism" and must be scotched. The publication of pocket-sized love stories is prohibited by the Prague régime. *Rudè Pràvo* urges as substitute reading such romance-whetting volumes as: *How to Fight a Kulak*, *The Lot of U. S. Negroes*, *The Coal Brigades* and *The Fraud of Catholic Miracles*.

Wholesale employment of movies, theater, music and art for Russian propaganda

Imagine what it would be like if all of your country's theaters, motion pictures, radio and other media of entertainment were nationalized by a Communist régime. Suppose that Communist Ministers of Culture and Art appoint and dismiss all executives and directors of these vast enterprises and also censor all programs. This is what the Stalinists are doing throughout Eastern Europe. Every film and other production is party-planned and controlled. Every performance or show must serve a party or a Russian propaganda purpose. The rulers hold an absolute monopoly on every audience, by eye or ear or both—everywhere. No foreign conquerors ever had it so good—or so easy. You don't like it? Then stay home.

In little Czechoslovakia the Reds claimed that more than one million persons attended showings of Soviet short films during 1950, that another 933,000 saw major Soviet features in the state movie houses. Even as early as April, 1950, Budapest reported that 76 per cent of its first-run theaters and 85 per cent of its second-run houses were showing Russian pictures. In these films Soviet life "radiates with consummate happiness"; people "are blooming . . . in the country of golden abundance"; and the heroines are "rosy-cheeked, 'new-type' girls, conscious of their importance." Hollywood at its worst was never so saccharine, nor so palpably make-believe. But people have nowhere else to go.

A very few non-Soviet foreign films are allowed. In this respect the Hungarian Reds made a major mistake—just once. Back in 1950 they invited movie fans to vote for the five films they liked best among those showing in a single month. For the first time in years people actually could cast a ballot secretly. By the third week Italy's *Bicycle Thief* was far in the lead, followed by another Italian movie, two Czech movies, and a Hungarian film. The Russian entries were all trailing far behind. But the final week's returns, announced by the Ministry of Culture, reversed everything: the Soviet films suddenly collected overwhelming numbers of favorable votes. There were no more film popularity contests.

The Soviets produce such celluloid caricatures of reality and such extravaganzas of Russian virtues that they often provoke a diametrically opposite reaction from those desired by Moscow. This happened with *Undaunted City*, a story about Warsaw's underground during Nazi occupation, which failed to mention the courageous uprising of General Bor's underground forces— about which the Poles, after all, are pretty well informed. And to top it off the hero of Warsaw's undaunted resistance was not even a Pole, but a Russian paratrooper! Whole audiences of infuriated Poles stalked out of theater after theater. This was probably the best propaganda for the West ever shown on a screen behind the Iron Curtain.

But when you keep throwing globs of mud at a wall some of it sticks. This is what the Russians do with movies and everything else. Puppet-state adults may brush 95 per cent of it off. Their teen-age children may not brush off more than 30 per cent today—and perhaps less than 5 per cent in another few years. Time works for Russianization—time and the strategy of saturation. Thousands of movie halls for workers now exist; thousands more in "Houses of Culture" and in youth centers. Hundreds of movie caravans tour satellite villages, together with theatrical, choral and dance groups. Nearly half of 180 documentary films shown in Hungary were Soviet-made. A similarly wholesale infiltration, glorifying everything Russian, occurs in every field of entertainment and artistic presentation.

The unforgivable crime of a Czech ballet master

When the Alexandrov Chorus opened in Prague, Sasha Machov, ballet master of the Czech National Theater, was ordered to present a special intermission number. Machov appropriately chose to honor the distinguished guest artists with a scene from the classic most beloved by all Russians—Tschaikowsky's famous "Swan Lake" ballet. It was performed superbly by the foremost Czech ballerina and her partner. The theater was shaken by prolonged tempests of applause.

The next morning Zdenek Nejedly, Czech Minister of Education, Science and Art, visited Machov's office. "Your 'Swan Lake' was premeditated sabotage," he screamed. "You have debased the matchless art of Russian ballet! You did it intentionally—in front of a Czech audience! You deliberately provoked an anti-Soviet demonstration! How else can such fantastic applause be explained?"

Ballet Master Machov was almost speechless with amazement. Stumblingly he tried to talk sense to a madman. He had conceived of the number as a tribute to the great Russian guests. The Communist Minister of Arts scarcely heard his explanations. "You have insulted the greatest living Russian artists!" he raged. "Don't you understand what we must do? We must be more interested in Russia's friendship than in the prestige of Czechoslovakia's ballet!"

Machov had been an idealistic Communist for years, but he was also a man of great artistic integrity. After this tirade he left his office in the National Theater and committed suicide.

Writers write as Moscow pleases.

"State orders for theater plays were signed on October 31, 1951, with the following authors," reports Prague's *Rudè Pràvo* on November 1, 1951. "V. Cach, for a play revealing the background of the Munich betrayal; Milan Jaris, for a play dealing with vigilance against the class enemy within the party; S. Turek, for a play disclosing the true nature of the Bata shoe régime; Frantisek Vrba [former cultural attaché in the u.s.a.:] for a play about the fight of the workers in America today."

This is how plays, movie scripts, radio dramatizations, novels and short stories are written in the puppet states, as in the Soviet Union. The writer submits a synopsis of his projected work to the proper Communist Party officials. When approved, or revised and approved, the state orders the work. Or it flatly rejects the idea. The state is theatrical producer, motion picture producer, radio producer, publisher and editor—rolled into one. The state orders the models manufactured. The writer delivers his model according to specifications—or no production! Every writer's output is state-planned, precisely as hydroelectric projects and tractor production are planned.

The Stalinists' literary assembly line was streamlined by the Politburo's late fire-eater Zhdanov. In a 1947 speech he elaborated the role of writers as "ideological workers" and imposed the "Zhdanov line," by which no literary activities can exist independent of propaganda. Top Stalinist literary bosses set the major themes and production targets for books, stories, plays, sketches—sometimes even for poems.*

The identical system has been exported into all Curtain countries. The Communists treat their writers like wild mustangs. They must be broken, branded and bridled; then lashed to work along rigidly fixed roadways, hauling specific cartloads. Because writers have unpredictable urges to jump fences, they are corralled into Writers' Unions or Federations for thorough training. The "breaking-in" process is organized to the last detail. Mrs. Soriana Gurian, who escaped to the West after attending the annual session of the Rumanian Authors' Society in January, 1949, tells how captive Europe's writers are put into Red harness:

* "Behind the Iron Curtain," by Michael Padev. *The London Times Literary Supplement:* August 24, 1951.

"The nationalized publishing house no longer accepts manuscripts that are not accompanied with a written recommendation of the (party-controlled) Authors' Society. To obtain this the novelist must submit to the Society—before he elaborates his book—the master idea of his subject and the broad outlines. He must take into account the Society's suggestions. When his first chapter is written he reads it before one of the Society's two weekly 'working sessions.' His colleagues make their criticism. At the next working session the author reads his revised first chapter, as well as his second. Only after the entire novel has been read and approved will the Society recommend its publication—and that the author be paid."

Schools for literary criticism, established by satellite ideological watchdogs, "give the pupils a proper orientation." So-called re-education courses help writers "to develop the necessary Socialist self-criticism and to rid them of the remnants of bourgeois influence." In "authors' universities," a recent innovation, the enrolled candidates are termed "writer aspirants"—underscoring the fact that you can really write only when you write to suit the party. In Czechoslovakia "aspirants" must write short stories, twice a month, on such assigned subjects as "a party congress, a trade-union meeting, Stalin's birthday"—whatever the Olympians of Soviet culture may designate as approved literary fodder. If the "aspirant" passes his exams, the party grants him a unique dispensation—he is actually permitted to write.

But any writer under Red rule has less security than a half-starved poet in a capitalist garret. He is in constant danger of finding that he has made eyelash deviations from fixed formulas. He must respect unceasingly a bewildering variety of taboos. Among these heresies are "bourgeois cosmopolitanism, formalism, naturalism and schematism"—if you follow me thus far. But, as Polish writers were recently reminded, every tinkerer with words must also direct them against "universalism, idealism and objectivism"—in order to achieve, at all costs, "Socialist realism." While dodging a dozen deadly isms to attain the only great Red literary ism, satellite writers must also unmask "the moral degradation of the United States and Britain," in particular, and the "decadence of Western culture in general." These themes have been hammered hard since 1950.

Suppose the author somehow runs the gauntlet of all the perilous isms and his book is published, what about his long awaited public acclaim? In pre-Stalinist Eastern Europe his work would have received dozens of reviews. Today it is disposed of by no more than two or three omniscient, party-line critics—and a single attack may end the author's career.

What is the effect of such intellectual prostitution on those who practice it? A Polish writer, still retaining a shred of inner honesty, tells frankly what has happened to him in a letter to a friend in exile:

"One never knows exactly how to write in order to be smiled upon. In a material sense I have never had such good conditions as now. We have a five-room apartment, sufficient earnings for a comfortable living, vacations at the seaside and a couple of weeks in winter at Zakopane. My wife has a mink coat at last, and a servant. For the first time in my life I have no debts; I even have a wine-cellar.

"As you see, it would be wonderful, if I could work. For two years now I prowl from one psychoanalyst and neurologist to another. Last year I spent four months in 'rest cures.' I don't know myself whether I've reached the end of my creativity, or if the present [political] climate does not agree with me. Probably it is both. Sometimes it seems to me that the lordly misery we knew before the war was a paradise in comparison with today's silken existence on a chain."

CHAPTER FIFTEEN

The Conquerors' Nightmares

HAVE THE RED CONQUERORS MOVED SO FAST in Eastern Europe that they are already unconquerable?

Thus far I have confined this report to what Russia's Communists are doing in the Curtain countries, and how they are doing it. The cumulative evidence is grim. But are the Stalinists as formidable as they appear? Before yielding to exaggerated pessimism or unthinking despair we must take a sharp look at the problems which obstruct and undermine the Soviets' efforts to make their new empire both attack-proof and explosion-proof.

Captive Europe proves once again that every tyranny sows the seeds of its internal disruption and ultimate destruction. The greater the tyranny the more intolerable are the strains and counter-pressures which it creates. There's also something else which Hitler and Mussolini should have taught us. Dictators and their super-policed, overgunned régimes are never so all-powerful as they usually look.

After the fall of Paris in 1940, the German Nazis appeared —superficially—to have won lasting domination of continental Europe. Yet when "Fortress Europe" was tested it fell apart; in big chunks and with amazing rapidity. Its seemingly invincible bastions were built on sand.

That lesson remains pertinent. It is as unrealistic and self-defeating to overestimate Soviet strength as to underestimate it. In some respects the Red Colossus may be girded with steel but its feet are of clay. Some of its afflictions are incurable; most cannot be eliminated in less than a generation. The Stalinists both confess and advertise this by the desperate speed with which they attempt to diminish the weaknesses within their system.

The truth is that *the men in the Kremlin have more acute fears and long-term anxieties, more nearly insoluble problems, more incurable complications and more frightening frustrations than those of any other government on the face of today's earth.* The very creatures who rule by a slave-state system of organized terror are notoriously the victims of their own terror.

This is why most well-qualified authorities question whether the Soviet bosses would deliberately provoke a major war in any near future—unless by miscalculation, or through another Korea, where the instigator unexpectedly was held sternly to account. With an intimate twenty-six-year knowledge of Russia Maurice Hindus says: "On no possible count can Stalin *afford* war now. His Soviet system, inside and outside Russia, suffers from monumental weaknesses—political, economic and above all psychological." No conclusion can be solidly based unless it takes fully into consideration the extremely vulnerable "soft spots" in the Soviet system.

We must refocus the Stalinists' domination of captive Europe in the light of their great and enduring nightmares. These nightmares are of two kinds: those which are directly related to the Soviet Union itself, and those which Moscow has created by sovietizing the Eastern European countries. Consider first:

*The weaknesses of the Soviet Union.**

For our present purposes these can merely be summarized here. Each major subject, however, could be documented at chapter length. Perhaps I should add that the eight great difficulties of the Kremlin, which I outline under this heading, do not represent solely my own analysis. All whom I have been able to

---

* Based in part on "Stalin's Headaches," by Leland Stowe. *This Week* Magazine: March 18, 1951.

consult have agreed about the nature of these Soviet weaknesses and as to their importance.

1. *Inferior productive capacity*

Stalin's favorite dictum is: "Production wins war." Near the end of World War II he admitted that United States factory output sealed Hitler's doom. Then, in February, 1946, Stalin told the war-fatigued Soviet people: "We must achieve a situation whereby our industry is able to produce each year up to 50 million tons of pig iron, up to 60 million tons of steel, up to 500 million tons of coal, and up to 60 million tons of oil. *Only under such circumstances can we regard our country as guaranteed against any accidents.* This, I think, will require perhaps three more Five-Year Plans, *if not more.* . . . We must do it."

At the end of the first postwar plan Moscow published figures which placed Soviet production in 1950 at 19,350,000 tons of pig iron; 27,200,000 tons of steel; 260,600,000 tons of coal; 37,820,000 tons of oil.* After close scrutiny United States government experts decided that Soviet steel output was actually almost two million tons less than Moscow claimed.** Despite tremendous efforts, steel was still much below the half-way mark to Stalin's 1961-to-66 goal. By early 1952 the combined Soviet-*plus*-satellite steel production was estimated at approximately 35 million tons—only one-third that of the United States.

But through his Korean Communists' aggression Stalin had committed perhaps his greatest blunder; he had remobilized Western production. The relative gains of his first postwar five-year plan were being swiftly wiped out. Within three years, in fact, America's steel output—from a yearly level of 90 million tons—would be boosted by another 16 million tons or more; *actually, increased by more than 60 per cent of the Soviets' 1951 steel capacity.* In these same three post-Korea years, as Edward Crank-

* *The New York Herald Tribune,* April 18, 1951.
** *The New York Times,* April 19, 1951.

shaw, points out, the United States would spend "five times the entire British national income on her defense effort. And . . . this colossal output is reckoned to be only a third of what America could produce in time of war." *

Add to that of the United States the productive capacities of all Western Europe, Great Britain, Canada and the other Commonwealth nations and you get some indication of Russia's long-term industrial inferiority to the West.** For even though the Politburo can divert a far higher percentage of its steel production to military purposes than we can, the Soviets cannot begin to match the pace of Western industrial expansion. Stalin himself had thrown away most of the comparative gains which he had hoped to achieve by the early 1960's. The gap is widening again, instead of narrowing. This Number One bugaboo must persist through the lifetime of the Soviet's present leaders.

2. Internal insecurity

Men who rule by machine guns, block spies, police terror and slave-labor camps live in perpetual fear of betrayal, plots and assassination. Approximately one-tenth of Soviet Russia's population, the party members and police, hold nearly 200 million persons in line by armed force. All of these people suffer great privations. Most of them have intimate reasons for hating the régime; relatives or close friends who have been jailed, deported or liquidated. Countless millions are deeply outraged by

---

* Edward Crankshaw, *op. cit.*, p. 236.
** "The sum total of such [vital economic] facts show that—war or no war—*not until 1970 or after can Russia expect even to equal our present production of such basic materials as steel, electric power and petroleum.* . . . In 1950 Russia's estimated total output was greater than ever before. Yet in 1949 America actually produced almost 75 per cent more coal than Russia did in 1950, 145 per cent more pig iron, 160 per cent more steel, almost 300 per cent more electric power and 570 per cent more oil. These are the commodities that provide the sinews of modern war. . . . *If Russia could add Western Europe, and Great Britain, to what she now controls, most of our present economic advantage would be canceled.*" (From "Can Russia's Economy Support a War?" by Harry Schwartz and Herbert Yahraes, *Collier's Magazine*, May 5, 1951.)

personal injustices as well. So the men in the Kremlin cannot trust their non-Communist masses. But they also distrust, repeatedly screen and purge their own fellow slavemasters in the party. All the top Stalinists must be incessantly on guard against their own associates as well as the general public.

One Westerner who knows Soviet Russia most intimately assures me that, in his judgment, Stalin's chief worry is "intense preoccupation with the régime's internal security." This fact goes far to explain what makes the Kremlin a citadel of fear.

3. *Inferiority in atomic weapons*

Gordon Dean, chairman of the United States Atomic Energy Commission, stated in October, 1951: "Now we are entering an era when the quantities of atomic weapons available to us will be so great, *and the types so varied*, that we may utilize them in many different ways heretofore impossible—*an era when we can use atomic weapons tactically as well as strategically*." * Mr. Dean added that we now have the possibility "to meet the invading force in the field *with a fire-power that should cancel out any numerical advantage he might enjoy.* Not only does this provide that we can stop aggression once it has started, but . . . *it provides a real hope for peace.*"

Senator Brien MacMahon, head of the Joint Congressional Committee on Atomic Energy, declared: "In truth, we are on the threshold of a revolution in the production and profitable military use of atomic weapons—*a revolution in our power to deter the Kremlin.*"** But this stupendous upheaval in the relative combat strength and fire-power of modern armies cannot become a reality until the new tactical atomic weapons have been produced in large quantities. Senator MacMahon stated that there were "literally dozens" of models of atomic weapons under study and that atomic plants required about three years to produce such weapons.† This should be the case, then, by late 1954

* *The New York Herald Tribune,* October 6, 1951.
** *The New York Times,* October 26, 1951.
† *The New York Times,* September 26, 1951.

or early 1955. In the same period can Russia compensate, at least to a dangerous degree, by extraordinary progress in her own atomic weapons development?

We must first consider the only atomic weapon which it seems quite certain the Soviets do possess. How many atomic bombs may the Kremlin already have? As of autumn, 1951, America's A-bomb reserve was reliably placed at several hundreds; possibly even exceeding 1,000. But most Western experts estimated that Russia might then have no more than somewhere between 20 and possibly 50 or 60 A-bombs. In the opinion of such an eminent atomic scientist as Dr. Harold Urey, Moscow would need "about 200 A-bombs in order to launch a major war." Can she produce something like that number before 1955, when the United States' lead in many tactical atomic weapons should be enormously great?

On this most crucial point William L. Laurence, the Pulitzer Prize-winning atomic specialist of *The New York Times*, offers important evidence. He demonstrates that it is possible to estimate quite closely and scientifically the *upper limits* of Russia's A-bomb production.* We must bear in mind that only the United States of America and its allies have available the ore from the world's three largest known sources of uranium: that everything indicates that the Soviets' sources are very much smaller and chiefly of inferior ore. "We know," Mr. Laurence wrote in October, 1951, "that [Russian] plants have been in operation for close to 800 days. To produce 80 bombs in 800 days would mean a production rate of at least 20, possibly as high as 60, pounds of plutonium every ten days. . . . This would mean that they had several gigantic nuclear reactors operating at full capacity from the very start. . . . On these facts alone *it appears extremely unlikely that Russia could have produced as many as 80 atomic bombs since September, 1949.*"

Mr. Laurence then points out that for Russia to produce a bomb at the rate of one every ten days "she would have to process 132 tons of ore on the basis of 20 pounds per bomb, or

* *The New York Times*, October 7, 1951.

as many as 396 tons on the basis of 60 pounds per bomb, every ten days. *To achieve this rate she [Russia] would have had to build plants for refining uranium ore about 17 times the capacity of our uranium refining plants.*" It is extremely doubtful whether any qualified expert, familiar with the fantastic complexities and engineering problems involved in America's Hanford and Oak Ridge installations, would concede that the Russians could possibly have constructed similar installations *seventeen times greater* in capacity—even by 1951. The Soviets required nearly four years before their first atomic explosion, and approximately another two years before their second. Mr. Laurence concludes authoritatively: "*We are far in the lead and intend to maintain it.*" In this opinion he has the overwhelming agreement of Western atomic experts.

Thus, as of 1952, it is still extremely unlikely that Russia has either an A-bomb stockpile of menacingly large size, or that she can develop and put into mass production new tactical atomic weapons for use against land armies or fleets in any near future. Everything indicates that, as yet, the Soviets have not had the time, nor the technical and material resources, for such vast and highly complex developments. America's big lead over Russia was tremendously increased through the successful tests of atomic tactical weapons during 1951. In that same proportion the Kremlin's atomic nightmare was magnified. Its occupants must now face the prospect—terrifying to them—that their gigantic Soviet Army may be rendered largely obsolete somewhere between 1954 and 1956. An utterly unprecedented and incalculable deterrent to aggressive war lies directly ahead.

4. *The shortage of oil and high-octane gas*

Although Russia's postwar production of oil has reached an all-time high, it remains only one-sixth of United States production—and it is virtually eaten up by the Soviets' current mechanized needs. The democracies control about 90 per cent of present production and about 75 per cent of the world's estimated reserves. In fact, Russia and her satellites combined produce only an approximate 8 per cent of world output of crude oil, while the United States produces 52 per cent; the Middle East 17 per cent, and Venezuela 14.5 per cent.* In addition, the Soviets' best aviation gas is only 91 octane, much inferior to the Western product.

But Moscow's limited and inadequate oil output constitutes a large Achilles heel in another respect. Something like 60 per cent of all Soviet-satellite oil comes from the Baku, Maikop and Grozny fields in southern Russia and the Caucasus; or from Ploesti in Rumania; at least 42 per cent comes from Baku alone. Yet all of these "life-or-death" fields lie within easy range of Allied bombing bases in the Middle East. In the first days of any major war they would certainly be atomized.

Because of their equally exposed and notoriously insufficient transportation system the Soviets urgently need huge and widely dispersed stockpiles of oil—especially, in their view, as a security measure in event of war. J. H. Carmical of *The New York Times*, on July 1, 1951, reported that "by operating the Trans-Siberian railroad at capacity and moving only oil supplies it is estimated that no more than 300,000 barrels a day could be moved, or about the quantity of oil used *daily* by the U.N. forces in the Korean War." Nevertheless, Russia's continuing shortage of oil, and her technical incapacity to increase her own or the satellites' production on a large scale, prevent important stockpiling. If she can barely meet her most essential "cold war" requirements, what if a hot war should occur? Most experts are convinced that the Soviets could not fight a long war without large amounts of oil from the Middle East.

But even if the Soviet Army invaded the Middle Eastern regions, they could not move any vital amounts of this oil into Russia. Consider Abadan's gigantic refinery as safely controlled by a domestic Communist Iranian government (if without a

---

* Address to the American Petroleum Institute by Gustav Egloff, Research Director of the Universal Oil Company, reported in *The New York Times*, November 15, 1950.

general war and still unbombed). The Russians still would not possess the tankers to transport the oil through the Suez Canal and the Dardanelles. (They were reported to have less than two dozen tankers in 1951.) Western engineers state that close to three years, at least, would be necessary for the Russians to build an overland pipeline from Iran into southern u.s.s.r.—and they are also very short of pipe. Finally, as Mr. Carmical points out, "Soviet construction of refining capacity" (in the Middle East) to equal that of Abadan "would take several years and cost upward of $500,000,000, exclusive of the cost of pipelines." Moscow, therefore, must preserve peace if it hopes to get oil out of Iran or elsewhere in the Middle East—and in any case, could hope to get very little of it for some years to come. Stalin's war machine is faced with thin rations for a considerable time. If he and the Politburo are sincerely afraid of a war launched by "Western imperialists," that's another nasty nightmare. Even on no-conflict terms, it's a big and enduring one.

6. Food shortages

Since 1945 Russia's food production has improved considerably, but it's still far short of the Kremlin's "national security" requirements. Moscow's great problem is to keep farm products increasing in proportion to the growth of its industrial and other populations (which are extremely high)—and still stockpile food supplies against a wartime emergency. Along with many other close students Professor Philip Moseley, director of Columbia University's Russian Institute, finds the Soviets "bumping along on inadequate food standards, faced by great difficulty in building up reserves."

Europe's foremost agricultural experts published the results of a prolonged study of Russia's food production for the U.N. Economic Commission for Europe in November, 1951. They concluded that over the past 40 years (while the Soviet Union's population had increased by much more than 30 million persons) the increase in grain production "probably has not quite kept pace with the rise in population." * The U.N. specialists expressed their findings with marked diplomatic restraint. But despite 30 years of Soviet mechanization, collectivization and production drives, a stark fact emerges. The Kremlin is unable to feed the Soviet people any better today than they were fed under the czars.

On the basis of the Kremlin's own reports, the E.C.E. investigators also declared that Soviet figures on grain production exaggerate by from 17 to 20 per cent. Quite independently Edward Crankshaw offers this graphic summation: "According to the returns of the [Soviet] Statistical Bureau, which I know to be exaggerated by perhaps 20 per cent, the 1949 production of basic foodstuffs in the Soviet Union—*plus* the three Baltic states of Lithuania, Esthonia and Latvia, *plus* a slice of East Prussia, *plus* the Polish Ukraine and the Trans-Carpathian Ukraine, *plus* Moldavia and Bessarabia—has just surpassed *the 1940 production* of basic foodstuffs *for the Soviet Union without these additions. The allowance per capita is thus considerably lower than it was in 1940—lower still than it was in 1928, which itself had just about reached the 1914 level.*" **

In the next few years the Soviets may gain an almost imperceptible fraction over Russia's 1928 and 1914 food levels—but only by most painful efforts and without creating sufficient reserves for any prolonged emergency. Nor can they hope to achieve more than minimum requirements in the satellite countries. Under the Soviet system food shortages must remain chronic for many years, together with peasant resistance, hoarding and sabotage.

7. Rearming of the Western democracies

Through the Communists' Korean aggression Stalin blindly provoked the Western democracies into the world's greatest rearmament program, and committed the supreme blunder of his

* The Economic Bulletin of the U.N.'s E.C.E., as reported in *The New York Times*, November 8, 1951.
** Edward Crankshaw, *op. cit.*, p. 238.

career. The immediacy and dimensions of this Allied counter-action must surely have stunned the men in the Kremlin. How could they hope to match a combined Atlantic Pact preparedness project which must eventually exceed $150 billion—possibly by a wide margin? The Politburo's members must take this fearsome reality to bed with them for the rest of their lives, knowing that the Stalinist bloc can never meet such competition.

8. *Red China and Mao Tse-tung*

"At last the Soviets have got an *ally*," one of the West's best-informed authorities on Russia said to me. "But you can't treat an ally like a puppet." After all, the Chinese Reds rule some 450 million people—two-and-one-half times as many as the Kremlin rules directly. Stalin may say that control of Hungary's popula-tion "is only a question of box-cars"—for deportation. He can even ship several millions of the most unruly Poles into Central Asia. He can kick the satellite Red leaders and parties around as he pleases. But Stalin can never dictate flatly to General Mao, or whoever may be the top Chinese in Peiping.

It's nonsense to speculate about Mao or his successors be-coming "another Tito." *In Moscow's view the appalling thing about any big boss of Red China is that he might eventually become a super-Stalin!* That alarming possibility is bound to grow steadily with time; in direct ratio to the Chinese Communists' consolida-tion and development of power. If no foreign power has ever been able to subjugate permanently an inert and slumbering China, how can the Russian bear hope to control for long an aroused Chinese dragon? And this intensely nationalistic China has the world's longest common frontier—with the Soviet Union.

As of today, Red China may be strongly pro-Soviet, but its huge masses of inhabitants can never be reliably Russianized. They can never be swallowed up and digested by Russia. Who knows how the Chinese and their Red leaders will feel toward Russia and the Kremlin tomorrow? Or even how they may be starting to feel toward them today? Mao's victory also means that the Soviets no longer have a free hand in Asia. Neither, most assuredly, do they have an easy mind. . . . Suppose China's Reds should some day reject Stalinism as a betrayal of true Communism and the gigantic phony which it is? Suppose they should steal the idealistic Communist revolution? In the neurotically suspicious minds of the Politburo these longer-term possibilities must already exist as serious threats.

* * *

For the sake of space I shall not examine the enduring problem of the Soviet Union's grossly inadequate and under-equipped transportation problem, save to say that it must never be left out of calculation. For our present purposes the eight major Kremlin difficulties, here summarized, may suffice. It's true, of course, that the Western democracies are not immune to such potent worries as inflation, financial solvency, economic stability, the threat of falling standards of living, and others. But the twelve Atlantic Pact governments are definitely not confronted by eight such enormous, almost insuperable obstacles as those which harass the Politburo's members, and must continue to do so for some decades to come. Yet these are by no means all of the bugaboos which bedevil Red Russia's masters. They merely serve as the obligatory and only realistic framework in which to examine:

The satellite nightmares.

Some of these have cropped up in the course of this report, but I think their full meaning cannot be appreciated unless they are considered as a whole. What conditions in the puppet states make consolidation of the Soviets' conquest both difficult and hazardous, and also a long-term proposition?

1. The inextinguishable antagonism of the people

Somewhere between 70 and 85 per cent of the adult citizens of the satellite countries are strongly anti-Communist and anti-

Soviet, most of them bitterly so. Without counting the satellite
youth and children, who may be largely communized in time,
the older and anti-Stalinist puppet-state citizens probably exceed
50 million persons; perhaps considerably more. They are the
Kremlin's expendables, but they are also its *unconvertibles*. For
at least another 20 to 30 years they will constitute *the greatest
potential fifth column on earth*—provided that events do not
meanwhile transform most of them into fighting enemies.

At this page in this report I trust that no reader will inquire,
"But why don't the satellite peoples revolt?" The fairest answer
to that is, "Why don't you and your family commit suicide—
and immediately?" For if you lived under such organized and all-
inclusive armed terror as exists throughout captive Europe, *how
could you revolt?* It might be a noble gesture. But unless you did so
when Soviet Russia was engaged in a many-front war, your
sacrifice would amount to virtually nothing.

Since the invention of the machine gun, so far as I know, no
popular uprising has ever occurred against a totalitarian dictatorship—unless it was already deeply involved in war. Popular revo-
lutions simply *cannot* occur, of and by themselves, against
police-state régimes holding a monopoly of modern weapons.
After having worked as a correspondent in several of this century's most oppressively dictatorial states, including Hitler's
Germany and Russia, I marvel at the fact that even a few thousands of Eastern Europeans continue intermittently to commit
acts of violent resistance. If apprehended, they face certain torture and execution. Yet despite the Red régimes' armies of police,
militias and spies such acts, isolated but incredibly heroic, occur
in all the puppet states. I think a few incidents should be recorded
here. They are taken from underground reports obtained by
Radio Free Europe. Although I cite examples from only three
Curtain countries, identical types of underground warfare occur
in the others.

In Rumania: An expelled Greek resident stated that two
Soviet ammunition trains were blown up south of Jassy in early
June, 1951. . . . One hundred and eighty people were killed
when a Soviet military train was derailed near Feteshti in *July.*

. . . Eighteen Russians were killed when another Soviet ammunition train was blown up near Copsa Mica in *August*. . . . In the village of Piscul a militia captain and two of his men were killed by rebellious farmers. . . . Underground men joined the peasants in battling the militia at Fagarash and killed three government agents.

In Poland: The Soviets' famed Blue Express—Moscow-Warsaw-to-Berlin—was reported wrecked twice during 1951. High Russian officials no longer traverse Poland by train. In May President Bierut told the Communists' Central Committee that "sabotage and wrecking are increasing," and extreme police-control measures were taken.

In Czechoslovakia: Twenty-five tons of grain were destroyed at Nove Zamky in Slovakia, when storehouses were fired by resistance groups on *August 17, 1951.* . . . Radar installation plans were stolen from the Tesla electrical factory at Bratislava on *August 18.* . . . A resistance band seized 100 rifles and thousands of cartridges from an arms depot near Brno on *August 24.* . . . A military train was attacked near Pilsen on *August 27.* . . . Overhead power lines were severely damaged at Lobzy, near Pilsen, late in *August.*

Because mass rebellions would be suicidal, and weapons are extraordinarily difficult to obtain, puppet-state partisans can operate only in very small bands. In most cases they make sneak attacks after long planning. But in the mountainous regions of Eastern Europe small groups of guerrilla patriots unquestionably exist. Perhaps because Rumania has thousands of square miles of wild, almost inaccessible terrain I have found more armed activities reported thus far from that country. These include partisan units in the Moldavian Carpathians; in the mountains around Targu Ocna, Palanca and Piatra Neamtz; in those of Transylvania where one band, as of June, 1951, was reputedly led by a former National Peasant deputy named Boian; also others in the Wallachia and Oltenia regions. The Reds have sent large bodies of troops, including Russian units in some areas, against the Rumanian guerrillas. Many have been wiped out, but new groups form from fugitives who flee into the mountains.

The Stalinist régimes are likely to find it impossible to eradicate all partisan bands in the hilliest and most forested regions of captive Europe. Their existence and their occasional destructive raids spur resistance in the enslaved populations. The guerrillas and the widespread sabotage of peasants and workers create a tremendous security problem which the Red conquerors can neither solve nor ignore. If war should come, they know that the partisans—supplied by arms and food from outside sources—would swiftly swell into resistance forces numbering hundreds of thousands.

2. *The Kremlin's distrust of their satellite leaders*

When Marshal Tito and his Yugoslav party broke with Moscow in June, 1948, they became Communism's first successful heretics. Since then the Politburo has conducted a non-stop purge of the puppet-state parties, from top to bottom. Michael Padev, an exceptionally close observer of all satellite developments, reports that by December, 1951 "well over one million Communists had already been expelled," or between 20 and 25 per cent of the East European parties' memberships. Tens of thousands of these Reds were jailed or put into slave labor. "A sort of equality—*the equality of persecution*—is being established . . . the only kind of equality that exists behind the Curtain." *

In every national Communist organization the general secretary wields control of the party machine. That's how Stalin foiled all contenders for Lenin's throne—and he is still general secretary of the Russian party. In this light, consider what the Kremlin's satellite purge has already done. Out of six general secretaries of Eastern Europe's parties five had either been executed or were being held for trial and liquidation by early 1952. In Rumania Lucretiu Patrascano was killed in prison. Traycho Kostov of Bulgaria and Koche Xoxe of Albania were executed. Wladislaw Gomulka of Poland and Rudolf Slansky of Czechoslovakia, both awaiting trial, faced a similar fate. Hungary's

* "What's Behind the Communist Purges?" by Michael Padev. *The Toronto Star Weekly:* December 8, 1951.

Matyas Rakosi is the only general secretary of a satellite party to escape—but his private secretary and his closest associates have been liquidated. Lazslo Rajk, one of the original big four among Hungarian Reds and former Minister of the Interior, was also executed as a traitor. The satellite parties' chief liquidators were being liquidated themselves.

Of what "party crime" were these most fanatical Communists accused? Not only of totally unbelievable "conspiracy with Western imperialists," but also of "national deviation," which Poland's Hilary Minc defines as the supreme crime of "lack of faith in the effectiveness of the teachings of Stalin." Kostov, Gomulka, Slansky and the rest had failed to subjugate themselves to Stalin and the Politburo in every minute detail, or had merely become *suspected* of such deviation. In any event the satellite parties must be shown how any slightest verging toward "Titoism" will be treated.

Hamilton Fish Armstrong puts his finger on Tito's mortal sin: "The notion of *equality* of Communist parties and the *independence* of Communist states." Such conceptions are intolerable to Moscow, because they menace the Politburo's control of Communists all over the world. Most of all, Tito's example constitutes a deadly threat to Russia's absolute control of the satellite parties. Suppose they should follow Tito in revolt against abject servility to Moscow? The Kremlin would lose control of all Eastern Europe, as well as of six most strategically placed puppet parties.

This is one of the Politburo's deepest fears. But how to make such a disastrous development impossible? Only through unrelaxed terror. The psychopathic Kremlinites must confront their satellite stooges with horrifying examples of Stalinist discipline and vengeance. By killing off many of the puppet states' biggest Communists, every party member is reminded of what he may expect if he departs by an eyelash from the Moscow line. The loftier the victim's position, the more indelible the warning becomes.

Rudolf Slansky's case illustrates this most strikingly. Like

Bulgaria's Kostov he was a 100-per-cent "Muscovite"; had trained for years in Russia. He had controlled the Czech party's machine ever since 1945, and had been its most ruthless liquidator. An aircraft plant was renamed for Slansky in August, 1951. Prague's official Communist news agency, the с.т.к., circulated flattering comments on his new book on November 16. Just eleven days later the same news agency announced his arrest, stating it had been proved that "R. Slansky has been guilty of active anti-state hostile activities." Yet this same slit-eyed, hard-mouthed fanatic had done more to entrench the Kremlin's and Russia's control of Czechoslovakia than anyone in its party. Above all others, he had appeared to be unassailably in Stalinist favor.

On the night when Slansky's arrest was announced (November 27) the Minister of National Security, Ladislav Kopriva, made a revealing declaration in a public speech. As the new chief party executioner he stated: "It has been confirmed that the conspiracy activities of Sling, Svermova, Clementis, Husak [all previously arrested top Reds], *Slansky* and others are not an exceptional phenomenon . . . *that ours is a case of analogy with the subversive activities of Trotsky, Zinoviev, Bukharin, Rykov and others.*" * It is an astonishingly frank admission. All of these former old Bolshevik comrades of Stalin had been liquidated by him simply because they stood in his way to absolute power. So the real crime of Slansky, former Foreign Minister Clementis and the others was that Stalin no longer trusted them. In addition, while Slansky had been the Czech party's indisputable big boss, the Communists' entire five-year production program had bogged down in a fantastic mess of bureacratic mismanagement. Never mind Slansky's extraordinary record of loyalty to Moscow. Stalin needed the most prominent and shock-producing victim he could find in Czechoslovakia.

What do the satellite trials and purges of top Red leaders really prove? They prove, first of all, that the more powerful a satellite big Red becomes, the more suspect he also becomes

* *Rudè Pràvo*, November 28, 1951.

in the Kremlin's eyes. The one safe solution is to wipe him out—
on trumped-up charges of treacherous dealings with Western
agents—because his personal party control has become too great.
That party-machine power makes him a *potential* dissident, a possible Tito. Suppose he should swing the party machine toward
National Communism? Or craftily undermine certain Moscow
policies? Stalin's answer—before the event—has always worked.
If any satellite Communist chief is too capable, too personally
powerful or suspected of personal ambitions—kill him off! The
Kremlin's occupants fear such foreign-born Reds because they
are too much like themselves. Besides, Moscow needs unrelaxed
fear throughout the foreign parties' memberships more than it
needs a Slansky or Kostov.

What is the result of this pathological obsession? Unquestionably part of the Kremlinites' fear is genuine and incurable. They
keep purging and liquidating life-long puppet-state Communists
in an effort to reduce that fear. But the more comrades they
liquidate the more consuming their fear becomes. Suppose the
executions breed real plots and plotters? Whom can Moscow
really trust in each Curtain country's party? Only the most
craven conformists to the Stalin line; the bootlickers, the opportunists, the least sincere and the weakest. A system based
on terror cannot rid itself of the very terror which it creates.
Here is the Red conqueror's most ironic and perpetual nightmare.

3. *Lagging industrialization*

This is definitely a long-term anxiety. The painfully slow and
uneven progress of the five-year plans demonstrates this fact.
For many years to come coal, oil and hydroelectric power cannot be produced in amounts nearly adequate for the plans' extravagant quotas. Old machinery and equipment can only be
replaced in fractions, year by year. As green workmen and
women are recruited by hundreds of thousands, months and

years are required to train them into reasonably efficient performance. It will take much longer to produce legions of industrial technicians worthy of the name.

Compared with the past, it's possible that captive Europe's industrial production will be built up to a remarkable degree by the early 1960's. But even then its contribution to Soviet power must be far below Moscow's interpretation of its urgent necessities. Even by the year 2,000 the Soviet Union, Red China and the puppet states (if they are still that) probably cannot come within competing distance of the North Atlantic allies' productive capacity. Moscow cannot count on any puppet states' five-year plan registering an impressive success. But every delay, set-back or failure inspires profound doubts and suspicions among the Kremlin's highly impatient slave masters. They must always be tormented by the possibility, more often the probability, that the "hand of the enemy" is largely responsible. What to do? Look for another Slansky!

4. *Resistance and sabotage*

Of course the brutal conditions imposed on labor by the Stalinist system and the puppet régimes' feverish production speed-ups cannot be changed. For this very reason the workers are bound to remain overwhelmingly antagonistic. But they have in their favor the fact that high-pressured industrialization assures the protracted existence of large labor shortages. Therefore, because they are indispensable, satellite workers cannot be jailed en masse. For a long time they can continue slow-downs, absenteeism, job transfers, secret sabotage and other obstructionism.

Here, too, the Stalinist rulers are caught in a vicious circle. The more they drive labor, the more Eastern Europe's workers will be provoked into all forms of sub-surface resistance. They know they are being used, as their countries are being used, for the aggrandizement of Russian power. But this generation's patriotism and national consciousness cannot be destroyed. The workers' self-interest is bound indissolubly to their own countries' interests and long-term welfare.

Perhaps, in another decade or two, a younger and largely communized working generation may co-operate docilely with the Russian conquerors. But at least into the 1960's or 1970's satellite factories will remain centers of labor difficulties. The men in the Kremlin have no possible solution except their only solution—always more brute force. But they cannot take several millions of most essential men and women out of captive Europe's expanding factories, put them into slave-labor camps, and hope to maintain the imperatively needed pace of the five-year plans. Either the Stalinists do that and bog down their satellite production disastrously, or they blunder along against the heavy brake of millions of workmen in subversive revolt. Moscow has no choice. It cannot change its system. Nor can it change human nature; least of all, that of tough Eastern Europeans.

5. *The recalcitrant farmers*

After more than thirty years of Soviet rule just one source of serious resistance persists in the Soviet Union—the peasant-farmers. But Eastern Europe's predominantly agrarian populations are equally stubborn, and they have had what Russia's peasants have never known—personal experience of free organization and independent political action. Through their National Peasant Parties they have exercised a strong influence through most of their lives. Who can imagine that peasants with such traditions will struggle with less persistence and skill than Russian peasants have shown in opposing collectivization?

Not the men in the Kremlin. They have sworn to liquidate several millions of independent farmers (so-called kulaks) and their families by deportations or by confinement in slave-labor camps. Rakosi and others have also plainly indicated that several more millions of middle peasants, including families, are to be treated eventually as "sworn enemies." As pointed out in Chapter VII, this means a long-term Moscow objective by which approximately 18 million in captive Europe's agrarian populations would largely be deported, imprisoned or forcibly collectivized. But when, and how? On such a scale this must necessitate a ten- or twenty-year war.

Those families in the comparatively well-situated "kulak" category are certain to be given top priority. Initially two million persons or considerably more might be involved. But their Red rulers cannot tear them out of agricultural production all at once, or in a year or two. First, because such precipitous action would enormously aggravate the satellites' already serious food situation, thereby throwing their five-year plans out of gear. Second, because vast numbers of peasants cannot be deported until much greater transportation and other facilities are created. Third, because hundreds of additional slave camps must be built before an all-out clean-up of independent farmers can be launched. After that many millions of middle peasants would still remain to be banished, broken or absorbed into collectives.

Meanwhile those puppet-state peasants inevitably will continue to resist crop deliveries and to sabotage production. As foreign farmers they have double incentives to fight Soviet-style enslavement, and they fight for their children's independence as well as their own. Without abandoning collectivization the Kremlin cannot end this war, and it cannot renounce Stalinism's basic land policy. There is no discernible end to this bitter and frustrating struggle. Moscow cannot escape it—but it cannot hope to win it in less than decades.

6. *Can the Soviets destroy the religious faith of the people?*

It proved fairly simple for the Communists to capture control of every organized church, of every creed, in the Curtain countries. But they have by no means been able to extirpate the religious convictions and loyalties of tens of millions of lifelong adherents to the Catholic, Orthodox and other faiths. By widespread testimony, Stalinist persecution has greatly intensified the devotion of puppet-state laymen everywhere. Even though the Red régimes threaten to produce a largely atheistic younger generation by the middle or late 1960's, the adult populations remain firm. Moscow recognizes their religious ideologies as a most dangerous opposition. But how can it be broken down?

Whether Roman Catholic, Orthodox, Jewish or Protestant, most of captive Europe's adults will cling to their faith as their only source of spiritual strength; as their sole consolation under persecution and terror; as their chief inspiration to endure, to hope and to believe in ultimate liberation. This is an inner citadel of moral and spiritual resistance. The Stalinists cannot destroy it. But they must be constantly aware of its existence. In event of war they know that these deep religious convictions would feed the flames of patriotic resistance and revolt. The alliance of patriotism and religious faith must always be feared. It will continue to threaten the permanence of Red conquest throughout the lifetime of this satellite generation.

7. *The impossibility of Russianizing millions of Eastern Europeans*

The one truly cheering thing about the Kremlin's aggressive efforts to Russianize the Iron-Curtain peoples is that it is essentially self-defeating. What could be more absurd than Moscow's attempts to make a Russia-lover—in fact a Russian—out of a Pole, a Czech, a Hungarian, Bulgarian or Rumanian? Perhaps this may succeed eventually with the satellites' youth who are today under 15 years of age. But what about the older 80 per cent or more of their countries' citizens who grew up with intense pride in their separate countries' culture, history and traditions? Human beings are amazingly resistant in holding on to their own national identity, to the loyalties of their birthright, to the things in their own heritage which belong only to them. Conservatively, the Politburo can worry about this for the next twenty-five years.

8. *Too much, and much too fast!*

Ever since the first five-year plan was launched in the late 1920's, the Kremlin has driven the Soviet people at a killing pace. In February, 1931, Stalin told his party leaders: "No, comrades . . . *the pace must not be slackened!* On the contrary we must speed it up to the limit of our power and possibilities. . . . To slacken the pace would mean to lag behind; and those who lag behind are beaten."

Hitler's invasion of Russia proved that Stalin's analysis was sound. But the war years imposed a still more Spartan and Herculean effort. At the war's end the Soviet populations badly needed a respite. Yet they were compelled again to shoulder the production drives of three or four more five-year plans. I think it is accurate to say that no other people in modern times has been driven so hard; nor at such a minimum level of food and housing—and for nearly 25 years without interruption. And today they are still goaded "to the limit."

It is unquestionable that millions of workers and peasants in the u.s.s.r. currently suffer from strained nerves, dulled energies and excessive fatigue. Almost everyone is overworked; perhaps the Communist Party members most of all. Konstantin Simonov, one of the Soviets' playwright-propagandists, once told how he worked an average of 16 to 18 hours a day on four different major jobs. Despite his tremendous physique, he looked ten years older than his approximate 40 years. Abnormal demands take a heavy toll from party officials and Soviet citizens in general.

Can the Soviet people maintain this terrific pace for another 20 years without increasing breakdowns and loss of efficiency? How fast can they go, and for how much longer? Edward Crankshaw rightly stresses this far too ignored question. Stalin's hold is threatened, he states, "because . . . he has been forced to drive his all too long-suffering people too far and too hard." *

* *Op. cit.*, p. 262.

Even the Russians, whose folk-saying boasts that "a Russian can endure anything and everything," have limits to their endurance.

But the Eastern Europeans are being driven equally hard and in some respects at a faster pace. Everything in the puppet states must be sovietized at absolutely maximum speed—to build Russia's power, to beat what Moscow sees as an atomic deadline, to consolidate the Soviets' conquest before it is too late. Soviet Army officers are known to have told neutral foreigners, and their satellite girl friends, that "the Communists here are trying to do in five years what we have been unable to do at home in thirty years—and after all, we Russians are much more capable."

Can the Stalinists indefinitely drive enslaved *foreign* peoples as they drive their domestic population? Almost all of these people have known a better life—certainly a life in which they had much more freedom. Why should they punish themselves endlessly, or accept endless punishment, to make their personal chains more unbreakable? They know that another five-year plan means more intensified hardship, fatigue and exploitation. The harder and the faster they are driven, the more they must obstruct and slow down. The Kremlin's occupants may continue to defy this reality, but they cannot escape it.

9. *Russia's most deadly enemy—the truth*

Of all the fears which haunt the Soviet conquerors, the most incurable must be their fear of the truth. Consider how the world's second most powerful government reacted to a simple map—the American Federation of Labor's map of Soviet slave camps. Several hundreds of thousands of copies were being prepared for distribution in Austria by the United States Information Service. The Russians confiscated all copies, and arrested the Viennese bookbinder and his wife.* Even in little Austria the truth about Soviet slave camps was a deadly menace to the Soviet empire.

* *The New York Times*, October 18, 1951.

No other dictatorship, in any century, has ever expended such stupendous efforts and funds to pervert the truth and to bar "unprocessed" information from all its subject peoples. It is estimated that Russia and its satellite régimes spent *approximately $1.4 billion on all kinds of propaganda activities in 1950 alone*. Even at half that amount the sum would still be colossal and without precedent. Nevertheless it is perfectly comprehensible. For the Soviet system and its techniques of conquest are based upon deception, distortion, falsification and coercion. Therefore every untampered fact or free opinion menaces the Kremlin's power and rule.

But what its occupants can least risk and least tolerate is that truth should get *into* satellite Europe, or that much truth about satellite Europe should get *out*. This is so, especially, because the East Europeans are subjugated rather than, as yet, permanently conquered. Also because the Soviet imperialists have here unmasked both their methods and motives to a startling degree. What if free peoples everywhere should learn even 50 per cent of the truth about captive Europe? Truth is Stalinist Russia's deadliest enemy. It must be perverted, polluted or killed. It must be fought savagely, without quarter, day and night.

Every East European who escapes to the free world carries with him minute but potentially fatal particles of the truth about Soviet conquest. Those particles of actual fact are sufficient to terrify the Kremlin's tyrants. So they have transformed every puppet state's border regions into no man's lands of mine fields, barbed- and electric-wire obstacles, interspaced with watchtowers whose searchlights sweep nightly. Never before have entire nations been fenced in. Yet despite regiments of "shoot-to-kill" border guards, bloodhounds and all the rest, about 1,500 courageous persons reached freedom from satellite terror during each month of 1951. A dauntless Czech engineer actually drove his train through the Curtain which is called "iron" on September 11, 1951. Shortly afterward another group of Czechs drove a homemade armored truck through it. Nearly half of Europe cannot be made escape-proof, nor into a model Soviet prison. *The truth will out.*

The Kremlin may have conquered one-third of the earth, but it cannot conquer truth—only a portion of it, and only for a time. As we have seen in these pages, even the Stalinists' party publications are a dead give-away. It is totally impossible to keep every copy of every issue inside the Curtain. So the Red conquerors' printed words (indispensable for their own propaganda and for boosting party activities) backfire upon their originators. On every page they betray their falsifications, their bureaucratic muddles, their fears, their betrayals and the immensity of their problems. They *must* print lies. Yet the more lies they print, the more truth they reveal about themselves.

The Stalinists have not only proved that "you can't fool all of the people all of the time." In satellite Europe they have found that they cannot fool more than a minor percentage of the people *any* of the time. Although they spend hundreds of millions of dollars and unrivaled efforts they cannot blot out all of the light that reaches for men's minds. They cannot keep truth in and they cannot keep truth out. No men now living have such compelling reasons to understand that "truth alone shall make men free." No men living hold that fact in such terror as well as unwilling respect. In the words of Leonard H. Robbins, "Who keeps the truth from the people stands in the way of God!" There will always be light because, in the final reckoning, the light of knowledge remains indestructible. This indeed is the Kremlin's never ending nightmare.

*   *   *

Seventeen major nightmares of these dimensions are not to be underestimated. Not one of these ever present Politburo problems can conceivably be settled permanently or removed within the next ten years; most of them not for so long as the present Kremlin occupants may live. But these seventeen varieties of nightmares can be made still more terrifying for them over the next few years. We in the free West have the power and the opportunity to do this. *Free men alone can keep truth free—can make truth work for freedom everywhere.* At last we have made a start. We have no reason to be defeatist. Only now have we experienced the compulsion to use truth as it demands to be used—and we are learning. Let us consider how we are beginning to use truth as our deadliest weapon, and in what ways we should be able to use it more effectively.

CHAPTER SIXTEEN

Freedom Takes the Offensive

"WHAT CAN WE DO TO HELP SATELLITE Europe's people?" someone asks. But this is merely one aspect of a much bigger question: What can we do to defend all peoples, including ourselves, against Communist infiltration and Cominform conquest? How much are we doing? How much more do we need to do?

But we must first face up to the real meaning of Soviet Russia's "cold war" against the Western democracies. Moscow began this conflict by preventing "broadly representative" governments in Rumania and Poland, early in 1945. The Soviet leaders violated their Yalta pledges almost before the ink on them was dry, thus starting the cold war. For five years their offensive has continued and the cold war now threatens to last indefinitely. Unless we fight it much harder and much more skillfully, we can still lose it.

The Stalinists were able to monopolize the offensive in the cold war chiefly because they have had long experience in psychological warfare; the Kremlin's occupants have waged a struggle for men's minds ever since 1918. From the outset they clearly understood that *the cold war is a war of nerves plus a war of ideas.* For such a conflict they alone possessed the strategy, the tactics, almost unlimited funds and trained technicians in vast numbers.

Because we had little experience of a war of ideas, and even less of a war of nerves, the Stalinists caught the Western governments and peoples utterly unprepared. They were infinitely better organized and better equipped. They also had us out-generaled and—let's admit it—outclassed. Our defenders of fact and truth were further handicapped by their ingrained scruples. Finally they were tremendously outnumbered—which they still are in most sectors—and they had to learn from their defeats. As a result, the Kremlin's ideological tanks were smashing through and running wild much of the time from 1945 to 1950. Few things so incredible have happened in this fantastic century. The perfectors of the greatest and most successful political idea in history were taking a fearful beating in a war of ideas. This was largely because the Western democracies' citizens failed to demand that adequate appropriations be made for the necessary weapons and personnel. They remained strangely blind to:

The stakes in the cold war.

Even today most of us do not visualize these stakes clearly. We know the issue is democratic freedoms versus Communist enslavement. But do we yet grasp that this is a struggle without quarter and without armistice? Do we perceive the nature and the size of the battlefield? The Kremlin's targets cover the globe. Consider the sheer numbers of people at whom its missiles are aimed.

The Stalinist bloc now rules 760 millions or more out of the earth's 2.4 billion people. In North America and the English-speaking Commonwealth 221 millions may perhaps be regarded as temporarily safe from Communist conquest. But there still remain approximately 1.4 billion persons who are at present exposed to Communist seduction. All of these people are vulnerable due either to their nearness to Russia or to their low standard of living. They constitute the overwhelming balance of power in tomorrow's world. They are Moscow's immediate target—and they must also be ours. Whoever wins most of these 1.4 billion people commands the future.

Dr. George H. Gallup warns perceptively that *"what you don't know may destroy you."* It is what these 1.4 billion people don't know about life under Communist rule that makes them peculiarly vulnerable. Who is going to tell them, if not us? In Italy and France it is what 25 to 35 per cent of the least privileged citizens "don't know" about Stalinism that makes these key nations of Western Europe most seriously exposed to infiltration and eventual conquest. Throughout the Middle East, Asia, Africa and Latin America, it is what the illiterate, ill-fed and discontented masses don't know that prompts them to believe false Communist promises. What 300 million Hindus don't know—and as yet have fearfully slight prospects of discovering—makes it possible that India may one day go Communist. But if we lose India, we lose, in effect, all of southeastern Asia in a catastrophe that could decide the fate of the world.

Inside the Soviet slave state the party members are a highly privileged aristocracy created under the slogan of "to each according to his need." No greater hoax was ever perpetrated. But it's not difficult to sell such a slogan to ignorant or ill-informed people who have never had enough of anything in their lives. What comes through to a half-starved Iranian or Indonesian is not the colossal fraud of Kremlin imperialism, but the glittering promises of a "better life." Unless we offer the world's "have-nots" something equally promising, but more applicable to their daily existence, the Communists will win in the end.

Whoever feeds world hunger destroys Communism.

This is the extremely sound idea behind the United States' Point Four program: to improve the food production and health of the world's underprivileged through the introduction of American and Western technological methods; to help the more primitive peoples to help themselves. A county agent from Tennessee, Horace Holmes, introduced the American farming methods on the Indian Government's experimental "Etawah Project" with these results: the wheat crop increased 63 per cent and the potato crop 112 per cent. The wheat crop alone was worth ten times the project's annual cost. With Point-Four help and several dozen United States county agents, Holmes plans to train 60,000 Hindus to work as instructors all over India. In 1951 the Holmes pilot-project cost the United States the pittance of $75,733.*

In many different regions Point Four has already proved what life-giving improvements it can create. But it needs vastly greater sums, if it is to change the lives of scores of millions of people. It is also a painfully slow process at the outset. Will Point Four's democratic weapon be made big enough to save entire nations from Communist seduction? Can it lift enough people out of hunger fast enough? What might reasonably be accomplished in 30 or 40 years now must be done in ten years or less.

But the amazing discoveries of Western scientists may yet defeat the Communists' exploitation of the world's hungry masses. A new chemical named Krilium, developed in the United States, converts non-productive soil into productive soil in a matter of hours. William L. Laurence reports that extensive tests carried out by nearly 80 soil scientists "indicate that the new chemical—the first synthetic soil conditioner—will mark the beginning of a revolutionary era in agriculture, in which man-made deserts may be turned in a short time into blooming gardens. . . . Scientists expressed the view that [Krilium] might prove to be an even more powerful weapon against Communism than the atomic bomb." It should be available in substantial quantities, at less than $2 a pound, in 1953.** When we mobilize Western science and technology against world hunger in a vast effort—and if we do it in time—the Kremlin's hopes of winning the masses, from India to Latin America, will be doomed.

In the meantime, however, the lies of Stalinism must first be made evident. We cannot fight the war of ideas successfully until the majority of citizens in the Western democracies know the Soviet imperialists for what they are. This is why:

* *Life Magazine*, December 31, 1951.
** *The New York Times*, December 30, 1951.

Satellite Europe is both an invaluable warning and a unique weapon for the West.

In captive Europe the Stalinists have shown us how Red terror functions in actual practice. There the Soviets' methods of conquest are revealed. For the Stalinists, in the puppet-states, have proved:

1) That the Russian Communists are by far the most efficient political organizers in today's world.

2) That, once they have seized power, they can build large Communist parties amazingly fast.

3) That the Stalinists can win the support or the tolerance of millions of well-intentioned non-Communists—before the Kremlin unmasks its true character and objectives.

4) That, given time and power, the Communists can win a decisive majority in any nation's youngest generation.

5) That the Stalinists, up to now, have been superior to the Western democracies in waging a war of ideas.

Thus the sovietization of Eastern Europe shows what the Kremlin can confidently expect to achieve, in due time, among a majority of the world's underprivileged peoples—unless the free nations make far greater efforts to win the war of ideas. Until we employ equally effective organizations and techniques on an intensive world-wide scale we cannot even begin to hold our own. Until we outmatch the Soviets both in aggressiveness and skills we cannot hope to persuade the ultimately decisive legions in the world's ideological marketplace. Therefore our own widespread incomprehension is largely responsible for the confusions and frustrations which have bedeviled us in these postwar years.

We have now realized that a war of ideas must be fought from strength. Our first help to Eastern Europe's peoples is to make the Western democracies' armed forces unassailably strong, and to build unity in the West. In the meantime, we must keep the spirit of resistance alive in the Curtain countries in the hope that some day we may be able to bargain with Moscow for the withdrawal of her armies from the captive nations. If that can be achieved—and it should be possible when the Atlantic allies are strong enough—Eastern Europe's nations would have much better chances of eventually breaking the Kremlin's chains. In the strength and unity of the West lies their only hope.

But the growth of that hope depends upon Western nations taking the initiative in the struggle for men's minds; upon our wholesale unmasking of Stalinist practices and deceptions for what they are. We cannot win ideologically without putting freedom's long neglected weapons to maximum use—and at last we are mobilizing and using these weapons so that their real power is being felt.

America's Campaign of Truth

In April, 1950, President Truman replied to Moscow's virulent "hate-America" campaign by declaring: "We must make ourselves known as we really are—not as Communist propaganda pictures us. We must make ourselves heard round the world in a great campaign of truth." After a perilously protracted case of the stutters Uncle Sam had found his tongue.

By the end of 1951 the State Department's international broadcasts increased from 29 to 48 daily program hours, in 45 languages (an increase of 21 during the year). Letters from Voice of America listeners totaled as many as 40,000 a month. The United States Information Service distributed nearly 80 million pamphlets, photo booklets and leaflets from its 145 offices in 78 countries; thousands of newsreel and documentary films were sent abroad; 150 film libraries were operating in 85 countries in the first nine months of 1951.*

This is the opening phase of a much bigger effort that must be made and permanently maintained. The campaign of truth came too late to dissuade millions of Koreans from supporting the Communists' invasion; too late to prevent a major strategic de-

* *The Campaign of Truth: The International Information and Educational Exchange Program, 1951.* Department of State publication, 1951.

feat for the democracies in Iran. And compared with Soviet
Russia's immense, high-geared propaganda offensives it is still
relatively small. Consider how the Stalinists are waging the war
of ideas.

While all American information agencies expended less
than $200 million in 1950, Washington officials estimate that
the Soviet Union and her satellites spent $1.4 billion. The Rus-
sians alone are credited with spending $840 million on broadcasts,
news services, films and financing of agitators; $48 million more
to train propagandists; $40 million for books and pamphlets.
The puppet-state régimes are estimated to have spent another
$481 million. The Kremlin's world-wide efforts are eight to ten
times greater in cost than those of the world's richest nation—in
personnel actively engaged, hundreds of times greater.

As an example of Soviet Russia's tremendous head start, take
France. If the Stalinists win France, they cut Western Europe in
two and capture the central defense base of N.A.T.O.'s armies.
By official estimates the Communists (Soviet, French and satellite) are spending about $150 million dollars a year on propa-
ganda in France. While the Voice of America sends about 15
hours a week into that country, Russian stations deluge it with
from 46 to 75 hours of broadcasts. With more than 500,000 members, the French Communist Party is said to have 14,000 cells in
French cities; 10,000 in rural areas; and 7,000 cells in industry.
More than 30,000 Communists are elected officials in municipal
governments; nearly 2,000 are reputedly enrolled in the Paris
police force.*

To combat this Stalinist menace the United States spends a
mere seven million dollars annually on information and propaganda work in France. The Kremlin's efforts are at least 20 times
greater than our own. The discrepancy is approximately as great
in Italy and in many other important countries. Anthony Leviero
reported in the *The New York Times* ** that Washington's policy-
makers "are belatedly aware *that the Soviet Union could win the*

---

* From a series of articles on the war of ideas, by Anthony Leviero. *The
New York Times*, December 13, 1951.
** December 9, 1951.

world without itself engaging in war. The question now is *whether truth . . . can at this late date meet adequately the sweep of the Soviet Union's world revolution. . . .* Has the United States conceived a strategy that will meet adequately the profound challenge?"

This problem prompted President Truman to assign Gordon Gray to organize a Psychological Strategy Board in 1951. Since its inception the P.S.B. has suffered from difference of top-level opinion in regard to its major policies and its degree of authority. It was limited by presidential directive to policy-making, with no direct operational functions. Thus its decisions must be turned over to the Departments of State and Defense, or other agencies, to be implemented. Of course the Kremlin's psychological-warfare apparatus has no such handicaps. Its strategists execute whatever policies are adopted. Their staffs are large and work full-time. Through their foreign parties the Cominform can strike with maximum speed anywhere in the world. After all, the Cominform *is* Stalin's P.S.B. After closely investigating Washington's groping approach to psychological warfare Mr. Leviero concludes: our campaign of truth *"is not adequate of itself to cope with the Soviet challenge."* *

The sobering fact is that we are still far from being in a position to win the war of ideas. The encouraging fact is that at last America has begun to fight this war; that we are finally building powerful weapons and perfecting effective techniques of our own. Among these weapons none is more important or more promising than the Voice of America and Radio Free Europe. They are doing two very big jobs, and they complement each other's efforts in remarkable ways. Primarily the Voice, speaking officially for the United States Government, presents American facts and America's case to the world. Because Radio Free Europe is a joint project of Americans and East European exiles, and is privately financed, it speaks to *and for* captive Europe's enslaved peoples.

These two dynamic organizations provoke screams of rage from the Red conquerors week after week. Their work is as

* *Ibid.,* December 15, 1951.

exciting as a detective story, yet most citizens in the Western democracies are still not informed of how v.o.a. and r.f.e., along with the b.b.c. and a few European stations, have become leaders in the truth offensive. To increase their effectiveness greatly, all that is needed is greater financial support by the United States Congress and from private citizens.

The Voice of America

During the first years after the war our policy made the Voice answer Moscow's vicious attacks, like a well-mannered gentleman, with strictly factual replies. Fortunately, that unrealistic nonsense has ended. v.o.a. now uses every effective weapon, including large doses of satire and ridicule.

Late in 1951 v.o.a. broadcast a series of talks, called "G. I. Ivan Speaks Up," about the personal experiences of Russian soldiers who had fled to the West. One soldier, speaking to the Soviet people, told how he and his comrades had listened to the Voice, "although we didn't know ourselves whether we should believe it or not. I heard on the Voice of America that America does not extradite fugitives. So I decided to cross into the American Zone. I was given new clothes and shoes. I get more food than I ever had in my life. I am allowed to listen to any radio station. I read any paper I choose, including Soviet papers. . . . Stalin and the entire Communist Party are cheating you."

These Russian-language programs were inaugurated by the Voice in February, 1947. Foy D. Kohler, chief of our international broadcasting operations, reports that even in its initial phase "all the evidence we could amass in Moscow *indicated that the Voice of America must have a regular listening audience of at least 10 million [Soviet] people*. . . . Our [current] monitoring indicates that the Voice can be heard 25 per cent of the time, even in Moscow, where jamming is concentrated, and 60 to 80 per cent of the time outside the capital." * Mr. Kohler cites evi-

* In an address before the Institute for Education, Columbus, Ohio, May 4, 1951.

dence "that we reach about 80 per cent of radio owners every day" in the Curtain countries; "that the Voice, with the assistance of the well-developed grapevine, can deliver an important message to practically the entire population of the satellite states within a matter of hours."

Moscow shows its fear of our truth campaign by its stupendous efforts to keep v.o.a. and r.f.e. out of all Stalinist-ruled regions. More than 250 Soviet jamming stations had been identified by early 1952. A single jamming station is very expensive to build and operate, yet the Russians are believed to be using 1,000 or more. It is estimated that they spend almost as much on jamming as Western governments combined spend on sending internationally.

Successful short-wave broadcasting from the United States into Soviet-ruled territories is restricted by geographical and climatic obstacles, but now what is called the Ring Plan is well advanced toward removing them. As an essential part of the campaign of truth, it was approved by Congress. Under it eight or ten powerful relay stations will be established around the entire periphery of Russia, the satellites and Red China. Thus the Voice of America will be able to reach almost anywhere in the world.

Three of these relay stations were completed and two more well along by early in 1952: in Munich, Tangier, Salonika, Honolulu and Manila. v.o.a. officials believe the Ring's entire relay network should be in operation by 1955. Thus Moscow's jamming war seems doomed to produce less and less results at ever mounting costs. There is, for example:

"Operation Vagabond."

A converted Coast Guard cutter, the 5,800-ton *Courier*, recently took to the sea as a new kind of raider. It is the v.o.a.'s first big floating radio station, with the most powerful transmitting equipment of its kind ever installed on a ship. The *Courier* will send Voice programs into Soviet or satellite countries from constantly shifting locations, which means that the Russian jammers can never keep its messages from getting through. The ship may broadcast from somewhere in the Eastern Mediterranean one month; from the Indian Ocean or the Far East a month or two later. Linked to shore-based antennae, it can go on the air in two or three months, instead of the 12- to 18-month delay stationary transmitters require for installation. If Congress provides the funds, the Voice hopes to use two more sea-roving "jammer-dodgers" later on.

Radio Free Europe

On September 11, 1951, engineer Jaroslav Konvalinka "tied down the throttle" of his train, which carried more than 100 passengers and "let her go"—straight through a Czech border station and on into Western Germany. Prague's Red régime was literally struck dumb for many hours. Of the train's occupants 32 elected to remain in the West, and 22 of them said they had listened regularly to Radio Free Europe's broadcasts. Chiefly because of relatives who would become hostages, 77 returned to Czechoslovakia. They were immediately forced to sign a declaration describing a United States kidnapping "plot" and their "brutal" treatment by Americans. That same night Radio Prague asserted that the train's passengers had "refused to the last man" to stay in Germany. Two passengers obediently broadcast a luridly falsified version of the incident.

In Radio Free Europe's Munich station a group of Czech exiles listened. At 30 seconds before 7 P.M. their speaker had made his usual announcement, but with a timely twist: "Now why don't you tune in on Radio Prague? Hear what it has to say about the Czechs who escaped by train today! We're going to listen, too. But tune us back in at 7:30. Then we'll tell you what really happened."

Precisely at 7:30 Engineer Konvalinka told his fellow countrymen: "The Communists are lying when they tell you that every passenger went back. Thirty-two of us have chosen freedom. If you don't believe I am here, go to my house. Here is the address. . . . Go to these other addresses. . . . You will *not* find one of us at home. We are all here in the West—and the climate is wonderful."

Another big Kremlin lie had been punctured as soon as it was uttered. R.F.E. has been fighting back in this fashion ever since its first broadcast in New York on July 4, 1950. It developed swiftly into an aggressive and effective instrument for getting facts to the peoples behind the Curtain; also for bedeviling their Red rulers. Today it is undoubtedly the hardest-hitting of all Western radio operations, for several reasons.

As a privately supported, independent operation, Radio Free Europe is not cramped by an official status. It fights Stalinist propagandists with every weapon. It strikes hard and often savagely on behalf of those peoples whose hands are chained. This is possible because its programs are planned, written and delivered by exiles from all the Curtain countries. Americans merely provide over-all guidance, co-ordination and certain techniques and technicians.

R.F.E.'s main objectives are to keep hope alive in the captive populations; to encourage their spirit of resistance; to build an audience of the most courageous anti-Communist citizens; finally, to make the Red conquerors' efforts in every way more difficult—to show them up for what they are. The results have already been remarkable. As President of the Committee for Free Europe, and chief administrator of R.F.E. in its second year, C. D. Jackson summed them up as follows:

"In our first six months of operations out of Munich R.F.E. became the most popular radio station, domestic or foreign, heard in Czechoslovakia. With our formula, which is actually a new one, we've *got* Czechoslovakia as an audience. We are getting Hungary. We will get Poland once we can go full blast— with one transmitter exclusively for Polish broadcasts. When you get people who want to listen, you don't have to worry about propaganda. That takes care of itself.

"How is Radio Free Europe different? Well, we started out to win an audience in just the same way as N.B.C. competes for an audience. We studied what the satellite Communists were offering on their stations. Then we met them, program for program—giving our competing number more appeal in every way we could, and also introducing American radio techniques wherever they proved effective."

Robert E. Lang, R.F.E.'s alert director, told me how this has worked out. It's an exciting story of radio pioneering; of mutual discovery and work with five different foreign psychologies; an effort toward a new kind of international teamwork, of pooling of ideas and experience, which the Communist opposition can never undertake.

"We thought it should be possible to use an American-style round-table discussion," Lang said. "But the Czechs were not at all sure. We had to convince them first. One night we invited eight Czechs and Slovaks to the Regina Palace bar in Munich. We had a recorder planted there secretly. We got them debating among themselves about the Schuman Plan. Then we played it back to them. 'You've done it, and in English!' we said. 'That's a lot more difficult than doing it in your own language. Why not do it in Czech?' That sold them on it. Next day we went back and they did it again—in Czechoslovakian. Since then we've had a round-table discussion as a regular feature."

By audience checking R.F.E. learned that the foreign-origin program with the biggest Czechoslovak following was a team of exiled comedians, Papa Snezek and Kohout, then on a Paris station. "We brought them to Munich and discussed a possible quiz show," director Lang reports. "It was new to them, but they agreed to give it a try. We put on a trial show at the big Valka D.P. camp. We offered radios, pens and nylons as prizes. Snezek and Kohout picked ten persons from the audience, and let fly with their questions. Within a few minutes it was a laugh riot. Now we record a Valka quiz show and have people laughing all over Czechoslovakia every week. Snezek and Kohout are as sure-fire as Fred Allen or Charlie McCarthy—and they work in a lot of powerful political stuff. Just simple questions; like asking an escapee, 'Where are your children?' They sting the Communists so hard it's a picnic for everyone else who listens."

Radio Free Europe throws everything in the book at Captive Europe's Red rulers. Its broadcasts constantly remind the enslaved peoples that they have powerful friends in the free world; that they are not forgotten; that their own free countrymen are defending their interests; that they themselves can help by smuggling out information and by their resistance; that Communist lies and crimes are being exposed; that they have reasons for hope. There are special programs for farmers, workers, women, youth—every vital segment in their populations.

In regular features known as "We Accuse" or "Messages Home" R.F.E. describes Red informers, torturers and other notoriously brutal party agents—ending with "*Your name is on the list!*" Many Communists get badly frightened and even begin to act unnaturally mild. The Hungarian broadcasts introduced a mythical reporter, Balint Boda, who always knows what's going on. Then listeners were urged to scrawl in every possible place the words, "Balint Boda was here!" Suddenly the taunting slogan popped up all over Hungary—on walls and buildings, in rest rooms and factories—with incensed Reds scurrying around to wash off the irrepressible Boda. The Hungarians had the rarest thing in their lives—a lot of fun.

Within six hours after R.F.E.'s first broadcast went out of Munich on May 1, 1951, Prague was trying desperately to jam it. Within a month the Czech régime handed a violent protest to the American ambassador, charging R.F.E. with "espionage, sabotage and other hostile activity." Later Prague put on two more jamming stations, and spent the remainder of 1951 building two others. But this also revealed that the Soviets definitely lack transmitter reserves. It indicated clearly that America can produce far more radio-war equipment than the Reds can muster. Despite their frantic concern over R.F.E. broadcasts, the Stalinists cannot blot them out.

Leaflets by balloon

"Winds of Freedom," a Radio Free Europe project, sent leaflets aloft by balloon and dumped a snowstorm on Prague and its environs on August 12, 1951. In the next six weeks more than 12 million messages were strewn by balloons across Czechoslovakia and Poland. Every fluttering piece of paper jubilantly announced: "A new hope is stirring! Friends of Freedom in other lands have found a new way to reach you. . . . Tyranny cannot control the winds; cannot enslave your hearts." For the first time in Soviet history scores of millions of *printed* words had hurdled the Kremlin's Curtain.

The immediate results were melodramatic, fantastic and hilarious. Eyewitnesses who are in the underground describe the frenzy with which the Stalinists reacted. Police motorcycle squads and trucks of Red militiamen dashed madly around the countryside. Police cordons in Prague and other cities surrounded the thickest squalls of bouncing papers as though they were death-ray invaders from Mars. In many places public loudspeakers blasted warnings to citizens that they would be severely punished if they so much as touched the little white truths. In other localities people were ordered to deliver the contaminating things to the nearest police headquarters. Thousands of Communist youths were mobilized to comb the gutters and hedges and scour the fields to round up the fearful rectangular strips.

Everywhere the police searched homes and factories, but thousands of leaflets kept appearing pinned by citizens on walls, fences or trees. For days the dreaded police were busy chasing leaflets. Nothing so magnificently ridiculous had happened since the Russians came. Millions of Czechs and Poles responded to the frantic spectacle with sheer delight.

By September 3, Prague's big Reds could no longer contain themselves. Prime Minister Zapotocky declared: "Our people will be affected still less by experimental balloons, filled with press manure issued by our exiles. . . . Everything brought to us by Western winds is just filth and dirt." Radio Moscow was so numb it could only remark that "these United States winds stink of Munich." The "press manure" had obviously struck supersensitive nostrils. Not long afterward 14 uranium miners crossed the border carrying the leaflets.

"Our 'Winds of Freedom' operation was simply a demonstration of a new kind of carrier," C. D. Jackson, President of the Committee for a Free Europe, says. "As a demonstration it was successful. The balloons went where we wanted them to go. The leaflets put the Communists in a great dither. The operation proved that balloon barrages are an effective carrier which cannot be jammed. It is also very inexpensive—in fact, terribly cheap. You can do a tremendous balloon operation for a few thousand dollars.

"But where this new carrier is going to come in very handy is this. We could prepare a small 'Air Magazine of Freedom' and send it into satellite Europe by millions quite regularly. But we could also send soap, aspirin or antibiotics. The day may come when it might be useful to send something a little heavier. We can make much bigger balloons and send a great many more— into a pretty specific area. You can lay a track across a target and plant the bulk of their cargo where you want it. Moscow can worry about that.

"Even with leaflets we can give the Communists a hell of a lot of trouble. It makes them ridiculous, and drives them half-crazy. If you immobilize thousands of Red police as white-wings for days on end, that in itself is a tremendous diversion. It keeps their secret police and thousands of other Communists away from their normal activities. For the future? Yes, there's a tremendous lot we can do."

What can we offer the peoples of captive Europe?

They need more than hope for tomorrow. Whenever and however liberation may come they will desperately need the cooperation and help of the leading Western democracies. For when our present war of ideas is largely won their own will merely begin, in poverty and chaos. What can we offer them?

The common experience of the staff members of Radio Free Europe points out where part of the answer lies. This is probably the first time that hundreds of East Europeans, of five different nationalities, have worked together freely in a great mutual endeavor. Actually, if inadvertently, R.F.E. serves as a modest but important basic training center for East European co-operation. There is nothing that Poles and Czechs, Hungarians, Rumanians and Bulgarians need more than this experience in teamwork.

The Soviet conquerors have also imposed a great deal of joint co-operative effort upon the puppet-state populations. Under Stalinist domination they have been forced to put aside their age-old antagonisms; they are united as never before in their common sufferings and their common need to liberate themselves from the common exploiters. Poles and Bulgarians and all the others share far more since the Red midnight descended—and have deeper sympathies for each other—than ever in their nations' long past.

But the Kremlinites have done much more than this. Through the five-year plans they have compelled an unprecedented economic integration of all Eastern Europe. The Curtain countries' tariff barriers have been lowered; their mutual trade vastly exceeds anything known before; all their governments are co-ordinating their economic planning. Politically, as well, Eastern Europe has been united—by force.

But a great deal of what has been established by compulsion has long been urgently needed, and could be retained, with some revisions, by the free option of all these countries. It is unthinkable that this can fail to happen after their liberation. Quite unintentionally, the Red conquerors have plowed the ground and sown the seeds for the creation of East European unity, both economic and political. They have also created the necessity for this enlarged, regional unity. This may well prove to be the one great positive contribution to emerge from Soviet conquest. This is also where both responsibility and unique opportunity present themselves to the Western democratic governments.

What the free West must offer liberated East Europeans is freedom of choice—but also something to choose.

That something cannot be a strictly American-type, British-type or French-type democracy. Even with restored and democratic self-government Czechoslovakia, Hungary and Bulgaria —to name three—cannot revert to strictly national economies and achieve any marked improvement in their standards of living. In any event, all the Curtain countries must emerge into freedom under conditions enormously different from any our Western democracies have ever known. Their resources will have been drained, though they will have hundreds of new factories, and their national wealth cruelly diminished. All the puppet states will return to freedom with tremendously changed peoples, having radically altered ideas.

As C. D. Jackson justly warns: "We must realize now what kind of people we are going to find there after liberation; otherwise, what we propose will be neither understandable nor acceptable. We are *not* going to find a middle class eager to accept American free enterprise." (We can't, because the middle class is already impoverished into proletarian status.) "We are going to find peasants, workers, soldiers, terrified government functionaries and a sprinkling of intellectuals. We will find a virtually unanimous refusal to accept from the West what [Eastern Europeans] have known in the past; namely, pre-World War I feudal capitalism."

What, then, can we offer liberated East Europeans? If we have learned anything from what is happening before our very eyes, we will offer them more of the extraordinary thing that is happening in Western Europe—the evolution of a federal system of national states. We Americans would be offering our experience with the great fundamental achievement of the American Revolution—a federal system. For nearly two centuries this has proved to be one of the most successful revolutionary ideas ever put into practice. It is not a Soviet experiment. It is an American fact. It is still profoundly revolutionary, so much so that it is revolutionizing the traditional relations of Western Europe's nations, right now.

Why are six European nations—France, West Germany, Italy, Belgium, the Netherlands and Luxembourg—turning toward a common federation, with a combined army and a super-parliament? First, thanks to the Kremlin. It would never have begun to happen without the threat of Stalinist imperialism. Slowly, for the most part reluctantly, these six governments discovered that separately they can neither protect themselves against Soviet aggression, nor can they separately *afford* to protect themselves. But in order to create and support a European Army they soon found that there must be an equally European government—even if restricted—a higher administrative authority with the power to collect the necessary funds for the proposed army, with a common defense budget, with a capacity to make and direct certain policies. In other words, a six-nation *federation*—the first concrete steps toward a United States of Europe.

The impoverishment and reduced living standards resulting from two World Wars in a generation should also force federation upon these countries. Europe's Missouris, Ohios, Michigans and Rhode Islands can no longer earn their living, or pay their way, as separate nations. By the grace of Providence and George Washington's Continentals, our Ohios and Missouris never had to try to do so. If they had, I wonder where we would be now.

But what is true of Western Europe's nations today will be equally true of Eastern Europe's nations tomorrow. After liberation their people will be understandably obsessed by fear of a possibly revived Russian imperialism; of a repeated Russian conquest and occupation. How can they protect themselves against that most terrible of possibilities? They *know* now that they cannot conceivably protect themselves separately; that their separate armies, differently organized and equipped, would never be adequate. If West Germany, France and Italy need a common army, the East European countries will need one a thousand times more. There is no way to get one except within a federal system. There is also no way for these nations' standards of living to be raised notably—no way for economic stability and hope of a durable peace to be realized—save by joining an all-European federation or, as a minimum, by starting with a regional federation of Eastern or East-Central Europe.

Out of satellite Europe's present torment must inevitably rise a new awareness of its peoples' interdependence, accompanied by new compulsions toward a federal union. The United States can provide immense, perhaps decisive support for unity and federation in Eastern Europe, as it already has in Western Europe. If liberation should not come for several years, Western Europeans may contribute most notably from their immediate experience with the peculiarly European problems of federation.

Those whom Soviet imperialism holds enslaved have a right to expect from us in the West one thing, above all others: That we understand and be true to democracy as a revolutionary idea. For much too long we have been blinded by the notion that Soviet Communism is revolutionary. But by their acts the Stalinists have proved themselves the extreme *counterrevolutionaries and reactionaries* of this century. On the contrary—especially in these postwar years—democracy has proved itself so revolutionary that it no longer is restricted in conception to the free choice and practice of individual nations. It is now offering an opportunity for groups of nations to form a federation, a more difficult, but also more audacious and potentially more rewarding achievement, than our original American model.

Federative and supra-national democracy is, in reality, the greatest revolutionary idea in today's world. The Communists would impose federation with slavery—a kind of one-party, federated autocracy jammed down upon national collections of real estate. The free peoples are taking the longer, infinitely more difficult way. But the free peoples would build federation *with liberty;* through trial and error—*by mutual consent.* Democracy is so revolutionary that it is moving up and moving out—up toward the higher plateau of international self-government; out to embrace, gradually and by their own choice, the peoples of the world.

The twentieth century's great revolution is ours.

We have only to see it, to understand it—and especially, to serve it.

* * *

Because pressures of time leave no alternative this report must stand as it is. No sizable body of information about satellite Europe today can be in any sense final, or absolutely accurate. I have now lived with this realization for many months. Communist controls and conditions in the satellites make a percentage of error unavoidable, often, undetectable. Therefore I cannot vouch for every item in every chapter, nor have I encountered anyone who could.

But I think I owe it to you to say this much. It is my considered conviction that the overwhelming mass of evidence in these pages is factually accurate. If the summations of Communist actions and policies in captive Europe were only 60 per cent accurate, as presented here, they would still constitute an inestimable menace to all free peoples. It is my belief that their percentage of accuracy is much nearer 90 than 60 per cent. In any event I *know* that the major aspects of Stalinist conquests and sovietization are presented here without distortion—that they are also based on irrefutable masses of confirming material from all five of the Curtain countries. What I can vouch for under oath is that the over-all portrait of Communist conquest by terror is undeniably true. It will stand the test of time. It will be further and incontestably confirmed—for how many years?— by future masses of evidence written in agony and bloodshed and enforced starvation; written in the abduction and perversion of millions of children's minds; written in countless betrayals and tragedies—written with the steel pens of the servitors of the man who goes by the name of Stalin (for steel).

There remains but one other question:

The matter of personal obligation—both mine and yours.

I think both yours and mine are inescapable.

My own seemed peculiarly so because I have been an American liberal, as well as an independent voter, all my life. I am also a reporter. Can a *reporter* shut his eyes to ugly and brutal facts?

Can any *liberal* ignore the violence done to those very liberties which he professes to value above all others? Can an *American* draw a veil across a vast process of enslavement which threatens both his own country and democratic freedoms everywhere? Some do. But they are neither reporters, nor liberals, nor Americans worthy of the name.

The truth is that liberals, above all others, have the obligation to defend the rights of man wherever they are undermined, denied or obliterated; that liberals, above all others, must oppose and expose totalitarianism in whatever form it may take. Many may have given Soviet Russia the benefit of the doubt in the first postwar years, as I did. Many may have withheld judgment out of mistaken hopes for improvement, as I also did. But who can rationalize or explain away the ruthless assassination of Czechoslovakia's democracy in February, 1948? Who needed to wait for the cynical Communist invasion of South Korea? Any self-styled "liberal" who refuses today to recognize the Soviet Communists, openly and categorically, for what they are, is no longer a liberal—or has never been one at heart. In addition to the liberal's duty as I see it, and as far as personal motivations in writing this report are concerned, I have had one beyond all others. The obligation to live with my conscience.

But in reality, and for whoever may read this book, this is in no sense a problem restricted only to some particular group in our democratic societies. It is *equally* a problem for conservatives and liberals, for middle-of-the-roaders, for "independents" and for individualistic radicals. Every citizen who professes to believe in the freedoms which we all enjoy in the West shares the same great and personal responsibility.

Either you stand with freedom—or you stand against it.

Either you defend the basic rights of free men—or you undermine them by your very indifference.

It's true that our "unconscious Fascists" remain a serious long-term danger to the preservation of democracy, in America and every Western nation. We shall have more Hitlers and Mussolinis, more Lavals and Huey Longs; and far more of the second-rate instinctual, spiritual Fascists who unreasoningly put Hitlers and Huey Longs into power.

But those among us who shut their eyes to the crimes of the Soviet slave system are equally "unconscious" allies of the Kremlin, and equally a menace to our way of life. *By their silence alone they serve as confederates of Communism and supporters of the mass enslavement of peoples.* Because an immeasurable burden of proof of Stalinism's true character and methods is already on record these silent allies are no longer pardonable. They are self-condemned.

In the final reckoning each of us must also be judged by our silence, by our indifference or by our acts of omission.

If you read such reports as this, and still find nothing to do about and for the free way of life—in your daily work, in the battle for freedom of speech and civil rights, in whatever you can contribute and however you can best contribute it—pray do not deceive yourself. For you will have taken your stand by default. You will stand among the parasites and dilettantes of the free nations—in the ranks of the conscious or the "unconscious" pro-Communists—another valuable ally of Kremlin conquest and of Soviet enslavement.

This war of ideologies will continue throughout our lifetime.

Already it is far advanced; and we, as yet, are still far from winning it.

The chips are down.

The roll call is now.

INDEX